The Strategic Board

WILEY NONPROFIT LAW, FINANCE, AND MANAGEMENT SERIES

The Art of Planned Giving: Understanding Donors and the Culture of Giving by Douglas E. White
Beyond Fund Raising: New Strategies for Nonprofit Investment and Innovation by Kay Grace
Budgeting for Not-for-Profit Organizations by David Maddox
Charity, Advocacy, and the Law by Bruce R. Hopkins
The Complete Guide to Fund Raising Management by Stanley Weinstein
The Complete Guide to Nonprofit Management by Smith, Bucklin & Associates
Critical Issues in Fund Raising edited by Dwight Burlingame
Developing Affordable Housing: A Practical Guide for Nonprofit Organizations, Second Edition by Bennett L. Hecht
Faith-Based Management: Leading Organizations that Are Based on More than Just Mission by Peter Brinckerhoff
Financial and Accounting Guide for Not-for-Profit Organizations, Sixth Edition by Malvern J. Gross, Jr., Richard F. Larkin, Roger S. Bruttomesso, John J. McNally, PricewaterhouseCoopers LLP
Financial Empowerment: More Money for More Mission by Peter Brinckerhoff
Financial Management for Nonprofit Organizations by Jo Ann Hankin, Alan Seidner, and John Zietlow
Financial Planning for Nonprofit Organizations by Jody Blazek
The First Legal Answer Book for Fund-Raisers by Bruce R. Hopkins
The Fund Raiser's Guide to the Internet by Michael Johnston
Fund-Raising: Evaluating and Managing the Fund Development Process, Second Edition by James M. Greenfield
Fundraising Cost Effectiveness: A Self-Assessment Workbook by James M. Greenfield
Fund-Raising Fundamentals: A Guide to Annual Giving for Professionals and Volunteers by James M. Greenfield
Fund-Raising Regulation: A State-by-State Handbook of Registration Forms, Requirements, and Procedures by Seth Perlman and Betsy Hills Bush
Grantseeker's Budget Toolkit by James A. Quick and Cheryl S. New
Grantseeker's Toolkit: A Comprehensive Guide to Finding Funding by Cheryl S. New and James A. Quick
Grant Winner's Toolkit: Project Management and Evaluation by James A. Quick and Cheryl S. New
High Impact Philanthropy: How Donors, Boards, and Nonprofit Organizations Can Transform Nonprofit Communities by Kay Sprinkle Grace and Alan L. Wendroff
High Performance Nonprofit Organizations: Managing Upstream for Greater Impact by Christine Letts, William Ryan, and Allen Grossman
Improving the Economy, Efficiency, and Effectiveness of Nonprofits: Conducting Operational Reviews by Rob Reider
Intermediate Sanctions: Curbing Nonprofit Abuse by Bruce R. Hopkins and D. Benson Tesdahl
International Fund Raising for Nonprofits by Thomas Harris
International Guide to Nonprofit Law by Lester A. Salamon and Stefan Toepler & Associates
Joint Ventures Involving Tax-Exempt Organizations, Second Edition by Michael I. Sanders
The Law of Fund-Raising, Second Edition by Bruce R. Hopkins
The Law of Tax-Exempt Healthcare Organizations, Second Edition by Thomas K. Hyatt and Bruce R. Hopkins
The Law of Tax-Exempt Organizations, Seventh Edition by Bruce R. Hopkins
The Legal Answer Book for Nonprofit Organizations by Bruce R. Hopkins
A Legal Guide to Starting and Managing a Nonprofit Organization, Third Edition by Bruce R. Hopkins
The Legislative Labyrinth: A Map for Not-for-Profits edited by Walter Pidgeon
Managing Affordable Housing: A Practical Guide to Creating Stable Communities by Bennett L. Hecht, Local Initiatives Support Corporation, and James Stockard
Managing Upstream: Creating High-Performance Nonprofit Organizations by Christine W. Letts, William P. Ryan, and Allan Grossman
Mission-Based Management: Leading Your Not-for-Profit in the 21st Century, Second Edition by Peter Brinckerhoff
Mission-Based Management: Leading Your Not-for-Profit in the 21st Century, Second Edition, Workbook by Peter Brinckerhoff
Mission-Based Marketing: How Your Not-for-Profit Can Succeed in a More Competitive World by Peter Brinckerhoff
Nonprofit Boards: Roles, Responsibilities, and Performance by Diane J. Duca
Nonprofit Compensation, Benefits, and Employment Law by David G. Samuels and Howard Pianko
Nonprofit Compensation and Benefits Practices by Applied Research and Development Institute International, Inc.
The Nonprofit Counsel by Bruce R. Hopkins
The Nonprofit Guide to the Internet, Second Edition by Michael Johnston
Nonprofit Investment Policies: A Practical Guide to Creation and Implementation by Robert Fry, Jr.
The Nonprofit Law Dictionary by Bruce R. Hopkins
Nonprofit Litigation: A Practical Guide with Forms and Checklists by Steve Bachmann
The Nonprofit Handbook, Third Edition: Fund Raising by James M. Greenfield
The Nonprofit Handbook, Third Edition: Management by Tracy Daniel Connors
The Nonprofit Manager's Resource Dictionary by Ronald A. Landskroner
Nonprofit Organizations' Business Forms: Disk Edition by John Wiley & Sons, Inc.
Planned Giving: Management, Marketing, and Law, Second Edition by Ronald R. Jordan and Katelyn L. Quynn
Private Foundations: Tax Law and Compliance by Bruce R. Hopkins and Jody Blazek
Program Related Investments: A Technical Manual for Foundations by Christie I Baxter
Reengineering Your Nonprofit Organization: A Guide to Strategic Transformation by Alceste T. Pappas
Reinventing the University: Managing and Financing Institutions of Higher Education by Sandra L. Johnson and Sean C. Rush, PricewaterhouseCoopers LLP
The Second Legal Answer Book for Fund Raisers by Bruce R. Hopkins
The Second Legal Answer Book for Nonprofit Organizations by Bruce R. Hopkins
Social Entrepreneurship: The Art of Mission-Based Venture Development by Peter Brinckerhoff
Special Events: Proven Strategies for Nonprofit Fund Raising by Alan Wendroff
Starting and Managing a Nonprofit Organization: A Legal Guide, Third Edition by Bruce R. Hopkins
Strategic Communications for Nonprofit Organizations: Seven Steps to Creating a Successful Plan by Janel Radtke
Strategic Planning for Nonprofit Organizations: A Practical Guide and Workbook by Michael Allison and Jude Kaye, Support Center for Nonprofit Management
Streetsmart Financial Basics for Nonprofit Managers by Thomas A. McLaughlin
A Streetsmart Guide to Nonprofit Mergers and Networks by Thomas A. McLaughlin
Successful Corporate Fund Raising: Effective Strategies for Today's Nonprofits by Scott Sheldon
Successful Marketing Strategies for Nonprofit Organizations by Barry J. McLeish
The Tax Law of Charitable Giving, Second Edition by Bruce R. Hopkins
The Tax Law of Colleges and Universities by Bertrand M. Harding
Tax Planning and Compliance for Tax-Exempt Organizations: Forms, Checklists, Procedures, Third Edition by Jody Blazek
Trade Secrets for Every Nonprofit Manager by Thomas A. McLaughlin
The Universal Benefits of Volunteering: A Practical Workbook for Nonprofit Organizations, Volunteers and Corporations by Walter P. Pidgeon, Jr.
Values-Based Estate Planning: A Step-by-Step Approach to Wealth Transfers for Professional Advisors by Scott Fithian
The Volunteer Management Handbook by Tracy Daniel Connors

The Strategic Board:
The Step-by-Step Guide to High-Impact Governance

Mark Light

John Wiley & Sons, Inc.
New York • Chichester • Weinheim • Brisbane • Singapore • Toronto

This publication is designed to provide accurate and authoritative information in regard to the subject matter covered. It is sold with the understanding that the publisher is not engaged in rendering legal, accounting, or other professional services. If legal advice or other expert assistance is required, the services of a competent professional person should be sought.

Library of Congress Cataloging-in-Publication Data:

ISBN 0-471-40358-X

Printed in the United States of America.

10 9 8 7 6 5 4 3

About the Author

Mark Light has twenty years of front-line experience as a nonprofit executive. He is currently President of the Arts Center Foundation, the Victoria Theatre Association, and the Dayton Opera. This performing arts alliance in Dayton, presents local, national, and international performers to an audience of 325,000 each season, owns and manages arts facilities, raises endowment funding for the arts, and provides shared services in administration and ticketing.

Mark's work in Dayton began in late 1989 as the Victoria Theatre Association's executive director. During his tenure, annual attendance for that organization expanded 1,400 percent, subscriptions increased 8-fold, sponsorship funding went up 5,100 percent, annual revenues were boosted 11-fold, and a $5 million endowment was built with budget surpluses.

Mark is a Tony® Awards voter and he is the first recipient of the Outstanding Achievement in Presenter Management Award from the League of American Theatres and Producers, the association representing Broadway theatre throughout North America and whose members vote on the Tony® Awards.

He is also President of First Light®, which is *Putting The Future Within Reach*® with client-centered services including the *Where To Go Tomorrow—What Gets Done Today*™ Strategic Board™ model of governance. He is a Board Development Associate for the National Center for Nonprofit Boards, the national organization dedicated to building stronger nonprofit boards, and he serves on its Council of Editorial Advisors. He has been published in *Board Member* and in *Nonprofit Management and Leadership*.

Mark currently serves on the board of the Ohio Association of Nonprofit Organizations. He has been a board member for Bank One–Dayton, the National Alliance for Musical Theatre, AIDS Foundation Miami Valley, and the Downtown Dayton Partnership.

He holds an MBA from UCLA and a BFA in theatre from Drake University. He and his wife, Joni, have three children, William, Michael, and David.

Preface

The chief limitations of humanity are in its visions,
not in its power of achievement.
—A. E. Morgan

INTRODUCTION

This book is a step-by-step guide to high-impact governance. It introduces the Strategic Board™ model of governance and shows how to turn an ordinary board into a strategic board: visionary about the future, explicit in delegating that future into the present, clear about the tasks that must be executed today, and disciplined about monitoring performance.

A strategic board is neither an operational board mired in the minutia of day-to-day detail or a rubber-stamp board controlled by the executive director, the board chair, or committees. A strategic board focuses its energy on making sure that the organization achieves its chosen destiny. This is the fundamental obligation of governance in a strategic board. The strategic board is a means to this end, not an end to itself, and the degree to which this promise is kept is the best measure of board performance. Nothing else is as important.

The Strategic Board model of governance gets the right answers by first asking the right questions:

- Where to go tomorrow?
- Who does what?
- What gets done today?
- Did it happen?

By addressing these four questions of great governance, the ordinary board becomes the strategic board and crafts a *Where to go tomorrow—What gets done today*™ Governance Plan™ to guide the work of the organization. This practical and common sense tool combines strategic and operational planning, governance, and monitoring into one simple and easy-to-use package that can be passed by the board in a single vote. Form follows function in the Governance Plan, with the focus on the critical few rather than the trivial many; those issues that will deliver the greatest results are the center of attention. Less is more; simple is better.

The strategic board has a clear job to do and it's *not* to do the job of the professional staff. Gone are the committees that simply mirror staffing operations; in their place, committees arise that help the board to do its job instead. In the strategic board, what counts is what the organization accomplishes, not the degree of satisfaction that the individual board member expresses. Board members are not customers who need a money-back satisfaction guarantee for their service; they are part of a team with a clear job to do. Serving on a strategic board is not a gift; it is an obligation that carries accountability and liability for the board member.

THE SEVEN REALITIES OF NONPROFIT BOARDS

Unlike Stephen Covey's *The 7 Habits of Highly Effective People*, which outlines the habits that all effective people want to have, the seven realities of nonprofit boards are ones that all boards wish they could change. A strategic board recognizes that these unavoidable realities shape the world for the nonprofit board.

First and most important, board members have limited *time* to give to the task, just over 11 hours around the board table a year on average.[i] Second, as a result of this limited time, board members possess imperfect *knowledge* about the organizations that they lead. No matter how hard he or she tries, the part-time board member will always be dependent upon the full-time professional executive for information. This creates a contradiction that is a constant source of confusion: The part-time board must lead an organization whose full-time professionals must follow the will of the board, but the professional staff must in turn lead the board in a productive way to ensure that the right direction is taken.

Third and fourth, *size* and *composition* are hit-or-miss as they are driven by needs often unrelated to governing the organization. From the board member's potential for providing influence in the external environment to the ability to give and get funds, a wide variety of qualifications control the recruitment process and number of board members. Unlike the for-profit board where executive experience is mandatory for its members, many nonprofit board members have no business experience whatsoever.

Fifth, there are few *consequences*, positive or negative, for the performance of the board member and board, which in turn leads to the sixth

---

[i]Richard L. Moyers and Kathleen P. Enright, *A Snapshot of American's Nonprofit Boards* (Washington, DC: National Center for Nonprofit Boards, 1997), p. 12.

reality of a constant struggle with *continuity* of the "voice of the board" from meeting to meeting that comes from uneven attendance by board members; the average nationally is 71 percent.[ii] Making matters worse are term limits that are a fact of life in almost all nonprofits.[iii] Along with the forced retirement of a sixth of the board members in their prime every year, board officers change frequently as well. At the same time that this great resource of tested wisdom is obliged to leave, an equal number of newcomers joins the board team. Add it all together and it becomes a given that the voice of the board will constantly fluctuate.

Seventh, the very information and guidance that the board is so dependent upon usually comes from first-time executive directors whose "once is enough" predecessors did not move on to another executive director position. Most of these *inexperienced executive directors* have five or fewer years of tenure.[iv]

In sum, board members are part-timers with limited time and imperfect knowledge of the organization. The size and composition of the board generally has little to do with the task of governing. Because there are few consequences for good or bad performance, the continuity of the board is difficult to maintain meeting to meeting. The full-time professional executives that might be a source of guidance in this environment are too often themselves inexperienced first-timers.

THE IMPACT

On their own, each of these issues (time, knowledge, size, composition, consequences, continuity, and inexperienced executives) might have little impact on a board's ability to be strategic. Together, however, it is a cascading mix that makes this very difficult. Size impacts composition and consequences, time affects knowledge, continuity influences executive tenure, and so forth in every conceivable combination.

Not all boards experience all seven realities at the same time, but it is a rare board that doesn't encounter a handful simultaneously. Under these circumstances, it becomes understandable why boards are ineffective, why they toggle back and forth between cheerleading the organization and subjecting it to inquisitions. As one respected nonprofit leader said at a recent governance conference, "To be irrelevant would be a step forward for many boards."

[ii] *Ibid*, p. 12.
[iii] *Ibid*, p. 5.
[iv] Top Position is One-Time Shot for Many Executive Directors, *Board Member,* November/December, 1999, p. 6.

These realities of a nonprofit board have a causal impact on many other aspects of governance and organizational life. Cohesion, the team spirit of the board, is affected by size, composition, and continuity. Fundraising results are highly sensitive to size and composition.

Some board members, executive directors, and governance experts want to believe that the world of nonprofit governance is different. Somehow, if the nomination process were better or the right meeting tool identified, if we did self-assessment or brought in outside counsel, some or all of these realities would be neutralized. Perhaps the seminar for executive directors and their board chairs would be just the ticket, even though it's only for the year or two that those particular executives and chairs are together. If we could just have a smaller board, a bigger board, more time for meetings, less time for meetings, more comprehensive meeting packets, less extensive meeting packets, meetings at noon, meetings at dawn, more discussion, less discussion, then somehow the situation would improve.

This is all wishful thinking in large measure. The better approach is to simply accept the fact that the seven realities of nonprofit boards exist and design a program for governance that embraces them, that works with the realities, not against them. The seven realities are relatively inflexible and interconnected. Fix one and another breaks. Reduce size and continuity improves, but funding erodes since fewer board members are available for solicitation.

Frustrating as these seven realities may be, understanding and accepting them is a better approach than expending precious energy and time trying to fix them. A strategic board recognizes these realities and works with them; an ordinary board is either oblivious to them, fights them to the point of distraction, or spends its time finding fault for its ineffectiveness. Pointing fingers and assigning blame is a waste of time. It's no one's fault, not the executive director's for failing to provide more information or the board member's for not reading materials thoroughly.

Under these conditions, the board cannot help but be reactive in its work, dependent upon outside stimulus for the call to action. There is nothing wrong with being reactive; in fact it is a significant asset to the board, but it must not be the board's only advantage. A board cannot react its way to a chosen destiny. It must decide that destiny first. In order to accomplish this fundamental obligation of governance, to become truly strategic the board must be both reactive and proactive.

Executive directors often experience the board's inclination to be reactive when coming up to their salary review anniversary. How many executives have waited patiently for their salary adjustment only to be placed into the uncomfortable position of having to ask for it? While no one should be put in such an awkward and uncomfortable position, it may be unreasonable to expect a loose collective to have the perceptive sensitivities that one individual would exhibit under similar conditions. A board is not a person and it doesn't think like a person. As one executive director observed, "The board is a human resource committee of 25 people with just one employee—the executive director." That "human resources committee" is generally reactive to the world around it.

Despite the difficulties and oddities in this strange world of nonprofit governance, the seasoned board member and executive know that a good board can be extremely helpful to the cause. Even though the board must be taught, coached, and sometimes indulged as board members reinvent the wheel and probe proven operations on the way up the learning curve, good boards can and do make a difference.

Many boards and board members contribute heroically to the causes that they serve, and for many people, serving on a board is one of the most meaningful experiences of a lifetime. That nonprofits are able to accomplish extraordinary, courageous work under the many challenges that beset the sector is nothing short of miraculous.

THE STRATEGIC BOARD

In a *strategic board*, it is the partnership between the board and its executive that yields superior performance. The strategic board is constantly engaged in learning about the organization in order to answer the four questions of great governance. The primary teacher in this continuing education is the executive director, who must distill the complexities of the organization into the critical elements that the board must understand. It is through this process that teacher becomes student, student becomes teacher, and a partnership is built that clarifies direction and makes dreams come true.

The strategic board knows that it cannot escape its accountability, but it uses its precious time and knowledge in ways that count. No board has the time or knowledge to watch over the shoulder of the professional staff every minute, but the strategic board decides what is important to monitor and then communicates it precisely. This way the professional full-time staff knows what is expected. Whereas the ordinary board forages about for things to watch over, often dummying down to micromanaging line items in the budget, the strategic board makes its time count.

The strategic board understands that there is a profound difference between the job of the board and the board member. The job of the board is to decide the four primary questions of great governance. The first and most important job of a board member is to make good decisions in support of the board's job.

The board as a collective adds the greatest value in the decision making that shapes the chosen destiny of the organization. These decisions include choosing the executive director and deciding the question of where to go tomorrow. Because these kinds of actions come along infrequently, the board must spend much of its time maintaining itself in a "knowledgeable state of readiness."

The board member as an individual adds the greatest value by participating resolutely in the decision making at the board level and in one-to-one exchanges that happen outside the boardroom. Whether soliciting a gift or writing a thank-you letter, celebrating the executive director's anniversary or writing a note of commendation for a fellow director's job well done, these exchanges can deliver tremendous positive results. Board members frequently miss the chance to have high impact because they dismiss the little things as being too small. In waiting for a chance to hit a bases-loaded home run, a turn at bat is missed that hits the game-winning single.

At the end of the day and despite the efforts that boards make, there will be members who miss meetings and who don't read advance materials. There will be disruptive members, those that are too involved with the organization, and those that are disconnected. There will always be inexperienced members and members who ignore the organization's annual fund appeal. The ordinary board is distracted by these challenges; the strategic board succeeds in spite of them.

William Bowen, President of the Andrew W. Mellon Foundation, writes:

> *Perhaps the overriding obligation of boards in both sectors is to require that* a sensible plan of some kind be in place *and that* it be monitored carefully. *It is surprising how frequently no real planning occurs, especially on the part of the nonprofit world. And it is even more surprising how frequently plans that were adopted are not tracked in even the most rudimentary fashion.*[5]

A strategic board fulfills this critical obligation while forging an extraordinary organization in the process.

BOOK ORGANIZATION

This book is organized in six sections. The first section is an introduction to the Strategic Board model of governance. The second, third, fourth, and fifth sections deal with the four elements of the Governance Plan. The last section is closing thoughts, which is followed by an appendix containing a complete Governance Plan.

Acknowledgments

If at first you do succeed—try to hide your astonishment.
—Harry F. Banks

My son William saw his first monster snowdrift when he was four years old. He was bundled up like the guy in the tire commercial, almost too bulky to move his arms. He was holding his little red plastic shovel when he surprised me in the garage. I was staring open-mouthed into the jaws of a six-foot wall of snow that had to be shoveled out of the way so I could get to work. In my frustration at the size of the job, I looked down at William and said, "What do you think you're doing?" "Gonna move the snow," he said.

"So, you think you can do it?" I said back to him. I should know better than to be gruff with a dreamer. Here was my son top-full of confidence and standing by my side ready to face the challenge. My response almost blew out the flame of his enthusiasm, just like leaders in organizations do sometimes, like I do too, with dreamers and novices. "You can't do that; never been done before; it won't work," we say to these adventurers.

Will looked up at me and said to my question, "I can do it, Daddy." "Oh yeah?" I said, "And just how do you think you're going to do that?" "Little by little," he said as he made the first cut at a snowdrift three feet higher than his head.

The Strategic Board is a "little by little" book; it has been in the works for almost a decade. The idea for the book grew out of my quest to find a practical method to help nonprofits in general and my organization, in particular, do a better job of thinking about tomorrow in a way that could make a meaningful difference in the work that gets done today.

Getting the book finished was a long haul and I owe a lot to the people who gave me encouragement: To my dear companion, Joni; to my beautiful children, who have always been supportive. To my brother, Paul, a much-published author and friend; to my colleagues at work who have suffered my relentless experimentation, especially Dione Kennedy and Sheila Spencer. To my friend, Denise Rehg, who proofed content; to my colleague, Jeanette Patton, who proofed grammar. To Rick Moyers, who gave early encouragement to me; to my friends at the National Center for Nonprofit Boards, to Maureen Robinson, who opened up the world of nonprofit governance to me. Finally, to the many boards that took a chance and allowed the model to be tested in their organizations; especially the Victoria Theatre Association and Dayton Opera boards.

Contents

The Strategic Board

Introduction to the Strategic Board

Imagine the desired result before you swing.
—Arnold Palmer

CHAPTER 1

Seize the Day

When it comes to governance, everyone is an expert.
—John C. Whitehead

1.1 INTRODUCTION

Somewhere there are effective governing boards. With over a million and a half tax-exempt organizations in operation today, the odds have to be favorable. Unfortunately, as many board members of nonprofits and for-profits know, great governance is tough to achieve. It's a bit like newborns that sleep through the night: You've heard about them, but it certainly didn't happen with your kids. Why can't boards do better? The seven realities of nonprofit governance help explain the answer.

1.2 THE SEVEN REALITIES OF NONPROFIT BOARDS

That boards want to be great but cannot make it happen is the endless puzzle of governance, which begins with the first reality: Board members simply do not have enough *time* to give to the task. According to *A Snapshot of America's Nonprofit Boards,* published by the National Center for Nonprofit Boards,[1] the average number of board meetings per year is eight, the majority of boards have meetings lasting two hours or less, and the average board member attendance is 71 percent. Do the math and the average board member gives just a touch over 11 hours per year around the table compared to the average executive director, who often works in excess of 3,000 hours during the same period.

The scarcity of *time* gives rise to the second reality of imperfect *knowledge* to make good decisions. That a board made up of part-time volunteers with limited time should have the final responsibility for the organization

3

creates a paradox of nonprofit governance. For the executive director, the paradox means that the executive must be an obedient follower while also being a visionary leader, often making things happen by sheer force of will. For the board, the paradox means that while the board is ultimately accountable for the organization, it cannot do this without the leadership of the executive. The executive and the board must be followers and leaders at the same time. It is a difficult act to maintain in balance.

Third, in the world of nonprofit governance, *size* matters. With half of all nonprofit boards having at least 17 members, and 19 being the average size,[2] it's no wonder that board members don't necessarily feel that they count. Furthermore, it's common sense that a larger group will have more difficulty deciding than a smaller group. Larger boards have more difficulties working together and accomplishing objectives than smaller ones. As team experts Jon Katzenbach and Douglas Smith say in *The Wisdom of Teams*, "Ten people are far more likely than fifty to successfully work through their individual, functional, and hierarchical difference toward a common plan and hold themselves accountable for the results."[3]

Fourth, making matters worse, the *composition* of the board is haphazard at best and generally has little to do with the task of governance. Sometimes board members are chosen because of access to political influence, and most of the time it's the capacity to "give or get" funding. In the nonprofit world, some board members lack even the most rudimentary skills that would allow them to understand basic financial statements or commonly accepted principles of delegation. Corporate executives accustomed to taking the bull by the horns and getting things done serve alongside grass-roots volunteers who practice the fine art of building consensus. Little wonder that common descriptions of the board include herds of cats and huddles of quarterbacks.

Is it bad that board members are chosen for reasons other than their skill at governing? Of course not. "Board members," says one board chair, "are one-quarter governance, three-quarters influence." A board member with the ability to raise significant funds or influence a particular outcome is worth her weight in gold. Ask most United Ways if they'd trade their 45-member campaign-driven boards for smaller, more effective governing boards and most would say, "No," especially those that have done just that and seen their campaign results sink.

Fifth, one would think that a poorly performing board or board member would suffer the *consequences*, but this is not the case. So what if a meeting is missed? Federal and state laws have arisen that make it extremely unlikely that a board member will ever be held accountable for simply not showing up. Are there any employees that could produce meaningful results if they were absent almost a third of the time, as are board members?

4

Not only are there few consequences for poorly performing board members, but the same holds true for poorly performing boards. William Aramony will be remembered for decades because of his role in the United Way scandal, but who can recall even one of the board members at the helm at the time? Whose picture ends up on the front page of the morning paper? Certainly not the board chair's. On the flip side, if things go well, the public rarely shares the success with the board at large. No downside for the board in poor performance, no upside in good performance.

Sixth, pulling the board together so that there is *continuity* of voice from meeting to meeting is tough since the organizational memory that provides the glue of historical and social context is short term at best. While helpful in terms of bringing fresh ideas to the board, term limits are the norm in the nonprofit sector and every year puts a sixth of the most seasoned board members into forced retirement. At the same time that these seasoned veterans leave, the same number of novices is welcomed into the fold.

With time and talent in short supply, the board lucky enough to attract a top-quality director will likely share that person with other boards. With most board chairs spending two years or less at the helm and new members arriving just as seasoned ones rotate off, the board is in constant flux, making it difficult at best for the board's voice to be consistent over time.

In fact the ratio of newcomers to seasoned veterans is one-to-one with almost half of all board members in their first, second, or third year of board service.[4] If we asked a championship NFL team to win by using a strategy of changing coaches every season and kicking out nearly 20 percent of the most experienced players, we'd be booed out of the stadium. Yet this is exactly the way that it's done on the nonprofit board.

Imagine for a moment that term limits didn't exist, that the board composition today is the board composition next year. Even if this were the case, the attendance habits of board members almost guarantee a different board at every meeting. Simple majority carries the vote for most nonprofits and quorum is generally set at half the trustees. With average attendance at 71 percent,[5] it takes only 40 percent of the board to change destiny. Is it any wonder that many board members complain of "déjà vu all over again" as precious time at meetings is taken up explaining the decision-making process from the last meeting for those who weren't in attendance?

Seventh, usually the full-time professional executive directors from whom the board so desperately needs support and guidance are themselves usually first-time executives with five or fewer years of tenure.[6] These *inexperienced executive directors* follow predecessors that left the top job because of burnout, a better opportunity, or poor board relations.[7] Having tried the sector, only

14 percent of these "once is enough" leaders go on immediately to take another top job with a nonprofit.[8] It's the blind leading the blind in many nonprofit boards. Helping to explain this "get me out of here" situation is that 80 percent of nonprofits have budgets of less than $1 million,[9] which makes money tight, executive salaries low, and tensions high in an increasingly competitive job market. Small organizations are magnets for novice executives who inherit the problems of the previous novice executives.

In summary, part-time board members have limited *time* and imperfect *knowledge* of the organization. The *size* and *composition* of the board are unlikely to have much to do with the task of governing. Because there are few *consequences* for good or bad performance, the *continuity* of the board is very difficult to maintain from meeting to meeting. The source of information and guidance that might provide some relief usually comes from *inexperienced executive directors*.

1.3 THE CHALLENGE OF INEXPERIENCE

Many first-timers on nonprofit boards have experiences reminiscent of the guy who found himself standing beside a swimming pool filled with alligators while attending a seminar at the opulent home of a success guru. The guru said, "Courage is the key to success. And if there's anyone here who has the courage to jump in this pool and makes it to the other side alive, I'll give that person anything he or she wants within my means." Since no one in the group jumped in, it was off to lunch. On the way inside, they heard a splash and turned to see a woman swimming for her life. After a few minutes of utter terror, she made it to the other side and pulled herself out, tattered clothes, bites, and all. True to his word, the guru said, "Whatever you want, it's yours." The woman replied, "Whatever I want? I'll tell you what I want. I want to know who pushed me in!"

One of the remarkable career advantages of the nonprofit sector is that young executives can get into top leadership positions very early in a career. It might not be a big nonprofit, but it's an organization nonetheless. Three years after graduating with my MBA, I was an executive director. My friends who graduated with me were still buried in the depths of their for-profit companies at the same point in their career development. The bountiful number of opportunities for young leaders is perhaps best explained by the fact that 80 percent of nonprofits have budgets of less than $1 million.[10] These small organizations can afford to pay only so much, which establishes an unappealing cycle of novice executives following novice executives. It's a wonderful opportunity to get a top job and a significant learning challenge early in a career.

The downside to getting top-level jobs early in a career is that you don't get the critical "learning by watching" opportunities that those in the for-profit sector receive. One day you wake up to find yourself in an executive director's job never having been to a board meeting or done a marketing plan or led anyone anywhere. In the for-profit sector, the care and feeding of executive talent is taken quite seriously. A young leader would never be given an assignment without having the skills to get it done. Attitude is important, of course, but so is having the abilities to get the job done.

In the nonprofit sector, attitude is everything; the necessary skills are much less important. This happens primarily because turnover is so high, the compensation is so low, and the working conditions are so difficult. That forces boards to look at younger, less-seasoned leaders for the top jobs. As William Bowen reflects, "Many nonprofits reflect the interests of individuals who are idealistic, committed to a set of nonmonetary goals and generally less experienced in some kinds of practical work than are those who live principally in the business world."[11]

John Whitehead, who gave a $10 million gift to Harvard University to be used for the development of a nonprofit curriculum, put his money where his mouth is on the issue. In announcing his contribution, he said, "Unfortunately, with some exceptions, nonprofit leaders have little training about how to run an organization and often are not good managers."[12] While Mr. Whitehead's words might have touched a nerve in many dedicated nonprofit executives, it does hit the mark. Many are the nonprofit executives who have followed four executive directors in less than three years.[13]

I'll never forget attending my first conference presented by Dance USA, the association for ballet and dance companies around the country. I remarked to the artistic director of another dance company that I didn't see very much gray hair in the executive directors around the room and it worried me. "What's to worry about?" he said to me. "No one is retiring from this field," I gulped, "They're all young." What I didn't realize is that many of these people would burn out before they had a chance to get some gray in their hair. After getting top jobs early in their careers, working in low-pay, understaffed conditions for boards that also lack much-needed training, is it any wonder that most of these early-career leaders leave the sector after just a few years?

It's not as if the nonprofit industry is a small one. One person in 12 works in a nonprofit. Fifty-six percent of Americans, 109 million people, volunteer for these organizations. There are more than 1.5 million nonprofits in America accounting for annual revenues of nearly $700 billion, which is more than the gross domestic product of Brazil, Russia, or Australia.[14] One of the world's biggest industries has many inexperienced and untrained people at the helm, both on the board and in the staff.

1.4 THE BETTER BOARD

It is not always true that a poorly functioning board can severely damage an institution or that an effective board equals an effective organization; there are exceptions to every rule. However, despite the lack of definitive research on the causal relationship between boards and effective organizations, common sense would make it seem apparent that a better board can help the organization reach its full potential. A dysfunctional board can hold it back.

There are other reasons to care about the quality of governance. Some board members point with good reason to the advantage of teams over individuals in decision making. William Bowen, President of the Andrew W. Mellon Foundation, points out that "the exercise of collective responsibility through a board can slow down some kinds of decision making, but it can also dampen the enthusiasm of the aspiring autocrat. It provides checks and balances by adding layers of judgment and protections against abuse of power and some forms of self-dealing, self-promotion, and favoritism."[15]

Finally, even if the full board is uninterested in attending to its responsibilities, the individual board member's self-interest about personal liability should offer ample motivation. In many boards, directorships are bestowed upon the generous patron as a thank-you for unselfish giving. Unfortunately, trusteeship should not be considered a gift, but rather should be conveyed as a serious obligation that carries significant responsibility and accountability, as Leifer and Glomb remind us in *The Legal Obligations of Nonprofit Boards*:

> One reason for incorporating a nonprofit organization is to protect individual board members and officers against personal liability for organizational obligations. . . . Generally, as long as board members exercise ordinary diligence and care, they will not be held liable for actions or decisions that cause damage or injury, even if their decisions were the result of poor judgment . . . reasonableness is the principal test of ordinary care. . . . Clearly, the best way for board members to avoid personal liability is by fulfilling all of the obligations of the office. . . .[16]

1.5 THE PUZZLE

The simple truth is that nonprofit boards have always struggled with knowing how best to govern. It is not that nonprofit boards don't want to govern well; they just don't necessarily know how to go about it, because they, like their executive directors, are inexperienced. This leaves many at nonprofits without trust in the ability of their board. Richard P. Chait, Thomas P. Holland, and Barbara E. Taylor stated, "After 10 years of research and dozens of engagements as consultants to nonprofit boards, we have reached a rather stark conclusion: Effective governance by a board of trustees is a relative rare and unnatural act."[17]

The search for the root causes of this gloomy assessment starts with an investigation into the common complaints of boards. Peter Drucker says that there are just two: "Nonprofit CEO's complain that their board 'meddles.' The directors, in turn, complain that management 'usurps' the board's function."[18]

However, it is not just inexperience that leads to problems; part of the difficulty lies with the board's view of its role; the board members themselves question their effectiveness. *Improving the Performance of Governing Boards* lists four complaints:

1. "There's no red meat on the table." The issues before the board and its committees are little more than a mishmash of miscellany—trivial matters disconnected from one another and from corporate strategy.
2. "Board meetings are boring." Events are tightly scripted, outcomes are largely predetermined, and opportunities to substantially influence significant decisions are severely limited.
3. "We have plenty of information, but we have no idea what it all means." Board packets bulge with raw, uninterpreted data, and trustees suffer from a deluge, not a dearth, of information.
4. "The parts on this board sum to less than the whole." The trustees' individual talents are not harnessed to a collective effort. The board functions more like foursomes on the same golf course than like players on the same team. Each committee or clique engages in a self-contained event on a common terrain, largely oblivious to the activities of others.[19]

Should leaders at nonprofits care that meetings are boring or that there is no red meat on the table? Isn't this a bit like worrying about whether the pilot on a flight is bored with the job and wants more meaningful things to do at 30,000 feet than watch the auto pilot? What we're interested in is arriving at our destination in one piece, not in whether the crew is having fun in the cockpit. If job satisfaction will have an impact on safety, by all means deal with it. If not, why is it a consideration?

However, this view of the problem does not accurately reflect the true board-staff relationship. In an airline flight analogy, the board would not have the role of the pilot. The pilot would be the executive; the board would play the role of passenger. After all, it is the passenger, not the pilot, who decides where and when to fly. We all know that a flight can get into trouble when the pilot leaves the flight deck, but boards ask for this all the time. They want the executive to pilot the plane and be a flight attendant at the same time.

Some executives like this behavior because it gets them off the hook. They expect to fly in first class with the board as pilot especially when it comes to fundraising. What young executive director hasn't complained about ineffectiveness on the part of the board in fundraising? It's little wonder that executives overwhelmingly rank the development/fundraising committee as the least-effective committee of the board.[20]

Some of the complaints about boredom in governance are simply unavoidable. Reviewing financial audits, for example, is not the most interesting task for board members, but it is a crucial one. If the organization is performing as it should, perhaps some boredom is tolerable and even a welcome sign of an effective board. No one could reasonably suggest that the executive director of a successful organization manufacture a "crisis du jour" for the board simply to keep the members entertained and stimulated.

Attending to these complaints has merit, however. Being awash in meaningless information is a waste of time and resources. Having a group of 20 board members when just one could get the job done more effectively is foolish. And if every meeting is a sleeper, what is the point of meeting at all? Why have a board at all?

1.6 TOO MUCH REFORM

The seven realities of nonprofit governance would seem at first fixable. Upon examination, however, many of them are simply unaffected by any attempt to change them. For example, time is fixed; no amount of effort can make more of it. It can be used more effectively, but it can't be increased simply through wishing for more. It is possible to make a larger board smaller, but perhaps not without the trade-off of reduced funding because of a loss of influential "door-opening" board members.

The problem with denying these realities, with not responding to them, is that the board will forever be reactive, always be subservient to outside stimuli that can take the form of rushed, stopgap measures or trendy fixes. This can be especially true when it comes to reform movements that are frequently promoted in the name of organizational capacity building.

These efforts at reform can do harm if the board embraces them in a reactive manner, grabbing every movement that comes along without a clear sense of what their organization needs.

Paul Light, author of *Making Nonprofits Work* and my brother, uses tides as a metaphor for describing the reform movements that nonprofits must react to on a regular basis:

> *Like the tides of the ocean, the tides of reform will never cease. Even if the current pressure for reform were to suddenly calm, the tides would rise and fall regardless, bringing their periodic shifts in ideology to the nonprofit sector just as they have to government and private firms for hundreds of years. And like the tides of the ocean, the tides of reform carry a vast collection of treasure and waste, some which gets used by the nonprofits, some of which gets tossed back into the ocean in due course.[21]*

Light says that there are four major tides. The first is *scientific management*, based upon Frederick Taylor's one best way and "rooted in the long-standing belief that certain organizational practices constitute essentials of good management . . . and it tends to arise in the form of checklists, templates, and benchmarks that tell a given organization exactly how to do its work."[22] Standards and codes of conduct most commonly express scientific management, and its central assumption is that "a set of core practices makes all organization effective."[23] Light goes on to say:

> *The strength of such efforts is obvious: the nonprofit sector cannot doubt what is expected by way of improvement. Not only are most of the standards measurable, but progress also is easily assessed. An organization either has a performance appraisal process or it does not; its board either meets three times (Better Business Bureau) or six times (Maryland) a year or not. The weakness is that the recommendations reach well beyond the knowledge base on organization effectiveness.[24]*

The second tide of reform is *war on waste:*

> *Like scientific management . . . [it] is driven by a belief that there is a "right" number of people and organizations for doing a specific nonprofit job. What makes the war on waste different from scientific management is its general belief that the right number of people and organizations is always less. Built upon Taylor's vision of the one best way, the war on waste is motivated by the desire for cost savings, whether through downsizing, mergers, or the outright "obliterations," as Michael Hammer called it, of obsolete organizations.[25]*

War on waste is most commonly expressed by reorganization, downsizing, strategic alliances, and reengineering, and its central assumption is that "staff, processes, and subsectors can be organized to create maximum efficiency."[26] About its pluses and minuses, Light says,"The great strength of war on waste is its focus on cost savings and efficiency. . . . The weakness of war on waste is its focus on cost savings and efficiency as the core measurement of success and the possible reduction in innovation as a result."[27]

The third tide of reform is *watchful eye,* which is "one of the most powerful traditions in management reform of any kind. . . . The notion is that organizations will not behave unethically if they know that citizens and the media might be watching. By throwing open the curtains that have so long protected corruption, advocates of watchful eye expect shame, embarrassment, and citizen pressure to do the work that scientific management and its legion of rules fail to do."[28]

Watchful eye is most commonly expressed by transparency and its central assumption is that "making financial and performance information visible will allow competition to weed out inefficiency."[29] Its strengths are "openness, donor empowerment," while its weaknesses are "inaccuracy, manipulation."[30]

The final tide of reform is *liberation management.* "At first blush, liberation management appears to be the anti-tide, meaning that it represents a general effort to undo and dismantle the rules and structures associated with scientific management, war on waste, and watchful eye."[31] Light goes on to clarify his point:

> *Central to liberation management is the dual notion that (1) employees know best about what works and (2) that accountability resides in careful measurement of results, not endless checklists and oversight. Liberation management involves a clear trade-off between the old compliance accountability of scientific management and the new performance accountability of outcomes measurement. Employees, and the organizations in which they reside, can be free to do their jobs only if their work enhances results. . . .[32]*

Deregulation, outcomes management, and employee empowerment most commonly express liberation management and its central assumption is that "organizations should focus on results, not rules, and be entrepreneurial."[33] Its strengths are "focus on measurable progress toward mission" while its weaknesses are "potential loss of discipline, focus on wrong 'customers'."[34]

This is all very interesting, but what do the four tides of reform add up to? There is a constant washing ashore of one reform after another, year after year. This year, it's strategic restructuring; next year it's outcomes management; last year it was a process to credential organizations. In such an environment, a nonprofit without a sense of itself is going to whip from one side of the reform spectrum to the other, from one good idea to another.

Because of the difficulties that come about from the seven realities of nonprofit boards, many organizations search high and low for solutions. We want to believe that we correct all the problems and make governance effective. It is a search for symptomatic relief, however. We can make it all better if we have a smaller board or a bigger board, maybe more time for meetings or perhaps a shorter time requirement, more thorough advance materials or abbreviated information, meetings after work or breakfast meetings, an annual retreat off-site or no more retreats at all.

Take self-assessment, for example. Like the tides of reform that Paul Light writes about, this one has been washing ashore in recent years. Because the evidence that self-assessment "by boards of trustees are of questionable validity as accurate and objective measures of actual board performance and competence,"[35] we must assume that boards are using these tools to improve their effectiveness by identifying and then solving myriad operating problems. As the authors of *The Effective Board of Trustees* go on to note, "Perhaps some alternative approaches will overcome the limitations to self-evaluation that we and other researchers have encountered. In the meantime, though, self-studies are likely to be more valuable as springboards to discussion and as measures of self-perception than as reliable barometers of a board's effectiveness."

Self-assessment tools can be very effective in identifying and fixing problems that will improve the work of the board. Fortunately, there is abundant advice about how the work of the board can indeed be bettered. One of the best sources for this kind of information is the National Center for Nonprofit Boards, truly the "A-to-Z" provider for everything imaginable, whether it's how to evaluate the executive director or run an effective retreat.

No board should be without this sort of helpful advice, provided, of course, that everyone knows what the organization is supposed to be doing in the first place. That's often where boards and organizations get into a lot of trouble. They forget that the fundamental purpose of governance is to achieve the chosen destiny for the organization; it is not to improve its scores on the "smile sheets," the "how did we do today" questionnaires, that sometimes pass for performance assessments. If the board fails to deliver on the promise of achieving a clearly articulated vision, it doesn't matter if board meetings are stimulating or directors happy. The strategic board first gets the four questions of great governance answered, then finds the problems and fixes them. It's not the other way around.

Boards often overlook the obvious: The board of directors is a team. When it comes to teams, the biggest source of difficulty isn't with how long or short a meeting is or how big or small the size of the collective is. It lies with the fundamental purpose. Carl Larson and Frank LaFasto, authors of *TeamWork: What Must Go Right/What Can Go Wrong*, explain:

> *In the descriptions of ineffectively functioning teams the factor that occurred far more frequently than any other was very simple: The team had raised—or had allowed to become raised—some other issue or focus about the team's performance objective. Something was being attended to that had assumed, at least at that time, a higher priority than the team's goal. . . . Whenever we encounter a team that is functioning poorly we always ask first: What is it that this team is elevating above its performance objective?*[36]

Governance is not an end unto itself; it is a means to an end. The old approach of giving the board something to do, anything at all, to keep members engaged is wrong. The board does have something to do. Something vital, and it's making sure the organization succeeds at reaching its chosen destiny.

The proof of a great board is in the accomplishments of the organization it governs, not in how effective it is with recruitment and orientation of board members or the degree of satisfaction with meetings. These are means to an end, not an end in itself. As Peter Drucker so aptly says: "To build a successful team, you don't start out with people—you start out with the job. You ask: What are we trying to do?"[37] Whether or not the organization achieves what it is trying to do, its chosen destiny is the best single measure of board performance.

1.7 THE PROACTIVE BOARD

Stephen Covey's immensely popular book, *The 7 Habits of Highly Effective People*, lists being proactive as its first habit:

> *While the word proactivity is now fairly common in management literature, it is a word you won't find in most dictionaries. It means more than merely taking initiative. It means that as human beings, we are responsible for our own lives. Our behavior is a function of our decisions, not our conditions. We can subordinate feeling to values. We have the initiative and the responsibility to make things happen.*[38]

Covey goes on to say, "If you wait to be acted upon, you *will* be acted upon."[39] No one can deny the rationality of Covey's argument, but it is not easy to make the transition from being reactive to being proactive. Making proactivity come alive in an individual is difficult to cultivate; if it were not, Covey would have listed it as a footnote, not as the first habit of seven.

And as hard as it is for an individual to be proactive, there is added difficulty for a collective like a nonprofit board operating in a world where the seven realities of nonprofit boards are added into the mix.

The first point in W. Edwards Deming's Management Method, widely credited for turning around Japanese Industry and restoring American quality to world leadership, is to create *constancy of purpose.* This constancy of purpose does not originate in a reactive environment: "It is easy to stay bound up in the tangled knots of the problems of today, become ever more and more efficient in them," Dr. Deming notes. But no company without a plan for the future, he emphasizes, will stay in business.[40]

The tides of reform, the tangled knots of today's problems, and the seven realities of nonprofit boards will always be present. In such circumstances, a nonprofit board cannot possibly react its way to the chosen destiny. To achieve a chosen destiny, the destiny must first be chosen. In order to become a truly great board, one that is strategic, the board must be both reactive and proactive. If a board is not proactive, it will be buffeted by every trendy reform movement that comes along. Not all of these reform methods are bad; however, nonprofits must be proactive in deciding which ones are for them. The board must be capable of reacting to the unseen and the unanticipated, but it must have a sure sense of its direction.

1.7 THE STRATEGIC BOARD

This book will show how to use the Strategic Board™ model of governance and build a high-impact board. To build a high-impact board and organization demands a process that must answer Peter Drucker's question: What are we trying to do? Any process for answering such a vital question must meet extraordinary requirements. First, it must be quick since board members and the staff do not have much time to give to the task. Second, it must be simple because the levels of experience are going to vary from member to member and within the professional staff itself. It must be user-friendly.

Most importantly, the process to build a strategic board must ultimately build a great organization that achieves its chosen destiny. It must be able to answer the four questions that build a strategic board:

- Where to go tomorrow?
- Who does what?
- What gets done today?
- Did it happen?

When a board answers these questions, it delivers on its promise. And in doing so, a great board and organization are the naturally occurring by-product.

While there are systems and processes that generate responses to some of these questions, most take an inordinate amount of time to craft and then implement. Making things worse, the processes are often very complicated and confusing to the very people who must use them on a day-to-day basis. After reviewing many different approaches and failing to find a satisfactory process, it becomes clear that a new approach is needed. That new approach is Strategic Board™ model of governance.

Rather than giving the right answers, the strategic board asks the right questions. It does not insist upon predetermined responses or specific prescriptions. It does build a dynamic, flexible, and durable framework for asking and then answering these questions. A strategic board produces a comprehensive plan containing four elements that answers the questions of great governance:

The Governance Plan

LEADERSHIP PLAN
Where to go tomorrow?

DELEGATION PLAN
Who does what?

MANAGEMENT PLAN
What gets done today?

VIGILANCE PLAN
Did it happen?

This combination of four elements is called a Governance Plan™. This, however, is not to suggest that the plan is solely about governance. The Governance Plan is a *Where to go tomorrow—What gets done today*™ practical and common sense tool that combines strategic and operational planning, governance, and monitoring into one simple and easy-to-use package that can be passed by the board in a single vote. Form follows function in a Governance Plan where the Leadership Plan is akin to a strategic plan, the Delegation Plan is a comprehensive set of job descriptions and guidelines of conduct, the Management Plan is similar to an operational plan, and the Vigilance Plan is a monitoring schedule.

If the Governance Plan looks simple, it is because it is meant to be simple. As Albert Einstein said, "Everything should be made as simple as possible, but not simpler," and this is the first rule of the Governance Plan. The Governance Plan gets much of its simplicity by using the 80/20 rule, which is formally known as the Pareto Principle. Pareto was an economist who declared that in any group of objects, 20 percent of the objects would account for 80 percent of the group's entire value. For example, 20 percent of the donors contribute 80 percent of the funds in an annual campaign. In the process of building a Governance Plan, it is important to focus on those issues that will have the most significant impact, the 20 percent that will deliver the 80 percent.

The second rule is that everything in the Governance Plan should ultimately make a difference in the work that real people do in the here and now. Nothing should be included in the Governance Plan unless it informs the work that gets done today. If it is confusing or extraneous, it's not in the Governance Plan. Period.

How involved the board is in each of these components depends upon the particular circumstances of that organization. Some boards will be very involved. They will participate in setting the goals for staff departments. Other boards will be concerned only about the work of the board itself. Some boards will delegate the crafting of every element of the Governance Plan to staff; other boards will be involved in every detail.

The degree of involvement on the part of the board in the day-to-day operations of the organization is fluid and depends upon a host of variables including the experience of the executive, the amount and depth of staff, and resources available. A grass-roots organization with a budget of less than $100,000 and no full-time professional staff will answer the four questions differently from a $10 million foundation. A board with 50 members will probably need an executive committee, a board of 12 might not, either of which is certainly agreeable. The point here is that the strategic board focuses itself on the four questions and derives answers that are appropriate at its particular place in time.

From the board member to the front-line staff, the Governance Plan is to be used on a daily basis. Gone are the long-winded mission statements and impossibly complicated documents that few can understand. The focus is on the critical few rather than the trivial many; those issues that will deliver the greatest results are the center of attention. Less is more; simple is better. This is all in keeping with what Tom Peters and Robert Waterman observed in the early 1980s:

> *The project showed, more clearly than could have been hoped for, that the excellent companies were, above all, brilliant on the basics. Tools didn't substitute for thinking. Intellect didn't overpower wisdom. Analysis didn't impede action. Rather, these companies worked hard to keep things simple in a complex world.*[41]

Relying on the rule that "What gets measured, gets done," the Governance Plan has a strong bias for accountability. It contains built-in, clearly stated, and quantifiable success measures in the Leadership Plan, explicit duties and behavior guidelines in the Delegation Plan, a comprehensive monitoring schedule in the Vigilance Plan, and specific goals for the short-term in the Management Plan.

Building a Governance Plan can be done quickly or it can be done at a more moderate pace. Whether it is a quick process is a matter of choice; what matters is that it gets installed. The fastest installations have taken just 13 hours of board time and seven hours of staff time. The slowest have taken about 27 hours total.

Most organizations decide to be quick about things in deference to the seven realities of nonprofit boards. The cost for speed is that the Governance Plan will have less refinement, but that can be balanced by making it an ongoing endeavor of the board to polish it. The Governance Plan puts a roof over the organization's head; polishing it over time makes it a home and becomes the perpetual work of the board. As the saying goes: A good plan today is better than a perfect plan tomorrow.

Recognizing that if the people who will be doing the work have a say in the decisions about that work, acceptance of the Governance Plan and its goal will be higher. If the process for building a Governance Plan is inclusive as opposed to exclusive. The more people involved including key staff, the better.

Not all organizations will involve the whole board or all of the key staff in the process of building a Governance Plan, however. A board of 50 people and 10 key staff can be a handful to manage and it becomes attractive under these circumstances to convene a smaller group. If this is the case, however, making sure that the smaller group contains the key board members and key staff is critical.

Form follows function in a Governance Plan. Instead of the old "we've always done it this way" approach, the strategic board builds its Governance Plan following the order of the four questions of great governance:

- Where to go tomorrow?
- Who does what?
- What gets done today?
- Did it happen?

Quicker installations can be better than drawn-out ones for another reason. Because of the modest investment in time, the Governance Plan is a home that no one will feel sad about renovating or selling or rebuilding from scratch. It isn't a palace that people are scared to live in.

A Governance Plan is not just for organizations that are already strong. In fact, it can be extremely valuable for those in dire circumstances. After all, once there is a plan of action, climbing out of a hole is easier than fighting your way out without any idea of where to go next. For the new executive director, no matter what shape the organization is in, the first thing that should be done is to see if the answers to the four questions exist. If the answers aren't there, get them quickly.

The Governance Plan is big-picture first, details next, and is inherently optimistic about the future. Since the success measures from the Leadership Plan are tied seamlessly to the Management Plan, where real people have bottom-line responsibility and authority for implementation, a feedback loop exists that moderates excess optimism. The Governance Plan can be upbeat about the future while at the same time absolutely down-to-earth realistic about what gets done today.

Boards can bring a wealth of value to the organization, but the fact of the matter is that any discussion about the assets and liabilities of a board is purely academic. Boards are a fact of life and a better board will always have the advantage. The way to build that better board? The Strategic Board model of governance.

CHAPTER 2

The Case Statement

We can't cross a bridge until we come to it; but I always like
to lay down a pontoon ahead of time.
—Bernard Baruch

2.1 INTRODUCTION

A board and executive director that are considering building a strategic board for their organization can understandably and justifiably become concerned about the investment of time and resources it will take to craft and implement a Governance Plan. Questions will arise about whether there is value in having a framework at all.

It would be hard to find an executive director or board member who would disagree that the fundamental obligation of leadership is to ensure that the organization achieves its chosen destiny. To do this, the organization must be strong and stable while at the same time quick and innovative. Given the extraordinary pace of change in the world today, the successful organization must adapt quickly and be comfortable at the edge of chaos, while at the same time be steady in delivering high quality results. The job is complicated and often contradictory, according to Paul Light in *Sustaining Innovation*:

> *Organizations are supposed to be simultaneously loose (that is, decentralized into relatively autonomous units) and tight (strongly controlled from the top); big (possessing extra money for good ideas) and little (with everyone having a stake in the organization's success); young (characterized by new people and new ideas) and experienced (stocked with seasoned professionals who know what they are doing); highly specialized (with individual employees and units focused on narrow pieces of the organization's overall job) and unified (with everyone sharing in the mission).*[42]

Building an organization that can achieve a chosen destiny within the turbulence of such opposing forces is a perplexing challenge. The people who push the envelope for innovation chafe under the very structure required to support the innovation once born. In this contradictory environment, the value of imposing the structure of any disciplined approach to thinking about the future is often debated.

This is not to say that executive directors and boards eschew the idea of exerting some control over the destiny of the organization. Everyone wants to have some certainty that what gets done today has some connection to where to go tomorrow. It is simply that no one wants to waste time.

Those that do not want to invest time in building a framework for planning often recollect their own personal experiences that were painful and led to little or no impact on the organization. They remember the exquisite misery of working for months and months on plans that were never utilized. As one trustee said, "I can still recall the endless hours of meetings with the consultant pounding away at us about strengths and weaknesses. It led to a document so thick that it made for a better doorstop than a plan of action. The bulk of the board didn't understand it, that was okay, but what really hurt was that the staff didn't understand it either. They simply discarded it and went about their business just as they had before we began the process."

One executive recalls vividly the installation of a new planning method that took so long and was so difficult that the board members who began the process actually were retired from the board when it was concluded. Board members involved could not recall when the process began and some had to be replaced because of sheer boredom with the pacing.

In addition to a fear of a drawn-out process from the board members' perspective, there is often real concern from executive directors that engaging in any process with the board will lead to an increased workload and invite the very micromanagement that the staff want to avoid. Furthermore, many opportunities that arise cannot be anticipated in formal planning processes. A competitor loses its executive director and thus creates a chance for merger. A foundation board changes its focus in a way that invites a new program. Why not just wait for these sorts of opportunities to come up and then seize upon them?

2.2 THE VALUE OF PLANNING

Does establishing a disciplined framework for thinking about the future have to be painful? Is it true that the thicker the document, the more successful the outcome will be? Does any disciplined approach to planning, building a Governance Plan or not, have any real value? James Collins and Jerry Porras give their answer to the question of whether the best companies really make their best moves by brilliant and complex strategic planning in their highly regarded *Built to Last:*

> *Visionary companies make some of their best moves by experimentation, trial and error, opportunism, and—quite literally—accident. What looks* in retrospect *like brilliant foresight and preplanning was often the result of "Let's just try a lot of stuff and keep what works." In this sense, visionary companies mimic the biological evolution of species. We found the concept in Charles Darwin's* Origin of Species *to be more helpful for replicating the success of certain visionary companies than any textbook on corporate strategic planning.*[43]

The concern of this statement is in the word *some* from the first sentence. If visionary companies make only some of their best moves by experimentation, what do they do about the rest of their moves?

This concern has not stopped the for-profit sector's love affair with experimentation as a valid approach to strategic thinking. Try a lot of things and see which one works. See what others are doing in your field, imitate, and improve. Don't try to control the world; let the world control the organization.

A reactive approach to thinking about the future has validity. Take the case of the Child Care Clearinghouse, a fictional name for an actual nonprofit organization. Two of the biggest strategic changes in recent years occurred serendipitously and were not anticipated as part of any plan. The first was an appeal for assistance to the Clearinghouse's executive director from the board president of another, smaller agency with a similar mission. Ten months later, a new joint program between the two agencies was launched with an annual price tag of $1 million. The program was executed by the smaller agency and promoted by the Clearinghouse and it dramatically changed both organizations. It is still operating four years later.

The second change for the Clearinghouse was even more surprising and coincidental and involved another agency in the same business. On a beautiful spring day, the executive committee of the Children's Referral Service called to express interest in discussing a possible alliance with the Clearinghouse. That the Children's Referral Service delivered an outstanding service and was one of the treasures of the community was not in question. That the Children's Referral Service was going through the most difficult period in its history and was teetering on the edge of financial collapse was also not in question. After just one balanced budget in seven years and a steady decline in activity, the board recognized its precarious situation and entered into a management alliance with the Clearinghouse that very summer.

Unfortunately, the alliance came too late to avoid a deficit of $250,000 for the Children's Referral Service, its biggest loss ever. Client placements hit a rock-bottom low and came off a high in the late 1980s that earned the organization the status of the state's best. The condition of the organization just 10 years later was a stunning reversal. Under these circumstances, the organization had no choice but to reduce its activities to exclude children above the third grade.

Fortunately, the community of funders applauded the alliance. Through an intensive effort, enough money was raised to pay off Children's Referral Service's accumulated deficit, cover losses for a few years as it worked its way out to a balanced budget, and create a cash reserve. At the same time, the new alliance built capacity throughout the two organizations and improved strategic position.

Both of these changes for the Child Care Clearinghouse occurred as a result of luck. No visioning process anticipated these opportunities. No strategic planning process covered the possibility of such high-impact opportunities.

Even though these two major changes to the Child Care Clearinghouse occurred as a result of luck, the third change came about as a result of carefully thinking about the future. Beginning with market research that concluded, "Families represent the greatest potential for future market growth," the Child Care Clearinghouse began planning to launch a new referral and shelter service for families. The new service was initiated in a test fashion a year later with full funding and rolled out in a full launch two years later, again with full funding guaranteed for the first three years.

So, which way is best? Is it the reactive approach in which no planning is good planning? Or is it the proactive approach, the one in which the organization tries to anticipate, as articulated by Karl Albrecht:

> The old success premise of "Get a good product, produce it at low cost, and sell it hard" is just too simplistic now. You have to know who you are, what you're really good at, what your basic business logic is, and what value-creation premise will win the business of your customers. In short, you have a vision for your success and a direction for getting there.[44]

There are those who will throw up their hands in the face of organizational complexity and the quickly changing world around them. They will complain about the plan that gathers dust on the bookshelf and they will strenuously avoid wasting time in any exercise that attempts to think about the future. Meanwhile, other people are doing real work. Whether consciously or not, each one of those people is making assumptions about the future.

No matter what leaders may wish, actions today have impact on to-morrow and when leaders deny this reality, it does little to help those people who must do the work of the organization. You either make a choice about the organization's destiny or someone else will. As Stephen Covey says, "If you wait to be acted upon, you *will* be acted upon."[45] That someone acting on the organization may not be a board member, may not be an executive director, but no matter; someone, somewhere is going to give direction. Does the executive director or board president really want the marketing director to set the "vision du jour"? Give direction by default or do it by design, but one way or another direction is going to be given.

It's one thing to have opportunities arise. It's another thing to recognize those opportunities and take advantage of them. How can an organization make itself ready for opportunity? It must start by being organized, by understanding its business, its structure. It must be able to answer the four questions that build a strategic board:

- Where to go tomorrow?
- Who does what?
- What gets done today?
- Did it happen?

An organization that can and does answer these questions with regular discipline will be ready for the future, whether it comes as planned or presents itself by accident. Having a framework, any framework at all, that deals with these important questions instills a discipline into an organization that can provide a welcome infrastructure that is hospitable to opportunity. The Yogi Berra leadership school of "You've got to be very careful if you don't know where you are going, because you might not get there" clearly applies here. If you don't know what business you're in, how can you make effective decisions about that business or new ones that you might enter?

The Child Care Clearinghouse alliance may have arisen by luck, but to manage the opportunity, to make it successful, required a systematic way of thinking. How could the Child Care Clearinghouse team handle the Children's Referral Service, which was in such deep trouble? How could the board of the Children's Referral Service, which was known for micro-managing its operations, become more helpful? These questions would have been sorted out over time one way or another, but the Strategic Board model of governance allowed them to be answered in short order.

One way or another, we must have some idea of the direction that the organization should move in. Either that direction is going to come in an orderly fashion through some process or it will be made up as it goes. Actions always indicate the plan behind them or the lack thereof. That plan is either articulated or not, well thought out or random. When everything is said and done, people have taken action. The question is whether that action fits a clearly articulated direction or is simply the whim of the individual.

Child Care Clearinghouse would not have been successful in managing its major projects without the Governance Plan framework. If an organization uses a Governance Plan, a level of discipline will develop that will allow for seizing the random opportunity successfully while at the same time making realities out of its plans.

Paul Light, in his book, *Sustaining Innovation*, studied 26 nonprofit organizations as he searched for common characteristics that would make the sporadic act of innovating a regular occasion. He identified four broad characteristics, including critical management systems that must serve the mission of the organization, not vice versa. About these management systems, he says:

Rigorous management systems cannot be taken as a given and are essential for sound innovation. They also make the single act of innovation less an act of courageous defiance and much more a natural act central to achieving an organization's mission.[46]

In the final chapter of his book, Light goes on to note:

There is no substitute for good management systems as a precursor to high performance and innovativeness . . . there is also no substitute for a focus on mission. Without exception, the Sustaining Innovation organizations centered on mission—they talked about whom they served, why they existed, how to know when they were succeeding. They could measure outcomes, for example, because they knew what the valued outcomes were. They could celebrate success because they knew when it occurred. Without a strong sense of mission, nonprofit and government organizations cannot long sustain innovativeness. They will have no basis on which to say either yes or no.[47]

Organizations are in some respects like long-distance runners who must build up muscle and endurance for the challenge of the race. That training, the mundane, day-to-day sweat and pain that prepares the athlete for the eventual race, is part and parcel of what it takes to win. It's not glamorous, but it is necessary for success. An organization that uses a Governance Plan builds the necessary organizational muscle to win. The discipline required assures the board and the staff that essential systems will be in place that can give the organization the foundation for achieving its chosen destiny, whatever it may be.

There will always be people who believe that planning of any sort—long-range, strategic, short-range—is a waste of time. "The world changes so rapidly, all that can be done is react," these people claim. Faced with the question of whether to act or react, do both. Invest in a process that will give the security of direction, but don't invest so much time and effort that changing course as conditions warrant becomes more difficult. Have a roof over your head that's flexible, one that invites addition, modification, or outright abandonment, but don't have a palace that must be worshipped and preserved because of its cost.

Any framework for thinking about the future and bringing it back to the present should be both specific enough to move the organization forward and loose enough to be able to react to changes that are needed or opportunities that present themselves. Loose-tight, structured-flexible; Albrecht creates a very likable metaphor for this balance when he writes:

> *Every leader needs bifocal vision—the ability to perceive accurately things happening further out toward the horizon that will inevitably affect the enterprise, as well as the ability to focus on the more immediate, pressing events in its environment. This ability to see the far field as well as the near field, and to deal comfortably with both, is relatively rare.*[48]

With a Governance Plan, the strategic board gains the ability to see the far field as well as the near field. The investment required is modest, which makes the process flexible. It is easier to strike the right balance between loose and tight, structured and flexible. Along the way, other benefits arise beyond building a board and organization that can achieve the chosen destiny, including more money being raised.

2.3 MORE MONEY

An organization with a Governance Plan finds a treasure trove of fundraising opportunities that make fundraising more effective and efficient whether it is in sponsorship funding or annual giving. In order to be successful in fundraising, a strong case statement always needs to be made. As a recent article from the National Center for Nonprofit Boards' *Board Member* magazine observes:

> *Board members need a solid understanding of the organization's mission in order to be good fund-raisers. "That's part and parcel of building a board," says Jane Couch, a Washington, D.C.-based consultant. "In order to be full participants in fund-raising, board members need to be thoroughly versed in the organization's*

programs and mission," she says. . . . Beyond the mission, the board needs to have a vision of the future a few years down the road, and board members need to be able to articulate what direction the organization is taking, says Guia Sandler. "If board members can talk only about the current year, it doesn't show good planning."[49]

This is especially true for startup nonprofit organizations:

When nonprofits make a pitch for a donation, they describe their longest running programs, show how well they manage money, and tout their success stories. But when start-up organizations look for seed money, they can't point to their achievements. To compensate, they must have a well-thought-out plan, something in writing that they can show prospective funders.[50]

The competition is fierce for the donor's attention, and the case statement, the reason why the donor should respond, must be compelling. That case statement should originate with the organization's mission statement. The very questions that a strategic board must answer are those that form the text of any credible case statement:

- Where to go tomorrow?
- Who does what?
- What gets done today?
- Did it happen?

All contributors want to know that their support is making a difference, that their dollars count. It is a fundraising fact that people give to people, not to organizations. Identification of the beneficiary of the donor's gift is a key tenet for successful fundraising. Furthermore, knowing what life-changing difference will be made is the core of a motivating appeal. The good news is that an organization with a Governance Plan answers these questions in a way that reassures the donor. From board member to front-line staff, the organization knows exactly the ends it wants to achieve and whether they are being attained.

As funds get tighter and funders get more concerned about organizational capacity, the nonprofit with a Governance Plan can prove beyond a shadow of a doubt that it has all the elements in place to address any questions about strategy, operations, and governance. The inclusion of a Governance Plan in a funder packet engenders confidence. It is an impressive document, which shows the potential funder that the organization takes its business seriously.

In a world in which general operating funds are increasingly difficult to identify, much less to secure, being able to build strong project-oriented proposals is a must to garner sponsorship support. A frequent claim from nonprofit organizations is that they are not project-oriented, especially in the human service area. It is often a surprise to those very organizations when they find that there are indeed programs and services that are fundable from a sponsorship standpoint.

Sponsorship is all about giving a sense of ownership to the sponsor. It starts with a careful review of the organization's strategies, which are the lines of business of the organization, its key programs or services, its major products. These strategies by themselves merit sponsorship support. By breaking them into the various program components, most nonprofit organizations can create a sizable inventory of attractive sponsorship opportunities.

A housing development organization, for example, that puts the American Dream of a home within reach for people with low to moderate incomes, found that it had a wide variety of sponsorship projects as part of the process of building its Governance Plan. The organization has three primary strategies, with two of these further defined:

1. Construction—*Building the American Dream for inner-city neighborhoods*
   * Rehabs—*Bringing neighborhoods back to life*
   * New Homes—*Raising the value of neighborhoods*
2. Rentals—*Renting the American Dream to low- to middle-income people*
3. Sales—*Making the American Dream happen for low- to middle-income people*
   * Lease Purchase—*Working toward the American Dream*
   * Straight Sales—*Realizing the American Dream*

Each of these strategies carries with it a customer-outcome statement that makes clear what difference the strategies are intended to make for what customer. In total, the housing development agency has seven distinct sponsorship opportunities, which can be "sold" to sponsorship prospects. In addition, five of the opportunities, Rehabs, New Homes, Rentals, Lease Purchase, and Straight Sales, can be further divided. New Homes, for example, can be subdivided into more sponsorship opportunities by neighborhood, by street, and even house by house.

Any organization can do the homework to develop a roster of sponsorship opportunities and the necessary case statements for general fundraising. The difference between fundraising in an organization that uses a Governance Plan and one that doesn't is that proposals, solicitations, and opportunities for giving are driven from a carefully considered process that answers the question of where to go tomorrow, a question that every donor wants explained.

A capable fundraiser must do the very legwork that a Governance Plan automatically generates, but the advantage of a Governance Plan is that it already has the blessing of the board, which a credible development professional would most certainly require. A strategic board provides this essential information on a regular basis as a natural output and without the constant bother of the development director.

All people who raise money face the inevitable funder inquiry about programs that received support: "Did it happen?" Especially in the case of general support funders is the need for an annual report outlining the results of operations for the fiscal year. Sponsors demand detailed reports about the funded project and government agencies require compliance summaries. Whatever it is called, whether it's compliance or assurance, *accountability* is the underpinning. Rather than waiting until the last minute to produce the report of accomplishments based on cobbled-together activity logs, data, and statistics, the Governance Plan has the needed information readily accessible and with a crystal-clear evidentiary trail to the mission.

Making fundraising even more effective is the existence in the Governance Plan of a well-thought-out executive summary, which summarizes the major points of interest of the organization's Governance Plan. It is an outstanding platform for the annual report that addresses the results of both the most recent fiscal year and the coming new year.

2.4 MAGIC BULLETS

A Governance Plan is not a magic bullet for improving board meetings or achieving impossible dreams. It won't fix intractable problems on its own. It won't mend the unmendable. It is a tool—nothing more, nothing less. There will still be board members that fail to live up to their obligations or executive directors that deliver disappointing performance.

John, a five-year veteran of a strategic board, comments that the Governance Plan "Bozo-proofs an organization and its board." It creates a context, a way of doing things, for governance so that the difficult decision or difficult board member, for that matter, can be confronted effectively. It works with and embraces the seven realities of nonprofit boards as opposed to working against them.

Bozo-proofing an organization by giving it a framework for consistently and capably managing itself is a sensible thing to do, but it must be a framework that is practical, one that doesn't take a two-day orientation seminar to grasp. The Strategic Board model of governance answers the need, but it isn't an "add water and watch" approach. It requires effort and time on the part of the board and staff to build the first Governance Plan and then a modicum of energy to put it to use over time. Boards find that the method can be easily maintained as a part of the regular annual agenda; the staff finds that it becomes a very effective way to manage important work on a day-to-day basis. Simply put, a Governance Plan becomes the way that things get done in the organization.

From this point forward, the focus of this book is on the Governance Plan, which is the output of a board using the Strategic Board model of governance. The Governance Plan is the way to answer the four questions and become a strategic board. The important point is that the strategic board answers the questions and achieves its chosen destiny as a result. As Cyril O. Houle says in his *Governing Boards*, "A board must ultimately be judged not by how it follows procedural rules, but by how effectively it achieves the mission of its institution. . . ."[51]

CHAPTER 3

The Governance Plan

*It's amazing what ordinary people can do if they set out
without preconceived notions.*
—Charles F. Kettering

3.1 INTRODUCTION

I am a practitioner, not an academic, and not a consultant. As I write this book, I have a day job in which I report to three different boards as President of the Arts Center Foundation, the Victoria Theatre Association, and the Dayton Opera. The consortium of these three arts groups creates a multivenue arts center organization that owns and manages the 1,139-seat Victoria Theatre (circa 1866), reopened January 1990; the Metropolitan Arts Center, opened in April 1992 and home to a 228-seat theater, public radio station, offices for nine arts groups, rehearsal studios, classrooms, and a restaurant; and the $82 million Schuster Performing Arts Center scheduled to open in 2003. The group provides programming activities that enrich life by making the customer the star for over 325,000 people each season through eight core programs: Broadway, off-Broadway, family, education, film, children's festival, cultural diversity, and opera.

When I started, the organization was just two months away from moving back into the Victoria Theatre after a $17 million renovation. Way back in late 1989, the Victoria's budget was about $500,000. The customer base of subscribers who buy packages of shows was less than that of the local college. Just 22,000 people were attending. Having shared an executive director with the local ballet company for many years, I was the first full-time professional executive for the organization in its then-15-year history.

Like many nonprofit organizations, the hiring of the executive director was the biggest and most important decision made by the board. Because many companies expect the new executive to be the source of inspiration about the future, the determination of the full-time professional executive director can be the mother of all board decisions, coming before that of choosing the destiny to be pursued. Logic dictates that the board should know the answer to where to go tomorrow before it hires an executive director, but many boards do it in reverse.

As with many nonprofit organizations, the answer to the question "What's the plan?" is "What plan?" In the first few days at my new job, I was overwhelmed by the sheer magnitude of problems that had to be confronted. From the installation of seats in the theater to the repair of the Mighty Wurlitzer Organ that had been left out in the rain, I hardly had time to think about where the organization should be going in the future.

Despite the intense activity, the board and I could not dodge decisions that would have a long-term impact on the company. One way or another, we had to have some idea of the direction that the organization should pursue. Either that direction was going to come in an orderly fashion through some process or we were going to have to make it up as we went along. From my office, I had to decide what shows would be chosen for the season coming up nine months later, technology systems and offices had to be furnished with some idea of what work would be done. "What's the plan?" became an immediate question that had to be answered. That's why the only order of business at my first board meeting was addressing the question of where to go tomorrow.

Our efforts then were crude compared to what we now use, but I vividly recall the long and hard debate about whether the organization was going to be "a" regional performing arts center or "the" regional performing arts center. The discussion about the choice of this single word in the mission statement was dramatic because the outcomes required substantially different levels of risk and effort.

If the organization were going to be *the* regional performing arts center, it would require a big gamble and expose the organization to a significant downside that would certainly cause short-term operating deficits. Box office systems, for example, would need to be purchased with the expectation of high attendance; telephone lines would need to be expanded to handle the phone calls that currently didn't exist, people hired to take those calls, advertising purchased to generate demand, marketing staff employed to buy the ad schedules, and great shows in the lineup.

One of the hottest shows at the time was *Les Miserables*. It was the "world's most popular musical" for good reason, but its price tag matched its appeal and was as much as the Victoria Theatre Association's total budget for the year. The choice of whether to do the show instead of something less risky literally hinged on the decision between "a" and "the" in the mission statement. If the organization was really going to be *the* performing arts center, then a high level of quality would be mandated. In a real sense, the future of the organization hung in the balance. In that one moment, I learned the value of taking time to think about the future and why planning is most certainly not a waste of time!

The vote to go with "the" was not easy, but the board knew the risks and was firmly unanimous in the roll call. That season the number of subscribers for shows was about 3,500 people. A year later it was 8,000. Ten years later it was 27,000. The total audience base grew from 22,000 to over 300,000, revenues were boosted 11-fold to $10 million, and sponsorship expanded from $20,000 to nearly $1.1 million. The choice of "the" galvanized everyone and allowed us to become comfortable with substantial risk. I had learned the value of thinking about the future in a way that had meaning for today. And the germ of the Strategic Board model of governance had been planted.

3.2 BEGINNINGS

In the earliest iterations of the Governance Plan, only two of the questions that build a strategic board were answered:

1. Where to go tomorrow?

LEADERSHIP PLAN	
Where to go tomorrow?	
VALUES	VISION

2. What gets done today?

MANAGEMENT PLAN	
What gets done today?	
BOARD	STAFF

In developing these questions, the best tool was one that could be used by a lean nonprofit organization that went head-to-head every day with the seven realities of nonprofit governance: Part-time board members have limited *time* and imperfect *knowledge* of the organization. The *size* and *composition* of the board are unlikely to have much to do with the task of governing. Because there are few *consequences* for good or bad performance, the *continuity* of the voice of the board is very difficult to maintain from meeting to meeting. The source of information and guidance that might provide some relief usually comes from *inexperienced executive directors.*

Over the years and through installations at other organizations, the Governance Plan became increasingly effective, but a deficiency began to show itself. There was frequent confusion and conflict about duties, especially at the board and executive director levels. Complaints about micromanagement by boards were common among executive directors, while boards often complained about dull meetings and not having a great enough impact on the organization.

The real answer to the governance question turns out to be one large dose of common sense. Simply decide who does what and make sure that it happens. Thus, the final resolution to the question of governance was the addition of a third and fourth element to the Governance Plan.

3. The Delegation Plan delegates who does what.

DELEGATION PLAN	
Who does what?	
DUTIES	GUIDELINES

4. The Vigilance Plan determines whether it happened.

VIGILANCE PLAN	
Did it happen?	
BOARD	STAFF
Reporting Schedule	Reporting Schedule

The fundamental purpose of a *Governance Plan,* is to achieve the chosen destiny of the organization. It is results-driven and includes four elements: *Leadership Plan, Delegation Plan, Vigilance Plan,* and *Management Plan.*

3.3 PUTTING IT ALL TOGETHER

The Governance Plan puts first things first and works its way down from large to small. Let the Leadership Plan—which answers the question of *where to go tomorrow*—drive the Delegation Plan that answers *who does what.* Let those two elements drive the Management Plan, which answers *what gets done today.* Finally, let the Vigilance Plan—which deals with *did it happen*—provide the needed oversight to keep things on track. Form follows function in the Governance Plan:

LEADERSHIP PLAN
Where to go tomorrow?
Executive Summary

VALUES	**VISION**
Values	Vision Summary
Values in Action	Mission
	Strategies
	Imperatives
	Success Measures

DELEGATION PLAN
Who does what?

DUTIES	**GUIDELINES**
Board	Board
Committees	Committees
Officers	Officers
Board Members	Board Members
Executive Director	Executive Director

MANAGEMENT PLAN
What gets done today?
Department Map
Budget Summary

BOARD	**STAFF**
Success Measures	Success Measures
Imperatives	Imperatives
Goals	Goals
	Individual Plans

VIGILANCE PLAN
Did it happen?

BOARD	**STAFF**
Reporting Schedule	Reporting Schedule

The Governance Plan has its own distinct vocabulary that in some ways is familiar. It uses many words that are common to planning and delegation like *values* and *vision*, but these words may have different meanings for different people. A board member, for example, commented that the values statements in the Governance Plan weren't really values according to his experience. He felt that values should compel the organization forward and should be aspirational. In the Governance Plan, however, values are about behaviors and they are not about a vision for the future.

The meanings of words in the Governance Plan are going to be new for some people and these words are not hard and fast. If you are more comfortable using one word than another, simply take your pen and write in the word you like better. The Governance Plan is not about forcing a vocabulary on anyone; it isn't about demanding the one true answer. There are no right answers—just the right questions. The Governance Plan is about building a strategic board, one that achieves a chosen destiny by answering the four questions of great governance.

The Leadership Plan

If you can dream it, you can do it.
—Walt Disney

CHAPTER 4

Where to Go Tomorrow

Good things only happen when planned; bad things happen on their own.
—Philip B. Crosby

LEADERSHIP PLAN
Where to go tomorrow?

Executive Summary

VALUES	**VISION**
Values Values in Action	Vision Summary Mission Strategies Imperatives Success Measures

---

4.1 INTRODUCTION

Almost everyone has a story about the power of a dream. One of the favorites on the inspirational speaking circuit for years begins in 1952 on the fourth of July off the coast of California on a foggy morning. Some 21 miles to the west, on Catalina Island, Florence Chadwick, a 34-year-old distance swimmer, waded into the water and began swimming toward California. She had already conquered the English Channel, swimming in both directions. Now she was determined to swim the Catalina Channel.

Millions of people were watching on television. As the hours ticked off, Chadwick fought bone-chilling cold, dense fog, and sharks. Several times, sharks had to be driven away by rifles. Fatigue never set in, but the icy waters numbed Chadwick to the point of desperation. Straining to make out the shore through her swimmer's goggles, she could only see dense fog. She knew she could not go on. Although not a quitter, Chadwick shouted to her trainer and her mother in the boat and asked to be taken out of the water. They urged her not to give up, but when she looked to the California coast, all she could see was thick fog.

So, after 15 hours and 51 minutes of fighting the elements, she was hauled out of the water. Frozen to the bone and her spirit defeated, Chadwick was devastated when she discovered that she was only a half mile from the California coast. The fog had done it. She had been licked not by fatigue, cold, or even the sharks. The fog alone had defeated her because it obscured her goal. It had blinded her reason, her eyes, and most of all her heart.

Two months later, Chadwick swam the same channel, and again fog clouded her view, but this time she swam with faith intact—somewhere behind that fog was land. This time she succeeded. Not only was she the first woman to swim the channel, she beat the men's record by two hours.[52]

The Leadership Plan of a Governance Plan is, at its essence, the description of the chosen destiny for the organization. Complete with values to guide behavior and a comprehensive vision, the organization has an exceedingly clear picture of its chosen destiny.

4.2 MANAGER VS. LEADER

There is no question that a sense of purpose, or direction, can be a powerful motivator. There is also no question that providing direction is a fundamental responsibility of leadership:

> *The first responsibility of a leader is to define reality.*[53]
> **—Max DePree, *Leadership Is An Art***

> *Leadership deals with the top line: What are the things I want to accomplish?*[54]
> **—Stephen R. Covey, *The 7 Habits of Highly Effective People***

> *The single defining quality of leaders is the capacity to create and realize a vision.*[55]
> **—Warren Bennis, *On Becoming a Leader***

Most people, board and staff alike, want to be seen as leaders in their field of endeavor. Most of us, however, are managers who are effective at getting things done today as opposed to deciding where to go tomorrow. Despite the fact that we may like the idea of being a leader, most of us are far better managers. Management is getting things done. Its sensibility is in the here and now, what gets done today, right now. John Kotter in *A Force for Change* aptly describes management as having to do with planning and budgeting, organizing and staffing, controlling and problem solving, all with the desired outcome of producing predictability and order.[56]

Alternatively, leadership is about setting direction. It's based in the future. "Here's where we are going" is its essence. Kotter describes it as having to do with establishing direction, aligning people, motivating and inspiring, all with the desired outcome of producing useful, often very dramatic change.[57]

Regrettably, there aren't many people good at being leaders and managers at the same time. Kotter surveyed senior executives in successful U.S. corporations and found that over 95 percent reported having too few people who are strong at both leadership and management.[58] However, leadership and management need each other. They are powerless without each other. Stephen Covey lays it out clearly: "In the words of both Peter Drucker and Warren Bennis, 'Management is efficiency in climbing the ladder of success; leadership determines whether the ladder is leaning against the right wall.' "[59] Management does things right, leadership does the right things.

There are two basic ways to begin any process of thinking about and deciding a chosen destiny for an organization: management driven and leadership-driven. The management-driven way first asks, "Where are we today?" and builds the future from there. Leadership-driven planning begins with the question, "Where do we want to go?" Nothing gets done without both. Thomas Morris, executive director of Cleveland Orchestra, notes:

> It is my fundamental belief that leadership is different than management. In a funny way, leadership is all about destabilization. A leader needs to be constantly pointing to what appear to be difficult directions. One of my responsibilities with the board is to constantly push in different directions so that we're always trying to do new things. It's so easy to merely exist. Good leadership means keeping an institution slightly off balance while also making sure there is enough management machinery in place to avoid chaos.[60]

The order of questions in the management-driven model is standard:

- Where are we today?
- Where to go tomorrow?

Having answered these questions, reducing the gap that exists between the two answers becomes the focus of activity. Leadership-driven planning reverses the order:

- Where to go tomorrow?
- Where are we today?

In this case, the gap between the two answers may actually be larger, more aggressive, and certainly harder to close. Even so, starting with "Where are we today?" can be inhibiting to creativity and can lead to incrementalism.

One of the best analogies to illustrate the differences between management-driven and leadership-driven models concerns two NBA basketball players from the mid-1990s. The first NBA player is Shawn Bradley, who started out with the Philadelphia 76ers. He's seven feet six inches tall. Bradley is the tallest American-born player in the game. Imagine what question he was asked the most when he was growing up. Here's the perfect example of management-driven thinking. Where are we today? We're seven feet six inches tall. Play basketball; case closed. In no way does this suggest that Shawn Bradley is a lesser human being because it was an obvious choice for him to play basketball. He was born with great gifts; he made use of them.

Now take Muggsy Bogues. He doesn't have the physical gifts of a Michael Jordan. Bogues grew up in Baltimore's housing projects. He went to Dunbar High School where he was frequently laughed at because of his diminutive size although he became the MVP in his senior year. At Wake Forest, he led the league in assists and steals in his junior year and made all-conference. He was one of five in Wake Forest history to have his jersey number retired. He became a first round NBA draft choice. At five-foot-three, he is the shortest player in the history of the game. He's a full two feet three inches shorter than Bradley, but his assist-to-turnover ratio is among the best in the league.

What if Muggsy Bogues had started out with management-driven thinking? What if he had let his dreams be shaped by a process that began with the question "Where are we today?" For those interested, Bogues 1999–2000 season high for the Toronto Raptors was 24 points, 5 steals, and 12 assists; Bradley's with the Phoenix Suns was 26 points, 5 steals, and 3 assists.

History is filled with hundreds of wonderful, inspiring stories of people and organizations that started with an idea of where they wanted to be and not with an appraisal of what they could accomplish. When looking at nonprofits, people see companies characterized by the same courage. Nonprofits go where for-profits wouldn't dream of going. Nonprofits go where the help is needed. They drive against incredible odds. They bring society's conscience to life with action. The nonprofit sector is all about leadership-driven thinking. Leadership-driven is *sky-down*. This is why the question of where to go tomorrow leads the order of thinking in the Governance Plan.

The essence of management-driven thinking is that goals are set based on where you are. Because people don't like to fail, they frequently set goals below their real potential. The end result is incremental improvements. If you start with an evaluation of where you are today, you may end up with something tomorrow that is better, but not necessarily as brilliant as it could be. This is not to suggest that an organization can succeed as a superb visionary and be a failure at executing. The successful nonprofit organization must find a way to both lead and manage. The road to success, to achieving a chosen destiny, must start somewhere. Thus, it is a foundation of the Strategic Board model of governance that the decision of where to go tomorrow is the primary one and that all other decisions should follow from here.

4.3 THE FIRST QUESTION

The first and most important question of the Governance Plan is where to go tomorrow, which is answered by the Leadership Plan. The Leadership Plan is where the high-impact decisions are made about the chosen destiny for the organization. The Leadership Plan is the board's work, where its voice is the most important. The Leadership Plan concerns itself with the ends that the organization wants to accomplish.

A good Leadership Plan, which is akin to a strategic plan in some organizations, is generally no longer than a page without the success measures. It doesn't take a lot of time to build one; a typical organization using a quick approach will need just seven hours with the board and one hour with the key staff.

In Larson and LaFasto's study of highly functional teams, they identified the key ingredient for an outstanding board: "In every case, without exception, when an effectively functioning team was identified, it was described by the respondent as having a clear understanding of its objective . . . and the belief that the goal embodies a worthwhile or important result. . . ."[61]

In the Governance Plan, the Leadership Plan holds the answer in its three key elements: executive summary, values, and vision. The executive summary is just what it says and it provides the reader with a synopsis of key points in the Leadership Plan. The values outline key behaviors, and the vision contains the mission, strategies, and success measures. Together these components of the Leadership Plan clearly articulate the chosen destiny for the organization.

4.4 THE EXECUTIVE SUMMARY

The executive summary of a Leadership Plan is the first element encountered in the Governance Plan, but it is actually the last to be crafted in the process. This is because it condenses the major points of interest of the Governance Plan into a very readable short summary, usually no more than two or three pages. The executive summary discusses significant issues related to three major elements of the Governance Plan:

1. Vision summary
2. Strategies
3. Imperatives

Very similar to an annual report, it gives the reader with limited time a first look at the core of the Governance Plan. The executive summary stimulates thinking by identifying those major topics that the board member should be most concerned about. The chief concern about providing an executive summary is that it may be the only portion of the Governance Plan that is read. If this is the case, the executive summary will have proved its worth by alerting the reader to matters of greatest importance.

Executive summaries do not contain only negative information. Good news is just as welcome. The executive summary of the Governance Plan is essentially an annual report outlining notable ups and downs. It is typically written by the executive director and can be an opportunity to celebrate success and acknowledge failure or concerns. Here, for example, are the first two paragraphs from the Governance Plan for a chapter of Big Brothers–Big Sisters:

Big Brothers–Big Sisters finds itself at a crossroads. On one hand, the organization is enjoying a period of outstanding financial results and dramatic growth within some strategies that together have achieved an operating margin of nearly 7 percent in 1999, up over 80 percent from 1997. On the other hand, Average Total Matches has declined 13 percent during the same period to 234.

The focus for the next two years is on tackling goals that will achieve the result of increasing core matches especially in 2001. At the same time, the organization is working to improve various business processes in order to secure more core matches. Thus, the Vision Summary for the 2000 Governance Plan is to build a foundation to boost the core.

The executive summary is a snapshot of the Governance Plan and the reader should always be reminded that it doesn't replace a thorough study.

CHAPTER 5

Values

If you don't stand for something, you'll fall for anything.
—Steve Bartkowski

LEADERSHIP PLAN
Where to go Tomorrow?

Executive Summary

VALUES	**VISION**
Values	Vision Summary
Values in Action	Mission
	Strategies
	Imperatives
	Success Measures

5.1 INTRODUCTION

The Leadership Plan begins with values and values in action. Values, beliefs, ethical standards, principals, creeds, tenets, rules: They are all very similar, sort of like the car that you drive. No matter where you are, what road you're on, where you're headed or who's in the car with you, the car stays the same. Values endure and survive challenges, chaos, and changes. It's not what you do; it's how you do it.

Values are the "how you do business" of an organization. Most companies know the common purpose that describes what they do and near-term performance goals are usually known as well. However, when it comes to the values of how business is done, most organizations don't take the time to clarify them. Not surprisingly, many nonprofit boards and executive directors cannot wrap their arms around the values that are important to the organization. Many have simply never thought much about values. It isn't as though there is a great deal of urgency to answering the questions.

Why should the organization care about having a clear set of values? There are two simple answers: First, how can you test your actions against your values or those of your organization when you don't know what they are in the first place? How can you "walk your talk" if you don't know what the talk should be? How can you lead by example if you don't know the example you are trying to set? Like the folk saying goes, "If you plant crab apples, don't count on harvesting Golden Delicious."

Second, knowing the values helps to set the stage for building a worthy vision. If it is an organization value to always be the best, the organization should be more risk tolerant when it comes to the vision. Likewise, the value of being a team should lessen the degree of bureaucracy in the organization. Like the proverbial vegetarian in a butcher shop, values dictate things an organization should and should not do. Because it is impossible to think with your head without first knowing what is your heart, values and values in action are the first part of the Governance Plan to be built.

5.2 THE THREE TRUTHS ABOUT VALUES

There are three truths about values that are worth noting: First, not everyone shares the same values. Second, values impact final outcomes. Third, "values by clairvoyance" simply doesn't work.

That not everyone shares the same values should be obvious and is illustrated by the lack of insight shown in a quote attributed to Alexander Wiley: "The Jews and Arabs should settle their dispute in the true spirit of Christian charity."[62] The fact is that in an increasingly diverse workplace, people have grown up in different environments with different ethical standards. Obviously, people look at the world differently and there are few bridging devices such as religion to give a common vocabulary. That's why Star Wars creator Lucas gives the galaxy C-3PO, the protocol droid "capable of conversing in six million forms of communication,"[63] which is as many different languages as an organization's stakeholders seem to speak sometimes.

Whether we like it or not, and we often don't like it, many of the conflicts between people occur as a result of values clashes. These differences occur not only with customers and clients, but also with employees and family members. Values conflicts happen everyday. It is all about the assumptions we make. I assume that my five-year old son has the very same perspective I have when it comes to taking responsibility. I assume that our marketing director shares my dedication to serving school audiences when, in fact, she's dedicated to the customer who pays $36 a seat, not the kids who come for free. And these values clashes logically will impact final outcomes.

In reality, most of us have "value defaults" just like the word processing programs we use on our computers. I use Word with margins set at one inch, Times Roman font set at 12-point, footer set at 0.4 inch, tabs set every 0.3 inches, and page numbers at the bottom right. Anyone that uses my computer will get this document format because it is set as my default. Just like the default, I have a particular values set that governs my behavior. It's mine and mine alone, not yours, not my organization's. In the absence of direction from the organization, the people who work for the organization, the volunteers, and the board members will default to their particular values. Explicitly outlining values for the organization gives rise to the possibility that these people will adapt to these values, especially if the values are modeled at the top.

The challenge to values is that they are frequently given lip service as a fad of the day. You'll come into the office one day and find that a manager has put up a framed picture of an eagle soaring in the mountains with a pithy saying about teams. The values of a Governance Plan are different from this scattershot, stereotyped approach. They are meant to be lived and are evaluated at the one-to-one manager-to-employee level.

"Values by clairvoyance" makes an assumption that you know what my values are, that you respect my values, that you care about them. Leadership frequently falls into this trap. Leaders seem to believe that others can read their minds when it comes to values, that others should know that lending a hand without asking is important to the boss and it should be done. It just doesn't work this way. Employees are not mind readers. If the leaders of the nonprofit organization want certain values embraced in the workplace, they need to spell these out explicitly and then live by them.

5.3 BRINGING VALUES TO LIFE

The values of the Leadership Plan are culture building in texture and describe how business will be conducted. These values are not about products or services, but are about behaviors. It is common to see values revolve around issues like trust, teamwork, customers, and striving to be the best. After determining the three or four primary values, values in action are voiced so that it is clearly understood what specific conduct is required for each of the values. Values in action are simply the necessary behaviors that bring the values to life.

Once the values have been set, they are reduced to greater levels of detail with values in action. Values in action are the essential behaviors that describe the values and are akin to a code of conduct. If building trust is a value, for example, values in action for trust might include keeping promises, being actively truthful, taking responsibility for actions, and being fair. The values in action for an organization go to work at a variety of levels, including organizational, departmental, and individual.

A value statement like "We believe in integrity" has very different meanings for people and on its own has limited benefit because it is so broad and open to interpretation. It becomes much more specific and functional through the values in action, which might include keeping promises, taking responsibility for actions, being truthful without hidden agendas, and doing the right thing. Exhibit 5.1 gives examples of values and values in action from two different organizations.

Notice that the values and value in action in Exhibit 5.1 are very simple and easily understood. This is so that the people who must live them quickly grasp the desired behavior and remember it. This is in keeping with the guidepost of the strategic board that less is more, simple is better. An organization with five values is less likely to succeed at embedding them into the life of the team than if there are four values.

The board and key staff work together to construct the values, but as many of the employees as possible work as a team on the values in action. If the employees are expected to live the values, it is a good idea to involve them in the discussion about the values in actions that will bring them to life.

No statement of values and values in action is of benefit to any organization if it is not kept alive through example setting and communication. The easy work is to clarify the values and values in action. The hard work is living by them and regularly assessing performance. Fortunately, the attention needed is provided in the Vigilance Plan and through individual plans.

VALUES AND VALUES IN ACTION FROM A FUNDRAISING ORGANIZATION

Visionary	*Community-Centered*
Can-do proactive attitude.	Identify needs.
Best practices.	Set priorities.
Creative solutions.	Develop responsive programs.
Dedicated and perseverant.	
Team	*Integrity*
Listen carefully.	Fair.
Celebrate each other.	Honest.
Lend a hand.	Promises kept.
Win–Win.	

VALUES AND VALUES IN ACTION FROM A HOUSING DEVELOPMENT AGENCY

Excellence	*Team*
Proactive.	Encourage each other.
Innovative.	Optimistic.
Resilient.	Give-and-take communication.
Customer-focused	*Trust*
Make each customer special.	Fair–unbiased and consistent.
Understand the customer.	Promises kept.
Meet the need.	Truthful.

Exhibit 5.1   Sample Values and Vision Statements

5.4 VALUES AND VALUES IN ACTION

Constructing values and values in action is done in a direct and under-standable process. The question of what values should guide behavior is asked in a group setting. The brainstorming technique is used to generate as many answers as possible, which are written down on large Post-it® notes. There are five steps to brainstorming:

1. The central brainstorming question is stated, agreed on, and written down for everyone to see.
2. Each team member in turn gives an idea. No idea is ever criticized!
3. As ideas are generated, write each one in large, visible letters on a flipchart or other writing surface.

4. Ideas are generated in turn until each person passes, indicating that the ideas (or members) are exhausted.
5. Review the written list of ideas for clarity and to discard any duplicates.[64]

The best way to begin brainstorming is to imagine a potential team member being interviewed for a job in the organization. While it is clear to the interviewee what job needs to be done, she asks what it takes to be successful in the doing of the job: "I know what my job is, but how do you get ahead in this company?" It can also be helpful to ask participants what values they have tried to impart to their children as they have grown up. The only thing to remember is that the values are about what is desired for the organization and not necessarily about what is currently in place. The Leadership Plan is about where to go tomorrow and it should have an aspirational feel to it.

Answers tend to be similar from organization to organization as the results from Child Care Clearinghouse illustrate:

trustworthy, responsible, on task, on time, fair, honest, safety of kids, keep promises, follow through, reliable, committed to what you're doing, extra step, was it right, do job, responsible, fair, Golden Rule, listening on both sides, objective, consistent, honest, open communication, real, direct feedback, team, team player, cooperative, work with others, flexible, listen, patient, approachable, open, positive attitude, respectful, polite, involved, speak up, ask, two cents, open statements, compromise, empathy, interest in others, play hard, sharing credit (good and bad), humor, at ease, polite, optimistic, jovial, upbeat, positive, lend a hand, support, care, sharing responsibility, cooperate, pick up slack, be a leader, high standards, "I can" versus "I can't," self-confident, planning, organized, think things through, initiative, productive, energetic, creative, inventive (not satisfied with status quo), proactive, focused, never give up, persistent, committed, work hard, diligent, dedicated

Once the group is finished, a basic technique called affinity grouping is used to arrange the answers into common themes that become the final values and values in action. Affinity grouping makes sense of a large number of ideas generated by brainstorming. After generating the ideas, there are just two steps:

1. Sort the idea into related groupings. Post-it® notes make it easy to move ideas around.
2. For each grouping, create summary or header cards using consensus.[65]

Exhibit 5.2 shows an example of the pool of ideas from a brainstorming session that were then affinity grouped into values and values in action.

POOL OF IDEAS	VALUES AND VALUES IN ACTION
trustworthy, responsible on task, on time, fair, honest, safety of kids	**Trust**
keep promises, follow through, reliable, committed to what you're doing, extra step, was it right, do job, responsible	Promises kept
fair, Golden Rule, listening on both sides, objective, consistent	Fair
honest, open communication, real, direct feedback	Truthful without hidden agendas
team, team player, cooperative, work with others, flexible, listen, patient, approachable, open, positive attitude, respectful, polite	**Team**
involved, speak up, ask, two cents, open statements, compromise, empathy, interest in others	Involved (listening and speaking)
play hard, sharing credit (good and bad)	Celebrating together
humor, at ease, polite, optimistic, jovial, upbeat, positive	Optimistic
lend a hand, support, care, sharing responsibility, cooperate, pick up slack	Lending a hand
be a leader, high standards, "I can" versus "I can't," self-confident, planning, organized, think things through, initiative, productive, energetic, creative, inventive (not satisfied with status quo), proactive, focused, never give up, persistent, committed, work hard, diligent, dedicated	**Excellence**
good ego, visibility, encouraging, instill motivation, committed to excellence, know limits, independent thinking, positive self-esteem	Self-confident
willing to take risks, organized, open, knowledgeable, self-directed, outside the box, goals, don't plan air castles, expand themselves	Proactive
diligence, good example, accountable, don't delegate the hard stuff, push yourself, persistence	Persistent

Exhibit 5.2   Affinity Grouping of Values

By using Post-it® notes, affinity grouping and brainstorming are very fast and effective techniques for dealing with many of the elements of a Governance Plan. This is the "one-two" punch that saves precious time yet still invites considerable input and ownership. The only thing to remember in doing the brainstorming–affinity grouping combination is that word-smithing should never be done in the group setting; the person who is facilitating the process should do it. Word-smithing is a creative process that is best left to the artisan and then reviewed and revised later. By delegating the word-smithing to a single person, people are always surprised at how little time it takes to craft beautifully written and very clear statements.

CHAPTER **6**

Vision

He who has a why to live for can bear almost any how.
—Nietzsche

LEADERSHIP PLAN

Where to go tomorrow?

Executive Summary

VALUES	**VISION**
Values	Vision Summary
Values in Action	Mission
	Strategies
	Imperatives
	Success Measures

6.1 INTRODUCTION

As opposed to ambiguous dreaming, a credible vision should be very clear and actionable and go beyond public relations statements or team spirit clichés. It should contain very explicit elements that allow for an obvious understanding of what has to be done. "We will be the best" may be an exciting vision statement and a call to action that impresses donors and staff, but without specificity it will yield very little benefit to the organization once the pep rally is over. Burt Nanus, an acknowledged expert in visionary leadership, defines the vision succinctly:

> *Quite simply,* a vision is a realistic, credible, attractive future for your organization. *It is your articulation of a destination toward which your organization should aim, a future that in important ways is better, more successful, or more desirable for your organization than is the present. . . . Vision is a signpost pointing the way for all who need to understand what the organization is and where it intends to go.*[66]

Nanus goes on to define the characteristics of powerful and transforming visions:

- They are appropriate for the organization and for the times.
- They set standards of excellence.
- They clarify purpose and direction.
- They inspire enthusiasm and encourage commitment.
- They are well articulated and easily understood.
- They reflect the uniqueness of the organization, its distinctive competence, what it stands for, and what it is able to achieve.
- They are ambitious.[67]

Above all else, a good vision must be practical; it must be usable to guide action. In the Governance Plan, a vision cannot perform its work with a meaty statement alone. It must contain rock-solid elements that explicitly answer the question of where to go tomorrow. It will contain a vision summary, mission, imperatives, strategies, and success measures.

6.2 VISION SUMMARY

The vision begins with a summary that describes in a few words the focus of activities for the organization over the next two to three years. While vision summaries can become rallying points for an organization, they are created to simply describe the thrust of the vision. A strategic board using a governance plan doesn't use "leadership by axiom." There are no platitudes seeking to inspire the team with cheerful pictures of mountains or soaring gliders. Even so, a vision summary can be a quick reminder to the organization of exactly what its vision is all about. Rather than describing the whole vision in minute detail, a vision summary can be a quick check, a "Hey, I thought we decided to do this" statement.

Like the executive summary, a vision summary is never crafted first in the process, but is put together after all the other the elements of the Leadership Plan are complete. It is a creative process that is best done by the executive director or the facilitator of the process that builds the Governance Plan for review by the board. "Set the stage for 2003" is an effective vision summary for a performing arts center that will open a new orchestra hall in that year. "Build a foundation to boost the core" is appropriate for a Big Brothers–Big Sisters chapter that wants to improve its infrastructure including its fund-raising capacity so that it can generate more core matches.

6.3 MISSION

The mission is the bedrock of a Governance Plan. It is the fundamental element in a nonprofit organization's success. It is the *reason for being* for the organization, the *why* of its existence. The mission drives all of the other elements of the organization, its activities, and its governance and management structure. The mission takes a global view of the organization. With a properly crafted mission, the organization has driven a *stake in the ground* that can provide an extraordinary amount of guidance in decision making at many levels of the organization. A mission focuses the organization and gives people the cause they so fervently need.

There are many senior managers in nonprofits who believe that the key motivator in the workplace is pay. You may know some of these people. "I remember when a person got a dollar for a dollar's work," they say. "Their paycheck is enough motivation." However, while money is a consideration, it is not as key as we might think or hope it is when it comes to motivating people. Jerry Bowles and Joshua Hammond in *Beyond Quality* subscribe to the following:

> *Quality organizations understand that employees who feel appreciated work harder and produce better products and services for customers. Indeed, more than fifty years ago Western Electric's Hawthorne Works, conducting pioneering studies on the impact of work conditions on productivity, discovered the "Hawthorne Effect," which holds that simply having management pay attention— any kind of attention—to workers automatically increases productivity.*[68]

What can be missed in all this is the obvious fact that cause-driven people need a cause. They need to have it reinforced on a regular basis. When new employees are recruited to the nonprofit, they need to be given a clear understanding of the purpose and how important they are to helping deliver on it. And at every opportunity, the cause needs to be reiterated. The mission that the board creates can provide that clear understanding and purpose.

At about 40 words, the mission is like all the other elements of the Leadership Plan in that it is meant to convey actionable information to the people who will be doing the work. The more specific the answer, the better for the organization. Time is precious and the mission must communicate as precisely as possible so that the professional full-time staff knows what is expected. A tightly conceived mission statement isn't about marketing or public relations; it is a decision-making tool for the organization. From the mission statement will come the strategies, which are akin to lines of business, that bring the mission to life. The more information a mission statement provides, the more specific it is, the more likely that the programs and services that follow as a result will be appropriate. A well-crafted mission addresses the following five points:

1. Ownership
2. Customers
3. Outcome
4. Reputation
5. Summary

Ownership   The Community

Clarifying ownership is the first step in crafting the mission. In the publicly traded for-profit, the ownership is made up of shareholders. While board members usually own shares themselves, they have accountability to represent the interests of all the shareholders. And while customers are critically important, the board is not accountable to them for the performance of the organization. The board is accountable to the shareholders.

In nonprofits there are no equity shareholders, but there certainly are owners in a philosophical context. Whether it is the members who pay dues in a nonprofit association or taxpayers that pay higher taxes through tax-exemption of nonprofits, every nonprofit board has accountability to some ownership. Like its for-profit counterparts, the nonprofit is doing its work on behalf of someone. That someone is not the board or the staff. It generally isn't the funders, although they surely provide much-needed subsidy of services for the clients. It generally isn't the clients or customers themselves.

Defining the owners is critical because board members must not behave as though the organization belongs to them. They must not forget that they are holding the organization in trust for the owners and decisions must be made on their behalf.

A typical United Way has dozens of agencies it supports and it has direct clients who use its information and referral services, but these are not the owners of the United Way. It has hundreds of donors, some quite substantial in their giving, but these people are not the owners. The community owns the United Way. As simplistic as this may seem, clarifying the ownership of the nonprofit organization reminds the board and staff that they are not the owners and that they are beholden to someone other than themselves.

Once the board recognizes that it is accountable to owners, focus is improved. The board isn't working in a vacuum. It must work to stay in close communication with the owners to ensure that the performance of the organization meets with their approval. "What would the ownership want?" becomes a familiar refrain.

Customers

After determining the ownership, the next step is to decide which customers will be served. By beginning with this question, the organization ensures that its customers are its focus. While this is an elemental concept, it is often neglected and deprives the organization of the very focus it needs to be successful. No organization can ever do wrong by focusing first on customers. As Harvey Mackay so aptly says:

> Successful organizations have one common central focus: customers. It doesn't matter if it's a business, a hospital, or a government agency, success comes to those, and only those, who are obsessed with looking after customers.
>
> This wisdom isn't a secret. Mission statements, annual reports, posters on the wall, seminars, and even television programs all proclaim the supremacy of customers. But in the words of Shakespeare, this wisdom is "more honored in the breach than the observance." In fact, generally speaking, customer service, in a word, stinks.
>
> What success I've enjoyed in business, with my books, my public speaking, and the many volunteer community organizations I've worked for, has been due to looking after customers—seeing them as individuals and trying to understand all their needs.[69]

Even with all the evidence, boards frequently worry that if a specific customer is defined, it will be limiting to the scope of activity. Unfortunately, no organization can be all things to all people and defining the customers to be served makes it possible to concentrate effectively. The key issue is to answer the question with authority and explicitness. Youth and children is a good start for a customer description at a Big Brothers–Big

Sisters chapter, but 7- to 13-year-old children from at-risk, single-parent households is much better because it gives more usable information for the construction of strategies.

Deciding the customer question as specifically as possible in the mission statement is critically important. Later on in the Leadership Plan, strategies will be created to bring the mission to life and to serve the customers identified in that mission.

Outcome

The third step in building the mission is to clarify the outcome for the chosen customers. Whether it is health restored for a cancer patient or well-adjusted families for a family-service agency, the outcome is what the customer will experience and should always have the texture of a final destination. The outcome for the customer frequently describes why the organization exists, its reasons for being in business in the first place.

The outcome should always be crafted in the context of the customer, not the organization. What is different for the customer is the question to be answered, not what product will be delivered by the organization. At the mission level, the outcome is global and it is uncommon to see more than one. Later in the process, more detailed customer outcomes are articulated to form strategies, which are analogous to lines of business, products, and programs.

Outcome is used here to describe what difference will be made in the life of the customer served. What change will occur as a result of the work that the organization does? Outcome is not about the organization; it is about the customer. The typical mission statement tells us all about the products and services provided by the organization; its essence is the organization, not the customer. The mission of a strategic board in the Governance Plan informs us about the life-changing difference that will be made for the customer through the eyes of that customer.

Life at its fullest is an example of a customer outcome for a person affected with multiple sclerosis. A performing arts center could easily consider an *enriched life* as a viable customer outcome. After all, the customer isn't going to the theater to just see a play or hear a symphony. The performance itself is actually a means to an end. That end is the outcome that the customer will have, which begins with the telephone call for tickets and ends when they arrive safely home after the performance. That same performing arts center might also use *standing-ovation experience* as an outcome statement.

A Chamber of Commerce responds to the question of outcome with "We provide information and referral services to business, group purchasing opportunities, business counseling and education services, and programming which meets the needs of our members." This does not answer the outcome correctly, however, because it is about the programs and services that the Chamber provides, not about what difference is made for its customers. It would be better for the Chamber to first determine what difference it intends to make for its customers before it moves to the strategies that will cause that difference to happen. An outcome of making business more profitable, for example, may inspire much different strategies than those from an outcome of making business more efficient.

Save the Children's outcome is to make *lasting positive change in the lives of disadvantaged children*. While this is very broad and some might prefer more definition, this is a properly crafted outcome and one that can give rise to significant strategies that can bring it about. A Big Brothers–Big Sisters chapter outcome is to *build confident, competent, and caring young adults*. This outcome was distilled from the following outcome possibilities:

> *making a difference, improving kid's life, respectful of self and others, get along*
> *with others, making good decisions, more respect, better grades in school, higher*
> *self-esteem, confident child, values, understanding, productive adult, social*
> *responsibility, the same results of a two-parent household, the foundation to grow*
> *into a confident-competent-caring adult, safe-secure-supported, well-rounded child*

While the chosen outcome of a confident, competent, and caring young adult is somewhat ambiguous, there can be no mistake that the organization is engaged in making a fundamental difference in the lives of young adults.

Most Multiple Sclerosis Society chapters will produce programs to help the newly diagnosed, update education to keep those afflicted current, provide funding for research, direct disbursements for those without means, and provide support groups to help people network with each other. Not one of these programs and services belongs in a mission statement because they do not answer the question of outcome. These are all about what the chapter does, what it makes, what it sells, its lines of business, what a Governance Plan calls strategies. The chapter's outcome is best described with *Life at its fullest for people affected by multiple sclerosis*. The difference that the local chapter makes is that a person afflicted by multiple sclerosis lives life at its fullest under his or her particular circumstances. Once this outcome is defined, programs and services that make up the strategies of the organization become easier to formulate.

Reputation

The fourth question in crafting the mission is *What reputation?* What particular strength will the organization be known for, and what reputation will the organization gain? What edge will the organization have that other organizations cannot match? A United Way, for example, decided on *uniting the community in an efficient and accountable manner.* A performing arts center decided upon *making the customer the star.*

The answer to the question of reputation provides definition to the management of the organization about what central theme should flow through implementation. A Girl Scout council might choose *scouting for all girls* as an answer, thereby defining inclusiveness as a core theme. Often organizations will look to the values and select one above all others that will be brought into the mission as its reputation statement.

Every organization has a choice in what it becomes known for. This choice is about the edge that the organization will have over all others like it, the defining quality of its work. What do we want to be known for, respected for? A Big Brothers–Big Sisters chapter looked at the following possibilities:

> *proven results, ongoing end-to-end professional support, through a 1-to-1 match, protect kids, brand name, confidence in the brand, national standards, produce results, history*

They chose professionally supported one-to-one matches that deliver results. There are other mentoring programs in the community, but none that can match the professional support and the results that are delivered. An agency with the outcome of putting the American Dream of a home within reach for people with low to moderate incomes decided that being the "go-to organization" would become its reputation. No other agency in the community would be able to match its position for one-stop shopping, for the breadth of its knowledge and services. "Here is what we will be known for in the delivery of the outcome" is the essence of the reputation element in a mission statement.

Mission Summary

Even though missions are typically short, they are not brief enough to serve as succinct summary statements. As John Kotter says, "If you can't communicate the vision to someone in five minutes or less and get a reaction that signifies both understanding and interest, you are not yet done."[70] Because the outcome statement is usually four to six words long, it often becomes the mission summary, the "T-shirt" message for the organization, the letterhead footer. *People helping people in need today* is the mission summary of a United Way. *Life at its fullest* is the summary for an MS chapter. Fannie Mae uses *We're in the American Dream business.* The Big Brothers–Big Sisters chapter highlighted above with an outcome of building confident, competent, and caring young adults picked *Building young adults.* Some organizations will choose the reputation statement. *You are the star* is the mission summary of the Victoria Theatre Association; Lenscrafters® uses *In about an hour!*

The mission summary has great value to the organization, especially for people who will be doing the work. Even at only 40 words, a mission statement is difficult to remember. The mission summary takes the most important feature of the mission and distills it down into just a few words. It can become a rallying point for decision making and a constant reminder to board members, staff, and volunteers about the organization's mission.

Think about the mission summary as the gateway to the mission. If the front-line people doing the work can only remember four or five words as a guide to making the right decision, what words should they be?

Eventually, if an organization lives with the mission summary long enough, the odds are very good that everyone close to the organization, including its customers, will know it and hold the organization accountable to it. At that point, the organization will have become truly mission-centered. That is, someone, somewhere will need to make a decision and they will recall that short mission summary; it will give them guidance, and they will make the right decision, one that is aligned with the mission of the organization. This is what it means to be mission-centered or mission-driven. It's not that everyone can recite the mission, it is that everyone's work is driven by it.

The Victoria Theatre Association uses a mission summary of *You are the star.* It has been in place for many years, published on T-shirts, jackets, and stationery, and is prominently displayed in every place imaginable including tickets and lapel pins. It is mentioned in curtain speeches and in radio commercials. So well-known is this mission summary that customers will remind box office employees or ushers about it if things aren't quite up to standard. That's what it can mean to get the message of a mission out to the community: The customers know the mission and hold the organization accountable for delivering it.

In the following three examples of well-constructed missions, most of the elements have been effectively addressed, which provides the necessary information that can bring these missions to life through appropriately developed strategies:

Mission from a Fundraising Organization

Bringing the community together to provide resources that help. ⇐summary

On behalf of the citizens of our community, ⇐ownership

the Fundraising Federation brings the community together to provide resources that help ⇐reputation

people in need or at risk ⇐customers

solve their problems. ⇐outcome

Mission from a Housing Development Agency

A home within reach. ⇐summary

On behalf of the seven-county community, ⇐owners

we are the "go-to" organization ⇐reputation

that puts the American Dream of a home within reach ⇐outcome

for people with low to moderate incomes. ⇐customers

Mission from the Victoria Theatre Association

You are the star! ⇐summary

Enriching life ⇐outcome

on behalf of our diverse Miami Valley community ⇐owners

for adults, families and school children throughout our region ⇐customers

by making our customer the star. ⇐reputation

The inescapable question about these mission statements is whether they are too simple. That the missions are straightforward and elegantly simple is exactly the point. No one benefits from confusion about the mission of the organization. Meaningful action must be driven by an explicitly clear mission. As a core driver of decision-making, the complicated mission that no one can recall or understand serves little value to the organization. The simpler the mission, the better, and the more likely it will drive action on the front lines of work. Keep it short and simple, hammer away at it at every chance, and the likelihood is that it will come to life.

Boards that decide to use the Strategic Board model of governance sometimes struggle with letting go of old mission statements. They like the feel of the words or the historical context. There is no issue whatsoever with using previously created mission statements in a Governance Plan provided that the mission explicitly addresses the five points with authority. Take the comparison in Exhibit 6.1 of before-and-after mission statements from a

Big Brothers–Big Sisters chapter. Which of the two mission statements is better? The new mission has the edge because it offers more specific information to inform decisions. The strategic board has one chief obligation and that is to achieve the chosen destiny. This requires that every element of the Governance Plan be actionable, usable by real people who must get things done. Less is more; definite is better than ambiguous.

MAJOR ELEMENTS		
CURRENT MISSION		**NEW MISSION**
	⇐summary⇒	Building young adults
	⇐owners⇒	on behalf of the three-county community
children and youth	⇐customers⇒	7- to 13-year-old children from at-risk, single-parent households
committed to making a positive difference, assist them in achieving their highest potential, grow to become confident, competent, and caring individuals	⇐outcome⇒	builds confident, competent, and caring young adults
primarily through a professionally supported one-to-one relationship	⇐reputation⇒	through professionally supported one-to-one matches that deliver results

COMPLETE STATEMENTS	
CURRENT MISSION	**NEW MISSION**
Big Brothers–Big Sisters, Inc. is committed to making a positive difference in the lives of children and youth, primarily through a professionally supported one-to-one relationship, and to assist them in achieving their highest potential as they grow to become confident, competent, and caring individuals.	On behalf of the three-county community, Big Brothers–Big Sisters builds 7- to 13-year-old children from at-risk, single-parent households into confident, competent, and caring young adults through professionally supported one-to-one matches that deliver results.

Exhibit 6.1 Before-and-After Mission Statement of a Big Brothers–Big Sisters Chapter

Like the process for values and values in action, building a mission begins with ideas generated in a group setting, which are then distilled into a final result. The responses are unique to each organization, but the following results from a Big Brothers–Big Sisters chapter provides a useful illustration of how the process works:

POOL OF IDEAS	MISSION
tri-county community, taxpayers, donors-supporters, children-families, board, volunteers, the public	On behalf of the three-county community, Big Brothers–Big Sisters
primarily elementary-aged kids, 7- to 13-year olds at time of match, tri-county kids, single-parent household, at-risk	builds 7- to 13-year-old children from single-parent households
making a difference, improving kid's life, respectful of self and others, get along with others, making good decisions, more respect, better grades in school, higher self-esteem, confident child, values, understanding, productive adult, social responsibility, the same results of a two-parent household, the foundation to grow into a confident-competent-caring adult, safe-secure-supported, well-rounded child	into confident, competent, and caring young adults
proven results, ongoing end-to-end professional support, through a 1-to-1 match, protect kids, brand name, confidence in the brand, national standards, produce results, history	through professionally supported one-to-one matches that deliver results.

6.4 STRATEGIES

A mission statement is meant to drive strategies. Strategies are the lines of business for the organization, the programs and services, the products. Strategies are how the mission will be brought to life and represent the organization's major brands. In the vision, it's where the rubber meets the road.

Many nonprofits have difficulty at first thinking in terms of strategies. Having lines of business seems to be an acceptable idea for a car manufacturer, but it's a foreign concept when it comes to a housing agency or mentoring organization. It doesn't take long, however, for the organization to get the hang of things when the question is asked in the context of core programs or services.

Strategies are distinguished from other activities within the organization because like the mission, they are ends, not means. They must stand the customer-outcome test. First, there must be a specific and clearly articulated customer external to the organization that will be changed as a result of the strategy. Second, there must be an outcome, the life-changing difference that will be made for that customer.

Strategies are constructed within the context and order of the following three questions:

1. What strategies do we have *now?*
2. What are the opportunities for *new* strategies?
3. What strategies should *not* be done?

What Strategies Do We Have *Now?*

The first step for determining the organization's strategies is to understand the strategies now in place. Some people involved with the organization may profess little interest in generating a list of current strategies because "We already know what we do," but board members and staff alike are many times surprised to see the breadth of strategies. What they thought was a two- or three-program organization turns out to be much more dynamic. In the process, some companies decide that the array of strategies is simply too broad to sustain; other organizations choose to expand.

Drafting the list of current strategies is straightforward and takes very little time. The benefit for the knowledgeable board member is to see the wide array of strategies; the benefit for the new board member is to see them for the first time. A United Way quickly identified its 14 key strategies:

1. Research, problems identified and prioritized
2. Resource Development, investing for high-impact solutions
3. Resource Distribution, nurturing children
4. Resource Distribution, strengthening families
5. Resource Distribution, building communities
6. Resource Distribution, eliminating abuse and neglect
7. Resource Distribution, encouraging self-sufficiency
8. Management Services, Baby Steps, healthy infants
9. Management Services, Immunization Track, healthy preschoolers
10. Management Services, Preschool-Jump-Start, preschoolers ready to learn
11. Links, the link to high-impact solutions
12. Labor and Community Services, high-impact solutions in the workplace
13. Heartland, fostering high-impact problem solvers in nonurban areas
14. Outcomers, results-driven problem solvers

Fourteen strategies are not an uncommon number for an active United Way, but it is too broad to be comprehensible to most people, especially board members challenged by the seven realities. By grouping the strategies by theme, this particular United Way was able to reduce the group into four categories:

1. Research, problems identified and prioritized
2. Resource Development, investing for high-impact solutions
3. Resource Distribution, funding for high-impact problem solvers
   - Nurturing children
   - Strengthening families
   - Building communities
   - Eliminating abuse and neglect
   - Encouraging self-sufficiency
4. Initiatives, leading solutions for the community
   - Management Services, incubating high-impact problem solvers
     - Baby Steps, healthy infants
     - Immunization Track, healthy preschoolers
     - Preschool-Jump-Start, preschoolers ready to learn
   - Links, the web link to high-impact solutions
   - Labor and Community Services, high-impact solutions in the workplace

- Heartland, fostering high-impact problem solvers in nonurban areas
- Outcomers, results-driven problem solvers

The level of detailing within strategies, the number of strategies, should stop when it becomes difficult to develop reasonable customer-outcome statements. This will depend on many variables including size and complexity of the organization. Because this list is still too complicated, Exhibit 6.2 is used to make it more coherent. The value of such a simple format is that it makes it much easier for everyone to understand the work of the organization, the ends that bring the mission to life. This is especially important in light of the seven realities of the nonprofit board and the first guidepost of the strategic board that *everything should be made as simple as possible, but not simpler.*

In Exhibit 6.2, Initiatives contains five strategies including Management Services, which itself holds three strategies. While Baby Steps has a

Research	Resource	Resource	Initiatives	
Problems identified and prioritized	**Development** Investments for high-impact solutions	**Distribution** Funding high-impact problem solvers	Leading solutions for the community	
		• Nurturing children	**Management Services** Incubating high-impact problem solvers	**Heartland** Fostering high-impact problem solvers in nonurban areas
		• Strengthening families		
		• Building communities	• Baby Steps • Immunization Track • Preschool-Jump-Start	**Outcomers** Results-driven problem solvers
		• Eliminating abuse and neglect	**Links**	
		• Encouraging self-sufficiency	The web link to high-impact solutions	**Labor and Community Services** High-impact solutions in the workplace

Exhibit 6.2   Sample Strategies

customer-outcome statement of healthy infants, it is not shown in the illustration for two reasons. First, this conveys its place relative in importance to other strategies. Second, it is easier for the reader to comprehend the full scope of the organization without it. This is not to say that Baby Steps is unimportant, but it is to say that presenting information in a comprehensible fashion is more significant throughout the Governance Plan.

The best way to present the Governance Plan is on a regular sheet of paper in vertical orientation with comfortable margins and a readable font. This forces economy of thinking, which is very valuable to the board member with limited time. A perfectly accurate presentation that is mind-numbing in its detail or impossible to read is worthless. Choices have to be made about what is important and what is not, which includes the decision not to include a customer-outcome for Baby Steps. Later on in the success measures, Baby Steps will still be grouped within Management Services, but it will have its own success measures.

Some staff and board members become concerned about the relative importance of the strategies to operational areas. They wonder why marketing or fundraising aren't strategies, given their importance. No one would deny that raising funds is central to success in most nonprofits, but it does not pass the customer-outcome test and it is consequently not a strategy except for agencies like United Way. Under no circumstances does a strategic board diminish the importance of raising money or maintaining buildings or keeping accurate financial records. These are vitally important to the success of the organization. Nonetheless, these are means to an end, not ends in themselves, and they are not strategies.

What Are the Opportunities for *New* Strategies?

The second step in the process of building strategies is to consider the possibilities for new strategies. Information that can inform this discussion can be provided by forecasts, situational analysis, focus groups, and external information gathering including other companies in similar industries or with similar processes. Thinking about the strengths of the organization that can be built upon, niches that can be filled, and best practices from other, similar organizations all add up to possible opportunities.

As with many processes for thinking about the future, building a Governance Plan offers the chance to use the *SWOT analysis*, which is described by John Kay:

> *The best and most familiar example of an organizing framework is SWOT*
> *analysis—the definition of strengths, weaknesses, opportunities, and threats that*
> *the business faces. SWOT is simply a list. It conveys no information in itself but is*

a way of helping us think about the information we already have. For a busy manager, confronted by endless everyday pressures and unused to standing back to think about longer term issues, it is a particularly useful list, as demonstrated by its continued popularity.[71]

SWOT analysis is done in two stages. Strengths and opportunities are reviewed when thinking about new strategies. Weaknesses and threats are reviewed when the discussion occurs about what strategies should not be followed.

The executive director and professional staff members often are the bearers of the opportunities for new strategies. These professionals usually have the experience to be up-to-date and knowledgeable about the organization's field and they may have a better feel than board members for opportunities. Asking the staff to come to the discussions with a variety of possibilities already identified can be a very legitimate approach to begin thinking about new strategies. If time and interest are available, the homework on opportunities can be very open to board and staff joint investigations. Thinking about opportunities can also be a superb ongoing tool for board education. One board annually puts together a task force to travel to other cities and investigate best practices and opportunities.

It is particularly important to avoid management-driven thinking about opportunities. Remember that management-driven thinking asks, "Where are we today?" and builds the future from there. Leadership-driven planning begins with the question, "Where do we want to go?" The opportunities are paramount when thinking about new strategies, not problems. Looking deeply into all the current constraints and difficulties, the blemishes and wrinkles, comes later. Now is the time for sky-down thinking.

What Strategies Should *Not* Be Done?

Once a list of opportunities is developed and clarified, the usual approach is for the new strategies to be fleshed out by the staff and then brought back to the group working on the Governance Plan for the third stage of the process. This final stage decides what strategies should not be done and it includes a frank discussion of both the current strategies and the new opportunities. It includes three distinct elements: obstacles, criteria, and deciding.

Sometimes during the process of thinking about new strategies, staff can become defensive and concerned about "reinventing the wheel." Boards can be expansive about opportunities without recognizing the difficulties inherent in bringing new strategies on line. The possibility of adding something new to the mix can be quite unsettling to an already overburdened staff. Fortunately, unlike the search for new opportunities, which has a clear sky-down flavor to it, this phase has a very down-to-earth texture. Management-driven thinking is welcome here by the bushel.

Obstacles are about the realities of the organization, its weaknesses and threats, the problems that must be solved in order for the organization to succeed, its obstacles to success. This reflection about obstacles holding the organization back can go under a variety of names, including performance audit, vision audit, and capacity review. The central idea is to develop a clear understanding of the capacities of the organization to determine whether it can actually succeed at the strategies on the table, including both new and current ones. Therefore, there must be a sincere willingness on the part of the participants to look at those obstacles holding the organization back because strategies not based upon reality are delusions.

In a quick installation of The Strategic Board model of governance, looking at threats and weaknesses in a very brief review identifies obstacles. For organizations that have more time and that want to explore these concerns about capacity in more depth, the discussion can actually be extensive. Many organizations choose the quick installation and do more extensive investigations into capacity as a preview to building the next Governance Plan. Like the exploration for opportunities, a thorough exploration into the organization's obstacles to success can be a great education tool for the board. Obstacles should address three points:

1. Problems
2. Weaknesses
3. Threats

Exhibit 6.3 is a sample list of obstacles from a typical organization.

Even armed with a clear understanding of the obstacles, the process for deciding what strategies should stay or go is never easy. That's why time is taken to develop criteria for decision making. Since many of the ideas that could be used for criteria such as values and mission, strengths, weaknesses, opportunities, and threats have already been decided, it is common to see these included. The discussion of what criteria should be used for deciding strategies is often as stimulating as the search for opportunities and the understanding of obstacles. A list from a human service agency is as follows:

- Plays to strengths
- Growth potential
- Profitable
- Responds to threats

- Maintains values
- Minimizes weaknesses
- Achievable
- Something extraordinary
- Drives and motivates
- Mission fit

POOL OF IDEAS	OBSTACLES
lack of education about United Way, perception, lack of understanding of need, times are good, apathy toward giving, confusion of terminology, communication, lack of clarity, marketing and communication message	lack of clarity in the community about United Way
left behind by technology, stagnation of United Way	stagnation
inefficiency of not giving directly, community foundation, watch market share, competition for funds, give directly, unpredictability of donor choice	competition for funds
number of volunteers, quality of leadership, less volunteer time	availability of volunteers
county perspective versus regional perspective, changing employee base, lack of county involvement, limited service delivery	county perspective versus regional needs
changing companies, lack of corporate pledge increases, employer ratio, economic realities of community, lack of leadership giving expertise	economic environment
agency versus United Way attitudes	agency relations

Exhibit 6.3   Sample Obstacles

In the decision-making stage of what strategies should not be done, strategies that cannot be discarded or changed are removed from the discussion. For-profit companies may be adept at exiting strategies and selling off brands, but it would be unthinkable for most nonprofits to exit core strategies as skillfully. A United Way, for example, cannot simply decide to stop raising money; a suicide prevention agency cannot suddenly become a service provider to Alzheimer's patients and abandon its responsibilities to dependent clients.

Strategies open for consideration are ranked against the criteria and a go-or-no decision is made. Ranking tools go from a quick and simple method to more complicated approaches, including those that Burt Nanus profiles in his *Visionary Leadership*.[72] Exhibit 6.4 is the output from an actual discussion about strategies for a human service organization using a program similar to Nanus's.

An organization going for a quick installation of the Strategic Board model of governance would use the fast multivoting technique where a green dot equals three points, a yellow dot equals two points, and a red dot equals one point. Each person gets the three dots to distribute on any combination of strategies: They can put all their dots on one strategy if they want or spread the dots around. Simply adding up the dots yields a strong sense of priority. It isn't as rigorous as the other method, but it gets the job done quickly and the process can be revisited later in more detail when building the next Governance Plan or in a special session with the board.

Many organizations decide not to do anything different at all with regard to changing, dropping, or adding strategies and wait until the next cycle to confront these questions. Other nonprofits have an immediate reaction and finally make the difficult decision to terminate a strategy that has been troubled or take a leap of faith and launch a new one. One United Way, for example, decided to exit all of its direct services including its information and referral business to focus exclusively on fundraising opportunities.

The process of understanding current strategies, developing opportunities, and deciding which of these not to pursue is an exciting time and intellectually refreshing provided that everyone keeps an open mind and concentrates on issues as opposed to people. This is not a time for finger pointing about failures. As Deming says, "Workers are responsible for only 15 percent of the problems, the system for the other 85 percent."[73] Keep the focus on the organization and off the people. By doing so, confidence is maintained, enthusiasm boosted, and a common problem according to Deming is avoided: "Some people have the very nasty habit of saying, 'Why didn't you do it right the first time? Then you wouldn't have to do it over again.' That's a terrible detriment to progress, because you won't do anything. It's like asking why the Wright brothers didn't design the 747 first."[74]

STRATEGIES SELECTION CRITERIA	STRATEGIES								
	WT.	A	B	C	D	E	F	G	H
Plays to strengths	10	41	63	69	75	70	65	57	46
Growth potential	9	90	90	90	63	90	63	54	63
Profitable	10	60	80	50	40	90	20	40	40
Responds to threats	10	22	52	50	28	33	23	25	24
Maintains values	10	77	75	77	85	77	85	81	88
Minimizes weaknesses	10	25	36	36	30	38	10	27	27
Achievable	5	25	10	20	10	35	20	45	40
Something extraordinary	10	40	90	90	80	80	100	30	60
Drives and motivates	10	60	70	80	60	100	60	90	50
Mission fit	10	56	40	48	80	64	72	72	64
Total		496	606	610	551	677	518	521	502

Exhibit 6.4   Ranking Strategies

Once decided, all of the strategies are framed into customer-outcome statements by the following questions:

- Which customers?
- What outcomes?

These customer-outcome statements are very important for conveying expectations. Without the statements, the organization would have only a list of programs or services. With the statements, the people responsible for bringing the strategies to life have a clear understanding of what is expected through the eyes of the customer. Consequently, the strategies have a far greater likelihood of succeeding.

Exhibit 6.5 illustrates strategies from two different organizations. Notice in the performing arts center's strategies that a place has been made to carry forward ideas for future exploration.

Thinking about strategies lies at the heart of the board's ongoing work. If the mission is the key driver of the vision, strategies are the workhorse. Spending effort and time on strategies can be one of the most

VICTORIA THEATRE ASSOCIATION STRATEGIES

Broadway Series
Sit back and enjoy for adults

Star Extras
Blockbuster memories for adults

Next Stage
Theatre for the mind for adults

Young at Heart
Quality Play Time for families with children grades K–4

Hot Times—Cool Films
Remember when for older adults

Jubilee
A sense of belonging for everyone

Victoria Children's Festival
I had fun! for families with children ages 4–13

Discovery
Enriched classrooms for school children and teachers in grades K–8
• Education Series
• In-School Workshops
• Muse Machine Tickets

Arts Center Management
A downtown source of pride for the Miami Valley

• Main Street Theatre
• Community Arts Center

Strategies to Explore
Setting the stage for future audiences
• Summer Stages
• Dayton Comedy Festival
• Camp Broadway
• New diversity initiatives
• New education initiatives
• New hall management

MODEL MULTIPLE SCLEROSIS SOCIETY CHAPTER STRATEGIES

Connections
You're not alone for the newly diagnosed with MS
• MS Peer Connection
• Moving Forward
• Knowledge Is Power

Conferences
Staying current for those living with MS
• Fall Education Conference
• National Television Conference

Research
Ending the devastating effects for all those affected
• National Research Allocation

Support Groups
Living the fullest life possible for those living with MS

Direct Assistance
Solutions for those without means
• Equipment
• Direct Counseling
• Referral Counseling

Exhibit 6.5 Sample Strategies

exciting activities for board members and staff alike. It provides much of the "clear, elevating goal"[75] that Larson and LaFasto say is so essential to building an effective team.

6.5 IMPERATIVES

For a long time, many boards and professional staff have operated under the assumption that boards decide, staff implement. The idea that boards make policy and staff members implement it is as old as the sector itself. Boards decide what; staff decide how. Boards set policy; staff executes it. Cyril Houle observes this pattern in his *Governing Boards:*

> Many authorities on boards have enunciated a single, fundamental rule by which to define the function of the board as contrasted to the function of the executive. Most frequently they say, often with an air of profundity, that the board should determine policy and the executive should carry it out. Brian O'Connell has responded succinctly, "This is just not so" and has called that distinction "the worst illusion ever perpetrated in the nonprofit field."[76]

Houle's thrust is that the board has a broader scope of interest that may extend into the operations of the organization:

> Whenever the board can, it should stay at the level of generality and not specificity, consider categories of problems rather than individual difficulties, plan for long-range developments, and put the program in the larger perspective of the whole community. The executive, on the other hand, must recognize that hers is the immediate responsibility, that she must manage each situation as it arises, and that she should express the importance of her field of expertness in the application of general principles to specific cases.[77]

Thus, the board is general; the executive director is immediate. It is easy to say that the board's work is to decide the question of where to go tomorrow and that it is the staff's work to deliver on what gets done today. There will always be advocates of this sharp distinction between the board and the executive director where no questioning of operations is invited. Yet the Aramony scandal should have taught all nonprofits a lesson that the board does have an interest in the manner in which business is conducted, in the operations of the organization, and in the details that are customarily considered the purview of the executive director.

This causes an inevitable puzzle: How can the board stay at the level of generality and consider categories of problems while still respecting the chain of command so necessary to ensure accountability? There may indeed be a need to draw a clear line between the work of the board and that of the staff, between the ends to be accomplished and the means to get it done. At the same time, the board carries the ultimate accountability for the organization, including the values in action of its professional staff. If the board begins to probe into the organization's day-to-day operations, the executive director may very rightly perceive this to be a vote of no confidence.

Despite these misgivings, the board has an interest in the operations of the organization. No board wants to get into the business of managing the organization, but no board wants to create a vacuum between itself and the day-to-day operations. Take, for example, an organization that announces the departure of two senior staff members in six weeks, one a nine-year veteran, the other a four-year veteran. Shouldn't the board have interest in this? An organization with short staff tenures is going to have difficulty accomplishing its goals and thus merits the concern of the board. The answer depends upon many circumstances. How large is the senior staff? What were the circumstances? Is this a continuing pattern? What sort of tenures do the other senior staff members have?

The board has an obligation to ask tough questions about the organization and the executive director has an obligation to answer them with the "truth, the whole truth, and nothing but the truth," but the board must strike the right balance between asking and telling, asking and demoralizing, or asking and breaching the chain of command. The process of asking tough questions should allow sensitive issues to be put on the table in a meaningful, respectful, and reasonable way as opposed to the random, knee-jerk, often demotivating manner that so often characterizes the process.

The fact is that boards struggle with striking a balance between asking tough questions and being supporters of the executive director. Chait, Holland, and Taylor observe this contradiction in *Improving the Performance of Governing Boards:*

> *Both professional staff and the literature on trusteeship consistently advise governing boards to be objective stewards. Trustees are expected to rise above parochial interests and personal biases in order to make decisions that are in the best interests of the long-term welfare of the institution.*
>
> *At the same time, the professional staff want board members to be committed, psychologically and financially, to the institution. The trustees are encouraged to be ardent advocates and generous contributors; however, as the board's ardor intensifies, objectivity may decrease.*

In short, boards constantly wrestle with when to be "product champions" and when to be studied neutrals—whether to stand and cheer like rabid partisans in Congress when the President of the United States delivers the State of the Union address, or to remain seated and stone-faced like Supreme Court justices who may be called upon some day to decide the constitutionality of the matter at hand.

It's easy to support the executive director and the staff; it's much harder to ask the tough questions. The way to help everyone be comfortable with asking tough questions about operating issues that are essentially the purview of the executive director is by putting them on the table upfront in the form of imperatives. Imperatives in the Governance Plan are defined as the major obstacles that stand between the organization and its success.

By reviewing the obstacles of the organization created during the strategies process and selecting one or two to be imperatives, the board makes sure that these issues will remain in focus. It ensures that these issues will be discussed and updated throughout the year as part of a well-defined Vigilance Plan. A housing agency used the following as its first cut for its imperatives:

POOL OF IDEAS	IMPERATIVES
working alone, infrastructure in neighborhoods—who's doing it, social problems, no coordinated effort in neighborhood	no coordinated effort to make neighborhoods better
are we duplicating, duplication of services, competition, St. Mary's, competition for financing, compliance of funding, credit issues, sources of funding	competition
adequate staff	inadequate staffing
30 percent of board needs to be low to moderate income, time, new board, unknowledgeable board members, board structure issues	board structure issues
housing stock	housing stock

After this first round, the organization chose the following as the imperatives:

- No coordinated effort to make neighborhoods better
- Inadequate staffing

These two imperatives are in fact both obstacles and opportunities. The housing agency by solving the coordination imperative becomes the "go-to" source in the community. Dealing with the issue of adequate staff, a chronic obstacle for many nonprofits, will build organizational capacity to implement its strategies effectively.

For executive directors and staff members who are concerned about overreaching in the strategies, the imperatives give them the opportunity to put these major obstacles up on the radar screen for the board to see. Imperatives introduce realism into the Leadership Plan and help everyone to remember that tomorrow's dreams eventually have to become today's work.

6.6 SUCCESS MEASURES

If the shareholder wants to know how the for-profit company is doing, the measure is generally taken at the bottom-line. Whatever it's called, be it shareholder wealth, net profit, share price, or return on investment, for-profits depend on financial information as a fundamental measure of their success. Nonprofits, on the other hand, are almost antifinancial when it comes to measuring strategies. "There is no single measure of success, or even of progress, that is analogous to the proverbial bottom-line for a business,"[78] says William Bowen.

The bottom-line for nonprofits is that if the financial condition is reasonably close to balanced, it's often a nonissue. It's not that nonprofits don't have measures of success. It's just that most of them aren't financial and most aren't written down. Nonprofits often have success measures based in the quality of things, but this is very challenging because it's softer in texture. "How much" is much easier to measure than "how good" or "what good."

Given the seven realities of nonprofit boards, the more that is known about how success will be measured, the better it is for the board and staff. First, having an explicit understanding about success measures provides a common vocabulary for monitoring performance. Thus, people with widely differing viewpoints can be on the same page when it comes to evaluating the work of the organization. Gone is the muddle of trying to decide what should be evaluated every time the issue of performance comes up or worse, using purely economic measures only because they're easy to come by.

Second, the executive director and the board can understand exactly what it means to achieve meaningful results. In addition to giving all participants a level playing field when it comes to performance, success measures offer the board and staff an agreed-upon platform for celebrating success or correcting deviations and perhaps for incentive compensation provided that it is based on measurable results that the employee has control over. Even better, this platform of success measures is readily available and preapproved by the board.

Third, success measures provide meaningful information that can make fundraising harder hitting in the case statement and provide required data for compliance reporting. Are you looking for a list of things to highlight in the newsletter or annual report? It comes ready-made in the success measures.

Perhaps the most important asset of success measures lies in a quote by Maison Haire, "What gets measured, gets done." Having an agreed-upon set of success measures that the board and executive director are vigilant about monitoring creates a much greater likelihood of actually achieving the desired results. Later in the Management Plan, when the staff and board must decide on what gets done today to implement the Leadership Plan, the success measures provide valuable guidance on where to focus attention. These measures seamlessly connect the Leadership Plan of where to go tomorrow with the Management Plan of what gets done today.

By connecting the thinking about tomorrow with the work that gets done today, the likelihood of action is high and the chances that the Governance Plan will gather dust on a bookshelf are low. Instead of crafting a plan and throwing it over the wall to the departments where it will languish, the success measures force a feedback loop that is useful to everyone.

The benefit of deciding success measures often first comes from the discussions and inevitable soul-searching that arises in deciding which ones to use. Vitally important questions of priorities become apparent; issues about precious resources of money and time are verbalized. For many boards, deciding success measures often presents the first opportunity ever to think about what is truly important and what is merely trivial. Says William Bowen, "Efforts to develop key indicators can be the occasion for a nonprofit board to think seriously (perhaps for the first time) about what really matters to the organization."[79]

Exhibit 6.6 illustrates success measures coming from a performing arts center, which has been using the Strategic Board model of governance

MISSION

	'96–'97	'97–'98	'98–'99	'99–'00 Budget	'99–'00 12/31 YE Forecast	'99–'00 Final	'00–'01 Budget	'01–'02
Total attendance	279K	288K	284K	294K	292K	284K	269K	285K
Total income	6.17M	6.99M	7.75M	7.95M	8.38M	8.78M	7.76M	7.89M
Earned-to-contributed	76/24	79/21	80/20	81/19	80/20	81/19	78/22	78/22
Net income	148K	99K	−79K	0	164K	99K	0	0

STRATEGIES

BROADWAY SERIES

	'96–'97	'97–'98	'98–'99	'99–'00 Budget	'99–'00 12/31 YE Forecast	'99–'00 Final	'00–'01 Budget	'01–'02
Total attendance	107.3K	101.0K	104.0K	103.9K	104.7K	106.6K	106.5K	103.0K
Subscriptions	15,727	14,421	14,708	14,400	14,525	14,525	15,000	14,700
Single tickets	13,000	14,500	15,790	17,500	17,500	19,423	16,500	14,800
Intermission walkouts	.039	.035	.014	.020	.030	.047	.025	.025
Gross sales	2.60M	2.78M	3.07M	3.10M	3.39M	3.39M	3.62M	3.68M
Renewal rate	.86	.80	.90	.84	.85	.85	.87	.86

REGIONAL THEATRE SERIES

	'96–'97	'97–'98	'98–'99	'99–'00 Budget	'99–'00 12/31 YE Forecast	'99–'00 Final	'00–'01 Budget	'01–'02
Total attendance		24,509	25,336	18,650	16,985	16,720	14,900	15,300
Subscriptions		2,237	2,379	2,500	2,397	2,397	2,600	2,900
Single tickets		13,324	13,440	6,150	5,000	4,735	4,500	3,700
Gross sales		566K	691K	495K	412K	414K	359K	406K
Renewal rate			.70	.67	.73	.73	.63	.68

Exhibit 6.6   Sample Success Measures

EDUCATION SERIES

	'96–'97	'97–'98	'98–'99	'99–'00 Budget	'99–'00 12/31 YE Forecast	Final	'00–'01 Budget	'01–'02
Total attendance	81,002	91,118	73,736	74,500	76,175	61,240	71,910	80,000
Gross sales	169K	184K	160K	198K	182K	160K	192K	202K
Percentage paid	.52	.47	.56	.65	.65	.65	.65	.65
Renewal rate	.68	.71	.73	.75	.78	.78	.80	.80
Workshop attendance	240	1,920	2,010	3,000	2,250	3,000	3,000	3,000

Exhibit 6.6   Sample Success Measures (*continued*)

method for a number of years. These particular success measures are ready for presentation to the board of trustees at a meeting that will focus on strategies and imperatives for the new fiscal year. The format of success measures is self-explanatory with the exception of the current year, in this case the 1999–2000 season. The board approved the budget column in this three-column section when it passed this version of the Governance Plan. The 12/31 year-end forecast column was presented to the board at midyear as part of the Vigilance Plan Monitoring Schedule and represents a "Here's where we will be at year-end" projection. The final results in the third column are preaudit and will be presented to the board in the fall as part of the process for constructing the new Governance Plan. By having the three perspectives of budget, forecast, and final, the reader gets a clear view as to the ups and downs of the year, which leads to important questions and discussions that help the board member understand the organization and its work. Furthermore, the executive director has valuable information about her staff members' performance relative to budgeting. For example, is there a problem with planning that caused the steep drop in total attendance for the education series, is there excessive optimism, or is some other challenge causing the wide variance?

The amount of history shown in success measures is completely flexible. Four years is better than three, three years better than two. Anything less than two years makes it difficult to see trends. The number of years out in the future is a different matter altogether, with three being the maximum recommended length and two years being more common. The pace of change is too rapid to advocate anything longer.

Expectancy theory has much to do with setting the targets in the success measures. It states that unless a person believes that his or her effort will lead to some desired result, that person won't work very hard. How hard someone works depends on how difficult they perceive it will be to achieve the result. David C. McClelland of Harvard University and John W. Atkinson of the University of Michigan base expectancy theory upon scientific research. In a classic article written for the *Harvard Business Review*, J. Sterling Livingston reported:

> *The degree of motivation and effort rises until the expectancy of success reaches 50 percent, then begins to fall even though the expectancy of success continues to increase. No motivation or response is aroused when the goal is perceived as being either virtually certain or virtually impossible to attain.*[80]

The direct impact of expectancy theory on setting targets for success measures is clear: If the targets are set unrealistically high or low, the results will not be achieved. As Livingston reported, "The practice of 'dangling the carrot just beyond the donkey's reach,' endorsed by many managers, is not a good motivational device."[81]

To be effective, however, the 50 percent mark should be used in setting the target for the year furthest out and 80 percent should be used for the coming year. This way, the budgets that will eventually be built around the success measures will have an 80 percent probability of success.

Measuring the Mission

Success measures always include a section about the mission itself, which is followed by success measures for each of the strategies. The mission success measures are usually composed of no more than three or four success measures and they have a more global texture. It is quite common to see success measures related to financial condition and total number of clients served. These success measures offer an effective way to quickly ascertain performance and health of the organization. While the mission success measures offer a snapshot of the organization, they do not offer the full picture that comes from adding in the strategies success measures.

The mission success measures from the performing arts center illustration first convey a sense of history, which in this case is four years long including the 1999–2000 season. The measures also tell a story about the future. Beginning with the mission success measures, we know that attendance is flat. Income, on the other hand, has risen dramatically during the period profiled. The earned-to-contributed ratio has remained relatively stable and the organization has a history of operating in the black.

It looks like a stable, well-functioning organization on first glance. Compare the performing arts center with the same mission success measures from an opera company:

	'96–'97	'97–'98	'98–'99	'99–'00 Budget	'99–'00 12/31 YE Forecast	Final	'00–'01 Budget	'01–'02
Total attendance	30,427	26,020	23,830	13,500	16,634	17,781	39,200	43,400
Total income	1.15M	1.07M	1.22M	1.13M	1.17M	1.24M	1.34M	1.39M
Earned-to-contributed	50/50	49/51	37/63	45/55	43/57	42/58	45/55	45/55
Net income	6.5K	−66K	−189K	−68K	−54K	−23K	−35K	0

These measures tell a much different story. Attendance has been in sharp decline, while income has remained relatively stable. The earned-to-contributed ratio shows dramatic change from year to year and net income has been worsening as well. Looking forward, the organization seems to anticipate coming out of this very difficult period as it looks to balance its budget in the 2001–2002 season.

Looking at just the mission success measures, the two companies seem to be in radically different states of health: the performing arts center is healthy; the opera is in trouble. Upon examination of the performing arts center, however, it would seem that the regional theater series strategy is itself having some difficulty. Obviously a new undertaking that began in the 1997–1998 season, its attendance has been in decline, subscriptions in a maintenance mode, single tickets sharply down, gross sales falling, and renewal rate, a measure of customer satisfaction, much lower than the Broadway series. The education series is also experiencing change. Attendance has declined by a third from its top in the 1997–1998 season and gross sales are in sharp decline.

The story told in success measures is always open to interpretation; they are intrinsically neutral. Perhaps the performing arts center is in the pink of health with an emerging regional theatre series that is still finding its voice and an education series struggling because of the failure of a school levy or a bus-driver strike. Perhaps the organization is slowly sinking into complacency through an increasing dependence on its Broadway series. Perhaps there are problems in the marketing tactics. Possibly the opera is more dynamic and has suffered the inevitable chaos that comes from taking risks in commissioning new American operas. Which is better, and which is worse? Resolving the questions from the success measures is the perpetual work of the strategic board.

As an example of the neutrality of success measures, notice the percentage-paid success measure in the education series measures from the performing arts center. In 1996–1997 it was 52 percent of the audience, but it changed to 65 percent in the 1999–2000 season. More school children are paying for their tickets; fewer free tickets are being distributed to needy children. Is this a good thing or a bad thing? Again, this is open to discussion at the board level since that is where the success measures are selected, targets set, and results discussed.

Exhibit 6.7 is from a housing agency that recently finished its Governance Plan installation and is early in its fiscal year. It is a new agency with very little history, which explains gaps in data and "to be announced" notations. Not all organizations will show the empty columns, which will be filled in with information as the year progresses: It is apparent from these mission success measures that the rental business is expected to grow substantially over the next few years, while the number of homes sold is expected to decline from 31 in 2000 to 17 in 2002. Because of the newness of its operations, these success measures will be a work in progress throughout the year and will require ongoing interaction between the board and the executive director.

Outcome Measures

The Governance Plan is meant to be interactive between the board and the staff. It is a tool of empowerment in the truest sense of the word that gives the people who do the work full accountability for the work. The success measures are an important element in conveying explicit instruction, an essential in effective delegation. The Governance Plan invites discussion and input; it involves the board with the organization and vice versa.

The process of developing success measures is much simpler than that required of strategies. The question of how success should be measured is asked and then answered. First, list the customer-outcome statement. Next, generate a list of possible measures that would indicate success. Finally, choose the best three or four. As Philip Crosby, author of *Quality is Free*, notes:

> *There are innumerable ways to measure any procedure. The people doing the work will respond with delight to the opportunity to identify some specific measurements for their work. If a supervisor says her area is completely immeasurable, she can be helped asking how she knows who is doing the best work, how she knows whom to keep and whom to replace.*[82]

MISSION

	'98	Budget	'99 Midyear Forecast	Final	'00	'01
Homes sold: straight sales	1	0			5	5
Homes sold: lease purchase	12	31			17	12
Rental units available	113	0			210	410
Income ÷ expense ratio		TBA			TBA	TBA

STRATEGIES

NEW HOMES

	'99	Budget	'00 Midyear Forecast	Final	'01	'02
New homes built	7	10			20	20
Construction cost per unit	71k	80k			90K	90K
Construction days per unit		150			150	150

RENTALS

	'99	Budget	'00 Midyear Forecast	Final	'01	'02
Rental units available	113	0			210	410
Vacancy rate	.04	0			.05	.05
Rents: capacity collected	374k 360k	0 0			822K 781K	1.602M 1.522M
Satisfaction measures		TBA			TBA	TBA

Exhibit 6.7 Success Measures from a Housing Agency

In choosing success measures, an important criterion is that the measure be easy to use. As such, a success measure built around readily available figures is always preferable. There is very little point in having brilliantly designed success measures that require another full-time staff member to keep track of. A good success measure that can be easily used without cost is almost always superior to a great success measure that is expensive to utilize.

In the process of building success measures, there is a natural tendency to generate more ways to measure a strategy than can possibly be managed. The number and permutation of success measures is surprisingly broad and the board and staff must be regularly reminded that measuring success takes time and effort, resources that are limited in most nonprofits.

Most success measures have a clear activity texture about them. Financial results, number of clients, and frequency of interaction are all measures of activity. These measures may not be glamorous, but they are very important to a board. There is no strategy or mission that can be accomplished by an organization that is insolvent, which is why net income is extremely important and is almost always chosen for a mission success measure. A nonprofit must respect certain inviolable laws of business and the board and executive director have great interest in paying close attention to these laws through properly drafted success measures.

Measuring business activity is meaningful, but financial condition at the bottom-line does not paint the picture of whether the client has actually experienced the desired outcome articulated in a strategy's customer-outcome statement. An agency that has as its outcome healthy babies from teenage mothers cannot tell if it has achieved this outcome through its net income. The only way to measure this outcome is to determine if its babies are healthier than those from teenage mothers who didn't come into contact with the agency. Weight of the child and Apgar score at birth would be possible outcome indicators. To be completely reliable, the success measures should also follow a control group of babies of similar teenage mothers who were not a part of the agency's activities. Tracking both groups over a longer period of time, say six months to a year, would also be advisable.

For a smaller agency with limited staff and funds, this sort of measuring is very difficult to do as it is expensive and labor-intensive. Fortunately, many national associations already have significant research that might be useful at the local level, but this information is not always produced on a predictable schedule that would dovetail neatly into the Governance Plan's success measures. If reliable information is available from a national association or other sources, consider using it and avoid the costs of reinventing the wheel. Plan to discuss the results as they become available in a way that can inform the processes of creating next year's new Governance Plan. Choose more available activity measures in the meantime.

Outcome measurements is currently a major focus for United Way throughout the country, as Paul Light observes in his *Making Nonprofits Work:*

> *No national organization has been more engaged in the outcome measurement effort than the United Way of America. Its Task Force on Impact began working in August 1995 on strengthening outcomes measurement in the field. At the time, only twenty-five to thirty local United Ways were engaged in any form of outcomes measurement, which the United Way of America defines as an evolutionary process that starts with a general commitment to change and moves step by step through agency training, identifying program outcomes and indicators, collecting data, communicating with donors, using the data, linking program outcomes to indicators of community change, and measuring community change. Of those twenty-five to thirty, only two or three had enough outcome data to use for making funding decisions.*[83]

To measure the outcome of a strategy, indicators of that outcome must be found. These indicators should be easy to measure if at all possible. An agency committed to an outcome of healthy lungs for smokers can measure the number and percent of clients who say that they have quit smoking during the classes and six months after the classes. A shelter for runaway children could certainly measure the number of kids that return home and the length of time that they stay there. Over time, this sort of measuring is going to take discipline and time. The United Way acknowledges the challenge here: "There is tension between the need for technically sound methodologies, which can be expensive and time consuming, and the staffing, funding, and workload realities that constrain nearly all service agencies."[84] Even though outcome measuring is tough to do, a strategy that isn't delivering its outcome is wasting resources.

Outcome indicators often have a texture akin to survey research. It is not about how many took the class, but how many people are using the skills learned. Did you quit smoking? Have you reduced the frequency of risky behavior? How many people who took the class can demonstrate the skills taught at three months, six months, and one year after the conclusion of training? A Big Brothers–Big Sisters chapter uses the measures in Exhibit 6.8 for its core match strategy that include specific outcome indicator measures approved by the local United Way. The measures do not include data for some measures in 1997 and 1998, as these were the years in which the measures were being brought on line.

CORE MATCH

	'97	'98	'99	Budget	'00 7/5 YE Forecast	12/31 YE Final	'01
December total matches: Boys	144	134	133	150	150		160
Girls	121	125	118	135	135		140
Average new matches: Boys	4.0		6.25	5.0	5.0		
Girls	3.75		6.83	5.0	5.0		
Average active matches length			1.6	1.5	1.5		2.0
United Way outcomes initial:							
Bigs want to keep match		97.4%	98.4%	95%	95%		95%
Littles want to keep match		99.1%	99.5%	95%	95%		95%
United Way outcomes 6 month:							
Bigs-Littles goals set			94%	100%	100%		100%

Exhibit 6.8   Sample Success Measures Containing Outcome Indicators

Is the degree to which Bigs want to keep a match going after an initial period a good outcome indicator? This is perhaps debatable, but the organization also commissions a biennial survey at a reasonable cost that measures more significant issues such as liking self, school attendance, attitude toward school, relationship with friends, influence of friends, relationship with adults, and relationships with family.

Most human service organizations have less difficulty with finding outcome indicators to include in their success measures. Performing arts organizations are particularly challenging. How does one measure a standing ovation experience? Focus groups, empirically valid survey research, standing ovations after performances, the number of people that return a second time, and the number of people who leave at intermission are all possible indicators.

Despite the challenges noted above, the good news about outcome measurement is that many outcome indicators are perfectly suitable as success measures. They can be simple and effective. Outcome measurement interfaces well with the Governance Plan, but only as it supports the achievement of a chosen destiny, not as an end to itself. As Paul Light notes:

> Despite all the evidence the United Way of America provides, not the least of which is the use of outcomes measurement in accreditation processes, there is a certain "whistling past the graveyard" tone to the promotion. Anyone familiar with outcomes measurement knows that the idea has been floating through

government and the nonprofit sector for decades, occasionally rising in specific initiatives such as PPBS, President Gerald R. Ford's management by objectives (MBO), and President Jimmy Carter's zero-based budgeting (ZBB) only to fade again as hope confronts the difficulty of management.[85]

As long as United Ways throughout the country balance the requirement for outcome measurement with the reality of the organization's capacity to provide them, outcome indicators will be a valuable input to success measures. Coupled with important activity measures that are regularly reviewed and significant research generated by national associations, the board and executive can be sure that the organization is accomplishing what it should.

Effective success measures are made up of a wide variety of components including outcome indicators, financial measures, and measures of activity. Success measures do not tell the reader whether the company is doing a good job or is in need of corrective action. Success measures are measures, nothing more, nothing less. It is in the interpretation that judgment calls are made. Success measures are inherently neutral; it is the board that must decide and debate whether a particular result or trend is good or bad. If one of the most important jobs of a board member is to ask tough questions, success measures provide much of the information that helps the board member do just that and helps the executive director, who has the obligation to answer those tough questions, be prepared and knowledgeable.

6.7 LEADERSHIP PLAN SUMMARY

Board members and executive directors often mistakenly believe that a successful Leadership Plan must be complicated. How could a complex organization with so many dedicated people working on its behalf have it any other way? If the organization is to be successful, shouldn't its aspirations be complex? In fact, the more focused and clear the Leadership Plan, the more focused and clear the organization's board, staff, volunteers, and stakeholders. In keeping with the Strategic Board model of governance mandate of the critical few over the trivial many, the Leadership Plan itself should be no more than two or three pages including the success measures. The values and vision without the success measures should take just a page.

On occasion a well-meaning board or staff member will complain that the Leadership Plan shouldn't be made available to the public, that it is not a public relations tool. While this is most certainly true, the more accessible the Leadership Plan is, and the easier it is to understand and communicate, the more likely it is that it will be implemented successfully. The success measures and imperatives may indeed be difficult to convey succinctly to the broad community, but the rest of the Leadership Plan can be used as a communication tool.

There are many stakeholders who care about the strategies of the organization, and the board, staff, and volunteers must all understand exactly what needs to be done. Getting everyone on the same page is always a difficult challenge. Putting the mission summary on the letterhead, T-shirts, and lapel pins can make a dramatic difference in ensuring a common vocabulary about the organization. Proudly publishing the Leadership Plan wherever possible leads to astonishing results: People throughout the community will know what the organization is about, which inevitably helps to make the Leadership Plan a reality.

Exhibit 6.9 is a Leadership Plan summary from the Victoria Theatre Association, which is published in every program book for every performance. It contains the essence of the Leadership Plan, but not its details, there are no success measures, and imperatives are not discussed. Appendix 6.1 is a sample leadership plan.

Leadership Plan Summary
from the Victoria Theatre Association

VALUES
Our customer is the star. Trust. Win and lose together. The best we can be.

VISION

VISION SUMMARY
Set the stage for 2003.

MISSION
You are the star!
Enriching life on behalf of our diverse Miami
Valley community for adults, families, and school
children throughout our region by making our
customer the star.

STANDING-OVATION STRATEGIES

*Sit back and enjoy
for adults.*

*Quality Play Time
for families with children
grades K–4.*

DISCOVERY!
*Enriched classrooms for
school children and
teachers in grades K–8.*

*Remember when
for older adults.*

*A sense of belonging
for everyone.*

*Blockbuster
memories
for adults.*

*Theatre for the
mind for adults.*

*I had fun in Dayton!
for families with
children ages 4–13*

*Now that's Opera!
for adults.*

**ARTS CENTER
MANAGEMENT**
*A downtown source
of pride for the
Miami Valley*

**Exhibit 6.9 Leadership Plan Summary from the Victoria Theatre
Association**

Sample Leadership Plan

It's more fun to arrive at a conclusion than to justify it.
—Malcolm Forbes

This sample Leadership Plan from a Big Brothers–Big Sisters chapter illustrates a Leadership Plan from a nonprofit with a $400,000 budget. All Governance Plans are different and are the result of the particular circumstances of the organization at its unique place and time.

EXECUTIVE SUMMARY

VISION SUMMARY

Big Brothers–Big Sisters finds itself at a crossroads. On one hand, the organization is enjoying a period of outstanding financial results and dramatic growth within some strategies that together have achieved an operating margin of nearly 7 percent in 1999, up over 80 percent from 1997. On the other hand, Average Total Matches has declined 13 percent during the same period to 234.

The focus for the next two years is on tackling goals that will achieve the result of increasing core matches especially in 2001. At the same time, the organization is working to improve various business processes in order to secure more core matches. Thus, the Vision Summary for the 2000 Governance Plan is to build a foundation to boost the core.

STRATEGIES

Although the organization is concentrating much of its efforts on fixing problems, improving processes within departments, and "planning the plan" for boosting the core, many strategies for 2000 will show dramatic growth. Teen Mothers, however, will be phased out this year and no new strategies are anticipated coming on line. Highlights of success measures include:

About Core Match:
- December Total Matches will be up 14 percent to 285.
- Average New Matches will decline 24 percent to 5.

About Core Match—University Medical:
- December Total Matches will be up 50 percent to 33.

About High School Mentoring:
- December Total Matches will rise 27 percent to 84, which will be a more than fourfold increase since 1997.

IMPERATIVES

Imperatives are those critical issues that must be addressed in order for the organization to succeed. Imperatives are most often about structural issues that affect operations or about particular strategies that are in need of acute attention. Recognizing that the key to success in building the core is a growing body of Bigs and Littles, the organization has adopted as its single imperative to recruit more Bigs.

To this end, the chapter has recently hired its first Director of Mentor Development, whose fundamental charge is to address this imperative. Plans of action to improve recruitment of minority Bigs and to improve the number of Little Sisters will be implemented on January 1.

VALUES

Trust	Team	Excellence
Promises kept	Involved (listening and speaking)	Self-confident
Fair	Celebrating together	Proactive
Truthful without	Optimistic	Persistent
hidden agendas	Lending a hand	

VISION

VISION SUMMARY

Build a foundation to boost the core.

MISSION

Building young adults.

On behalf of the three-county community,

Big Brothers–Big Sisters

builds 7- to 13-year-old children from single-parent households into confident, competent, and caring young adults through professionally supported one-to-one matches that deliver results.

STRATEGIES

Core Match

Building 7- to 13-year-old Littles
into confident, competent, caring young adults.

Core Match

Community University

University Medical

High School Mentoring

Building 7- to 13-year-old Littles and 15- to 17-year-old Bigs
into confident, competent, caring young adults.

Teen Mothers

Building pregnant and parenting teens
into confident, competent, caring parents.

IMPERATIVES

Recruit more Bigs.

SUCCESS MEASURES
Mission

	'97	'98	'99	Budget	'00 7/5 YE Forecast	12/31 YE Final	'01
Average total matches	269	237	234	245	245		257
Total income	384K	473K	447K	451K	451K		450K
Operating margin percent	3.8	5.5	6.9	0	0		2.0

Core Match

	'97	'98	'99	Budget	'00 7/5 YE Forecast	12/31 YE Final	'01
December total matches: Boys	144	134	133	150	150		160
Girls	121	125	118	135	135		140
Average new matches: Boys	4.0		6.25	5.0	5.0		
Girls	3.75		6.83	5.0	5.0		
Average active matches length		1.6	1.5	1.5			2.0
United Way initial: Bigs want to keep match		97.4%	98.4%	95%	95%		95%
Littles want to keep match		99.1%	99.5%	95%	95%		95%
United Way 6-months: Bigs-Littles goals set			94%	100%	100%		100%

Core Match—Community University

	'97	'98	'99	Budget	'00 Midyear Forecast	12/31 YE Final	'01
December total matches	29	33	31	35	35		35

Core Match—University Medical

	'97	'98	'99	Budget	'00 7/5 YE Forecast	12/31 YE Final	'01
December total matches		15	22	33	33		40

High School Mentoring

	'97	'98	'99	Budget	'00 7/5 YE Forecast	'00 12/31 YE Final	'01
December total matches: North High				15	15		30
Catholic	13	27	21	24	24		24
Colonel	7	23	24	20	20		20
National			21	25	25		30
Program outcome evaluation						TBA 1.1	TBA 1.1

Teen Mothers

	'97	'98	'99	Budget	'00 Midyear Forecast	'00 12/31 YE Final	'01
Average total matches	6	27	18	10	7		0

PART III

The Delegation Plan

A courtyard common to all will be swept by none.
—Chinese Proverb

CHAPTER 7

Who Does What?

Even the best team, without a plan, can't score.
—Woody Hayes

<table>
<tr><td colspan="2" align="center">DELEGATION PLAN
Who does what?</td></tr>
<tr><td align="center">DUTIES</td><td align="center">GUIDELINES</td></tr>
<tr><td align="center">Board
Committees
Officers
Board Members
Executive Director</td><td align="center">Board
Committees
Officers
Board Members
Executive Director</td></tr>
</table>

7.1 INTRODUCTION

It was a beautiful late summer day outside of corporate headquarters. Inside the presidential suite, a group of five people sat together. Four board members and their new executive director were debating what to do next. The executive director wanted to know how the board intended to speak to him with a unified voice. One gentleman spoke up with frustration in his voice, "But we're speaking with you now, aren't we?" "Of course you are," replied the executive, "But you're only speaking as an individual board member. I can't take direction from 15 different people. I want to be sure that what I'm doing meets your requirements." Another board member spoke up, "Isn't this all spelled out in the bylaws?" "It is and it isn't," replied the head of the group. "Some issues are clearly defined, others are silent." "Maybe finding out what each of us is supposed to be doing is the best place to begin," another pointed out.

Even if the question about where to go tomorrow is solidly decided in the Leadership Plan, governance is often unsatisfactory simply because questions about who does what are left unanswered or are ambiguously stated. Board members end up confused about what their duties are and which guidelines should govern behaviors. As Karl Mathiasen III, author of *Board Stages: Three Key Stages in a Nonprofit Board's Life Cycle,* so ably describes: There is "a perplexing lack of clarity about what boards 'ought to do,' even when one can identify the organization life cycle and the board's stage of growth."[86]

The Delegation Plan explicitly deals with empowering the people who will carry the accountability for implementation: the full board, committees, officers, individual board members, and the executive director. The Delegation Plan provides the often-missing bridge between where to go tomorrow and what gets done today. It eliminates the unclear roles that cloud the effectiveness of so many nonprofit boards. It establishes guidelines of behavior, the "rules of engagement" for the board. The Delegation Plan answers the question of who does what and it is divided into two sections: duties and guidelines.

7.2 THE DIFFICULTY IN DETERMINING ROLES

The curious thing about governance is that there is so little written about it relative to other leadership areas. Yet, one only has to turn to a great body of literature on teams to find a vast amount of helpful advice. In many respects, the board is a team just like many other teams. It may have its own idiosyncrasies, but much about teams is applicable to the nonprofit board.

Carl Larson and Frank LaFasto, authors of *Team Work: What Must Go Right/What Can Go Wrong,* write that there are just two primary considerations concerning effective team structures. The first requires a determination of the broad objective to be achieved by the team, which in the Strategic Board model of governance, is answered by the Leadership Plan. The second consideration in determining an effective team structure focuses on those four features that are common success factors in the design of an effective team. These factors are largely dealt with by the Delegation Plan:

1. *Clear roles and accountabilities:* Each team member of any successful team must understand at the outset what he or she will be held accountable for and measured against in terms of performance.
2. *An effective communication system:* Whatever the system used for documenting issues raised and decisions made, the key ingredient is the discipline required to capture accurately the decisions made by a team on an ongoing basis.
3. *Monitoring individual performance and providing feedback:* Without knowing an individual's performance, it becomes impossible to determine, with any sense of accuracy and equity, how the individual should be regarded, what the individual's development needs are, and what increased or further responsibilities this individual might assume in the future.
4. *Fact-based judgments:* Whatever the database, it is important to base decisions on sound facts and to make sure that facts are interpreted with the harness of predisposition.[87]

A few years ago, two groups of people attending a national conference for nonprofit organizations gathered over breakfast on two different mornings to think about obstacles holding their boards back from being more effective teams. The attendees were from a wide variety of organizations—some were board members, some executive directors—and all were interested in the topic of the board team. The first task was to take a brief quiz built around the features of an effectively functioning team as profiled in Larson and LaFasto's book.

Seventy-two people took the quiz over the two days. A perfect score was 100 and within a range of 29 to 86, the average score was 66 and the median was 67. The results were not usable for any other purpose than to stimulate conversation by suggesting that the boards represented by participants were operating at only two-thirds of their potential.

Following the quiz, each participant wrote down three key obstacles to board team performance. The participants then worked in small groups to identify the top three from among these. These obstacles were then presented to the whole room and affinity grouped to reduce the volume of ideas to the following:

- Unclear roles
- Lack of accountability
- Inconsistent levels of individual commitment
- Poor use of time, lack of time
- Strategic direction
- Poor communication

- Personal agendas, ego
- Ineffective leadership
- Insufficient knowledge and training
- Inactive or absentee board members
- Poor interpersonal skills
- Poor board member recruitment

Finally, each participant voted on top choices. Leading by a wide margin was unclear roles, which was followed by lack of accountability and inconsistent levels of individual commitment.

While the exercise with this group cannot be viewed as statistically viable for all boards, it illustrates the key problem that most boards have when it comes to operating effectively: unclear roles. The job of a board member is tough enough to do even when duties and guidelines are clear, and even more difficult when operating within the seven realities of nonprofit boards. Add unclear roles to these characteristics and things become flammable; add uncertainty about values and vision and things become spontaneously combustible.

Board members in all fairness have a difficult job to do. They are expected to be members of a collective, individual board members, and volunteers, each with different expectations. Robert C. Andringa and Ted W. Engstrom highlight this puzzle in the *Nonprofit Board Answer Book* by using the metaphor of hats to describe roles:

1. *Governance hat:* Worn only when the full board meets, proper notice has been given, and a quorum is present.
2. *Implementation hat:* Worn only when the board gives one or more board members authority to implement a board policy.
3. *Volunteer hat:* Worn at all other times, when board members are involved with organizational activities as volunteers.[88]

The authors go on to note: "Problems arise when board members and/or staff confuse these hats or when board members assume that *individual* and *collective* board responsibilities are interchangeable. They are not."[89] They describe how they distinguish the authority vested in each of the three hats:

- *Governance hat.* An *individual* board member has no authority in governance. Governance is *group* action.
- *Implementation hat.* Occasionally the board delegates at least one of its members to act on its behalf. . . . Such authority is not automatic just because a person is a board member. It depends on the board's having given its authority, acting by resolution in an official meeting.

- *Volunteer hat.* As a volunteer, a board member has no individual authority simply by virtue of his or her position. When wearing a volunteer hat, the board member is accountable to another person. . . .[90]

Complicating matters is the fine line that exists between advice and instruction. A prominent board member, influential in the community and generous to the organization, pulls the executive director aside to ask a question about what insurance broker the organization uses and why. The executive director should certainly be able to answer these questions, but if the questioning were to continue, the executive director might begin to wonder whether the board member is instructing her. Perhaps the organization is not using the best broker; perhaps the board member wants a more thorough process. Advice becomes instruction and instruction dilutes authority and accountability, which are the building blocks of effective delegation.

Board members very rarely have a problem with confusing advice with instruction; it is the staff members that have the difficulty. "I work for the board; this is a board member, therefore I work for this board member" is the faulty logic, but it doesn't go away simply because it is wrong. This can be an especially difficult problem when it's the chair of the board, who carries great weight with the board. Board members have to be extremely guarded about how they interface with the staff, as Andringa and Engstrom highlight:

> *The most misunderstood and abused principle of governance is the requirement for group action. The chief executive and staff cannot serve two (or 22) masters. The full board sets policy, not individual board members who feel strongly about something and voice their opinions to the chief executive. Board members must be taught this principle, and staff must be reminded of it. Otherwise, confusion and conflict reign and board effectiveness is diminished.*[91]

No matter how hard the board member tries, the executive director is likely to interpret advice as instruction. This is especially true given the reality that most executive directors are first-timers in the job with limited tenure. Thus, when the time comes to measure results, the executive director may very well have cause to say that things would have been different if she had been allowed to do her job without interference.

Once the board gives instruction about implementation, the job no longer belongs completely to the executive director. Let's say that the executive director recommends that certain giving levels be increased for the coming year, but an influential board member pulls her aside and warns that the higher levels should not be adjusted. What should the executive do? Adjust the numbers and live with the results that may not meet expectation? Hold fast and risk the ire of that board member who is a member of the review committee of executive director performance? As Alexis de Tocqueville observed nearly two centuries ago, "When the government speaks it is difficult to ascertain the difference between a suggestion and a command."

How can boards and board members avoid these kinds of pitfalls? Start with explicitly outlined duties and follow them with understandable guidelines of behavior. After all, boards are made up of people who surely will perform better, wear their three different hats well, and be more satisfied in their service if they know what is expected of them. As Sharon Percy Rockeffer says:

> Boards have to know their role. They have to care a lot, and they have to be committed to the organization. For both the board and staff, the dynamics of that caring can be time-consuming, but worth it in the long run. . . .[92]

7.3 DUTIES

Duties are jobs, nothing more, nothing less. If left vague, many board members will confuse the duties of the board with those of the individual board member, and the executive director may have mistaken impressions of their authority. The duties of a Delegation Plan solve this problem by providing detailed job descriptions for the full board, committees, officers, individual board members, and the executive director. Job descriptions will vary from organization to organization but jobs are assigned only if they carry both full responsibility and full authority. Thus, only those duties that the board intends to hold itself accountable for should belong to the board.

As with other elements of a Governance Plan, it is important to answer the four questions that make the board strategic and remember that the answers will depend upon the particular needs and circumstances of the organization at its time and place. There are no right or wrong answers. While answers are indeed unique to each organization, common themes have arisen especially with regard to the duties of the board, board members, and executive director.

Most strategic boards include the following four board duties in the Delegation Plan:

1. Decide where to go tomorrow through the Leadership Plan.
2. Delegate who does what through the Delegation Plan.

3. Decide what gets done today through the Management Plan.
4. Determine if it happened through the Vigilance Plan.

There are boards that will add fundraising or government advocacy to this list. Provided that the board holds itself accountable for the results and uses its authority to get the job done, this presents no problem. Accountability and authority are inseparable in a strategic board, which can be helpful in deciding who actually owns the duty. For example, if the board holds itself accountable for the duty of fundraising, financial performance under the executive director's purview should exclude these results. If the board holds the executive director accountable for the bottom-line, including fundraising results, the authority for fundraising should be the executive director's.

Board member duties usually include at least these four:

1. Make good decisions.
2. Raise money.
3. Champion the organization.
4. Do the board's work.

The executive director commonly has two duties:

1. Implement the Leadership Plan.
2. Provide support to the board.

Most governance models embrace most, if not all, of these duties. The major advantage of using these typical board duties from a strategic board over comparable approaches is ease of comprehension and certainty of focus. When there are fewer things to remember it is more likely that they *will* be remembered.

Most of the duties and guidelines of the Delegation Plan are crafted using the brainstorming–affinity grouping combination of techniques and the rule of large to small. This rule states that the largest statement governing any matter is crafted first and that subsequent smaller statements must be derivative of that larger first statement. By following the rule of large to small in constructing a Delegation Plan, there is reassurance that a safety net exists that will cover anything that is left silent. Similar to building an outline, the board starts with the largest statement and drills down into the outline to the level of detail that it feels is adequate. Duties and guidelines can be as complicated or as simple as fits the organization. One board will list a board member's duties this way and let it stand:

• Make good decisions.

Another board will get into much greater detail:

- Make good decisions.
  - Keep the Leadership Plan in focus.
  - Know the business.
  - Attend at least 75 percent of scheduled meetings.
  - Participate resolutely and ask tough questions.
  - Vote conscientiously.

A board going to the deeper level is better off because this can inform actions more effectively, in this case recruiting and assessment of performance. Nonetheless, whatever works for the board, works. The answers and the degree of detail are completely flexible and unique for each board, which is just as it should be.

Once finished, many organizations use the duties contained within the Delegation Plan as a useful tool for cleaning up inconsistencies in the bylaws. Furthermore, because bylaws are usually difficult to change, many issues in the bylaws can be readily moved to the Delegation Plan where revisions are easier to accomplish.

7.4 GUIDELINES

Guidelines describe the standards of conduct within which the full board, committees, officers, individual board members, and the executive director intend to operate. Among guidelines typically included are how responsibility for implementation of the Leadership Plan is delegated to the executive director, how differences of opinion are managed, the focus of meetings, conflict of interest, attendance, and participation in fund raising. Here, for example are the board guidelines that are in place for Child Care Clearinghouse:

- Focus talent and time on important work.
- Be a give-and-take board that values the diversity and strength of all its members.
- Govern the organization—don't manage it.

These straightforward guidelines provide enough detail to give a solid framework for governance. If the board decides it wants to provide more detail in the guidelines, it is a simple matter to do so:

- Govern the organization—don't manage it.
  - Adhere to the Governance Plan.
  - Ensure that committees, officers, and board members are account-able to the board, helping the board to perform its duties effectively.
  - Respect the chain of command between the board, the president, and the professional staff.

As a way to keep the guidelines in focus, some boards make it an agenda item to review one or two sections of the Delegation Plan at each meeting. Other boards will build self-assessment around the duties and guidelines.

Because the greatest responsibility for Leadership Plan implementation is delegated to the executive director, the bulk of the guidelines are related to that individual. These guidelines often include treatment of customers, treatment of staff, financial planning and budgeting, financial condition and activities, asset protection, compensation and benefits, and communication and support to the board.

By spelling out these guidelines in advance, the board relieves itself of worry that the executive director might be conducting business in a manner at odds with the board's wishes. The strategic board understands that it cannot possibly monitor or approve every variance and every decision. Instead, the board sets guidelines that tell the executive director what boundaries he or she must stay within.

In a board meeting not too long ago when the executive director's guidelines were being developed, a participant insisted that the budget not vary at all from the final results. Once set, the budget was not to be breached under any circumstances. It took but a moment for other board members to confront the impossibility of this demand. "The second the budget is printed, it is obsolete," one board member commented. "It's senseless to expect perfect tracking—things change too rapidly."

As with the budget, the organization cannot be held in check waiting for approvals from the board. An approval-oriented board leads to management gridlock as the staff waits for board permission, or, even worse, insubordination as the staff takes necessary action without approval. Because the guidelines preapprove most activity, this allows the board to concentrate on more important work related to the Leadership Plan. Furthermore, well-constructed guidelines liberate the executive director to get things done expediently.

In keeping with the rule of large to small, all executive director guidelines begin with a statement similar to the following:

- The executive director will conduct himself or herself with the high-est business and professional standards at all times, never causing or

111

allowing any practice that is illegal or unethical or that breaches the values or vision contained in the Leadership Plan.

Most boards will not stop with this statement and will add sections including finance, personnel, communication to the board, risk assessment, planning, and fundraising. The following is an example of executive director guidelines related to finance:

- With regard to financial matters, the executive director shall:
    - Be allowed to make capital acquisitions of less than $5,000 without board approval.
    - Draw a maximum of 5 percent income annually from endowment investments.
    - Have and follow an audit-proof procedure for handling income and disbursements.
    - Receive a clean audit and comply with any recommendations outlined in the accompanying management letter.
    - Keep the organization debt-free including lines of credit.
    - Achieve at least a 2 percent surplus annually of income over expenses subject to the following provisions:
        - Income shall exclude planned gifts not budgeted and investment income from endowment funds other than the 5 percent annual draw.
        - Expenses shall exclude unfunded depreciation, any incentive package costs for management, and contributions to endowment funds by the organization.
    - Present budgets with a probability of occurrence of at least 80 percent.

Some board members might argue that this example is too detailed in some respects and not detailed enough in others. For example, it doesn't make mention of whether the organization can lend money to its employees in the form of payroll advances or interest-free loans. While each set of guidelines will be unique, the board cannot speak about every detail. The executive director must make decisions about matters that are not detailed in the guidelines or are not detailed at a specific enough level. That is why the controlling statement mentioned earlier is used as a safety net and the executive director guidelines should contain a section on reasonable interpretation similar to the following:

- With regard to interpretation of these guidelines, the executive director shall use reasonable interpretation, the same interpretation as an ordinarily prudent executive director would exercise in a like position and under similar circumstances.

A management issue that is essentially within the purview of the executive director, but is of legitimate concern to the board, can be dealt with appropriately within the executive director guidelines. A check-signing protocol is clearly the business of the executive director, but the board has every right to demand that a certain level of conduct about it be observed. Whether it is the insistence of a clean audit or that staff is treated with respect, the board has ultimate accountability for the organization and it should be clear about its expectations.

When given proper attention, guidelines become triggers for examination, but do not necessarily require action. For example, the executive director guidelines listed above require a 2 percent surplus be achieved annually. This does not necessarily mean that action should be immediately taken if the executive director is out of compliance. It does mean that the matter would need to be discussed in a timely fashion between the executive director and the board.

As opposed to an approach that could lead to board micromanagement, using the Strategic Board model of governance respects the board–executive director partnership while at the same time effectively dealing with the issues that could cause concern.

CHAPTER **8**

Determining Duties and Guidelines

A board member's role is simple: Ask why.
—Sharon Percy Rockefeller

DELEGATION PLAN
Who does what?

DUTIES	GUIDELINES
Board	Board
Committees	Committees
Officers	Officers
Board Members	Board Members
Executive Director	Executive Director

8.1 INTRODUCTION

Effective delegation means that the board can't have its cake and eat it too. It can't delegate accountability to an executive director but keep the authority to itself. The board must be willing to authorize its delegates to do their jobs and give them necessary authority. This chapter will look at the duties and guidelines for each position.

Boards decide; that's their job. Until the question is called, the board is simply a group of individuals. Boards decide what gets done and then must delegate to people who will do the work. Boards don't raise money; board members do. Boards may decide how much money needs to be raised, and may decide how to raise the money, but others do the work. Those others may include board members, staff, and community volunteers. That boards decide and then delegate is a key principle of what it means to govern.

8.2 BOARDS

All boards want to make a difference for their organizations. They want to avoid wasting time and talent. The common complaint of not doing important work is often a result of simply not taking time to describe exactly what that work should be. While everyone agrees that boards should be productive and meaningful, many people simply don't grasp that boards are means to an end, not ends to themselves.

Recognizing that board members have limited time to contribute to their respective boards, the board must focus itself on the key duties that add value. By design, using the Strategic Board model of governance guarantees that the four major duties of a successful board of directors are accomplished:

1. Decide where to go tomorrow.
2. Delegate who does what.
3. Decide what gets done today.
4. Determine whether it happened.

Constructing board duties is uncomplicated and uses the brainstorming–affinity grouping combination of techniques. First, answer the question "What are the duties of the board?" Most boards will give answers similar to those from a model organization:

> *planning, set future direction, give direction about future, initiate change, decide strengths—weaknesses—opportunities—threats, understand operations, needs identification, identify improvements to programs, prioritize and set goals, measure performance, strategic planning, allocate resources, hire/manage executive director, request action by staff, give outside expertise to management, problem solve, interface with staff, monitor programs, oversight, compliance, oversee finances, investigate problems, review strategies, updates on strategies, audit, identify gaps, report to each other, govern, new members, receive education, know the agency, learn about the organization, facilitate well, convene meetings, raise funds, coordinate special events, identify and oversee fundraising strategies, brain trusting, development, open doors to funding*

Second, make sense of the answers by affinity grouping them, as was done in Exhibit 8.1.

POOL OF IDEAS	DUTIES
planning, set future direction, give direction about future, initiate change, decide strengths—weaknesses—opportunities—threats, understand operations, needs identification, identify improvements to programs, prioritize and set goals, measure performance, strategic planning, allocate resources	Decide where to go tomorrow through the Leadership Plan.
hire/manage executive director, request action by staff, give outside expertise to management, problem solve, interface with staff	Delegate who does what through the Delegation Plan.
monitor programs, oversight, compliance, oversee finances, investigate problems, review strategies, updates on strategies, audit, identify gaps, report to each other	Determine whether it happened through the Vigilance Plan.
govern, new members, receive education, know the agency, learn about the organization, facilitate well, convene meetings	Decide what gets done today through the Management plan.

Exhibit 8.1   Sample Affinity Groups of Duties

Guidelines are just as easy to put together for a board as shown in Exhibit 8.2. These guidelines can be expanded to the level of detail that the board wants. They can stay simple as illustrated in Exhibit 8.2 or they can be broadened.

POOL OF IDEAS	GUIDELINES
do important work, support mission, be productive, on subject, stay focused, use time effectively, start/end on time, don't waste time, not boring	Focus talent and time on important work.
a proactive and give-and-take board, be active, evaluate committee reports, board participation, interactive, review status, respect each other, positive, be happy, no personal agendas, not constant confrontation, professional, feel valued, cooperate, respectful of each other, open, honest	Be a give-and-take board that values the diversity and strength of all its members.
don't meddle, remember board's role, board job versus staff job, respect chain of command, not involved in operations, value CEO's opinions, motivate executive director, love, nurture, follow up, hear what staff says, respect, staff experience, be consistent, be fair, set clear expectations	Govern the organization—don't manage it.

Exhibit 8.2   Sample Affinity Grouping of Guidelines

8.3 COMMITTEES

The usual approach to structuring committees is to duplicate staff departments. Personnel, facilities, marketing, and programming committees are good examples. This rarely leads to satisfactory results for either the committee or the staff. Rather than helping, board committees formed in this manner often unwittingly push the staff in directions that are ill considered and counterproductive.

This conventional approach can quickly become unwieldy: A typical board of average size can easily end up with 12 committees including development, executive, education, facilities, finance, marketing, nominating, personnel, planned giving, planning, program, and public relations. Assume that most of these committees will meet at least twice a year, that the executive committee and the board will meet six times each, and the total comes to 34 meetings. Most boards operating this way don't end up so lucky and have many more meetings; it's not completely uncommon to see a schedule of over 70.

Given the volume of activity generated by the conventional approach to committees, how can anyone be surprised that board meetings are boring as one committee report after another is presented? Or that there's no red meat on the table? Or that there's plenty of information, but no one can make sense of it? Or that the parts on the board sum to less than the whole? When will these organizations have time for truly important work?

What can get lost in all this is the cost of staff time to service committees. While a board or committee meeting may take only an hour or two, the preparation time and follow up can be significant. Executive directors, for example, report spending an average of eight hours per week on board-related issues. A board that meets monthly, and with five very active committees including an executive committee, can easily require 1,000 hours of staff time a year, which is equal to a part-time employee.

Because committees receive their authority from the board, members often feel that they must do something meaningful as a result. Staff members who are inexperienced with working with the board are completely powerless to refuse to do the work that these well-intentioned committees request. Staff complaints to the executive of "reinventing the wheel" go unresolved because the executive, after all, works for the board. In the end, staff members are pulled in two or three or even more directions, becoming servants of many masters.

While few executive directors or boards are in favor of whipsawing the staff, many encourage the staff department approach to committee structure. First, it is easier to use a committee of four to make a decision than to use the full board. The full board never really takes a stand on any matter of importance in deference to the hard work and recommendations of the committee members. How can the full board ever say no to a committee that has worked tirelessly on its recommendation? It is effective, but the end result is a rubber-stamp board.

Second, some executive directors like the protection from accountability that this approach to committees offers. If the committee reviews every detail about staff operations, then the executive director is protected in the event that things go the wrong way. What gets overlooked is the tremendous waste of staff and board member time and resources, which might be used for more productive purposes.

Whatever approach is used for committee structuring usually doesn't come about by design, but by default. No one really thought about it, other boards were doing the same sort of thing, and it made sense to copy the prevailing convention. Anyone who has ever served on a committee can appreciate the reason why Anthony Sampson says, "Muddle is the extra unknown personality in any committee."

In the Strategic Board model of governance, form follows function with committees structured to help the board do its job, not to help the staff do their jobs. While an organization would usually have a governance committee to recruit, orient, and assess board performance, it would probably not have a committee for marketing, which would generally be considered a staff responsibility. Three board committees are common:

1. The *performance assurance committee* is structured to recommend revisions to and monitor performance of the executive director's guidelines. Because so many of these guidelines are financial, the performance assurance committee usually includes all of the duties of a typical finance committee. The treasurer of the board usually serves as the chair of this committee.
2. The *executive committee* is chartered to serve in a wide variety of duties, including ensuring effective delegation from the board to the executive director. Generally, the committee is made up of just the officers of the board, with the chair of the board at the head. In smaller boards, this committee is often unnecessary.
3. The *governance committee* is set up to deal with issues such as the recruitment, orientation, and education of trustees and the assessment of board performance. The incoming chair of the board generally leads it.

Not all boards elect to follow the common structure, however. Some boards have fewer committees; others have more, including the development committee. The process for thinking about committees is interactive and involves open discussion. The question to be answered is what committees are needed to help the board do its job. The following are committee duties from a model organization:

- Executive
    1. Ensure effective delegation from the board to the executive director.
        a. Manage the selection process.
        b. Manage the individual planning process, including quarterly meetings.

    c. Manage the performance review process, including the compensation program.

    d. Mentor the president.

  2. Determine the board's agenda.

  3. Recommend committee membership.

  4. Recommend revisions to the President's Duties.

- Performance assurance

  1. Recommend revisions to the President's Guidelines.

  2. Assess the president's performance against the President's Guidelines.

  3. Serve as the audit committee of the board.

- Governance

  1. Recruit, welcome, and orient new board members.

  2. Recommend the officer slate.

    a. Nominate the chair.

    b. In concert with the chair, propose the other officers.

  3. Assess performance against the Delegation Plan, excluding the President's Duties and Guidelines.

  4. Recommend revisions to the Delegation Plan, excluding the President's Duties and Guidelines.

  5. Make sure that the accomplishments of the board are recognized.

  6. Ensure alignment between the Governance Plan and the bylaws.

- Development

  1. Conduct the board member portion of the annual fund campaign.

  2. Provide qualified prospects.

  3. Serve as a think tank for development innovation.

Because the committees and officers serve to help the board do its job, many boards will use a common set of guidelines for the board, committees, and officers, as shown in Exhibit 8.2 for board guidelines:

- Focus talent and time on important work.
- Be a give-and-take board that values the diversity and strength of all its members.
- Govern the organization—don't manage it.

Again, these guidelines can be outlined at a more specific level based on the needs of the particular nonprofit.

In some organizations, there is a need for board-level committees that are chartered to assist the professional staff. These committees mirror staff functions such as fundraising and marketing. They are especially prevalent in smaller organizations where the resources are too limited to fully staff these functions. Some large fundraising organizations like United Ways find campaign cabinets to be enormously productive for similar reasons. The people on these staff committees help the staff get their jobs done and should report to the staff person in charge of the particular committee. Because of the delicacy of having board members work for line staff, it is advisable to add a guideline governing conduct to ensure that staff committees are accountable to and support the work of the staff. Exhibit 8.3 is what a Big Brothers–Big Sisters chapter decided to do in describing board and staff committee duties.

Whether a committee is identified as a staff committee or board committee is largely by choice of the organization and driven by the particular duties of that committee. In Exhibit 8.3, the development committee is obviously not doing the work of the staff and it is consequently a board-level committee.

The desirability of having an executive committee is almost certain to come up with every board. Is it a good committee to have? F. Warren McFarlan has written much about this particular committee, including a recent article in the *Harvard Business Review:*

> Legally, the entire board is responsible for the health and governance of a nonprofit organization. But the executive committee provides the small-group atmosphere that helps members talk about problems on a more intimate basis. Members can discuss sensitive topics with less danger of damaging leaks and with greater likelihood of reaching a quick consensus on operational issues.[93]

McFarlan goes on to highlight the risks:

> But there's a big risk that an executive committee will turn into an "upstairs" board, whose members are in the know. Committee members get great emotional satisfaction out of this but it alienates the "downstairs" board who aren't on the committee.[94]

Whether a board has an executive committee depends on so many variables that it cannot be decided by fiat. A large board will have a greater likelihood of needing an executive committee than a small board. Some executive directors prefer having a carefully chartered executive committee that can be an intimate sounding board whether there is a large board in place or a small one.

The executive committee does its greatest disservice when it keeps the rest of the board uninformed. To learn that the executive committee has made a major decision without taking the counsel of the rest of the members can be very off-putting and worrisome. The frequent excuse for creating this committee is that it is needed in case of an emergency, but this

BOARD COMMITTEES—HELPING THE BOARD DO ITS JOB

- Executive
  1. Assure performance by setting and ensuring implementation of the vigilance plan.
  2. Ensure that the executive director is selected, supported, reviewed, and managed.
  3. Act for the full board in the event of an emergency in which the full board cannot be effectively convened.
  4. Act for the full board on routine matters during months when the board does not meet.
  5. Determine the board's agenda.

- Development
  1. Recommend fundraising policies.
  2. Raise the board portion of the annual campaign.
  3. Serve as the board's think tank for innovation in fundraising.
  4. Provide qualified prospects.

- Governance and Nominating
  1. Recruit and orient new board members.
  2. Ensure that the board is educated.
  3. Make sure that the accomplishments of the board are recognized.
  4. Recommend the officer slate and committee membership.

- Special Events
  1. Bowling for Kids
  2. Old Time Fun
  3. Gourmet Dinner

STAFF COMMITTEES—HELPING THE STAFF DO ITS JOB

- Program
  1. Ensure visible mentoring programs, that appropriately respond to identified community needs.
  2. Provide services to waiting-list children.
  3. Ensure agency program compliance with the highest professional standards and the national Big Brothers–Big Sisters standards.

- Marketing
  1. Improve community awareness of and exposure to the Big Brothers–Big Sisters program.

- Recruitment
  1. Increase the recruitment of adult volunteers, especially minority males.

Exhibit 8.3   Sample Board and Staff Committee Duties

simply doesn't wash. If it's an emergency, shouldn't the whole board be notified and involved? Says McFarlan,

> In some cases, "downstairs" board directors are so out of the loop so much of the time, they never hear anything but the official line, . . . I know one case in which a "downstairs" board member of a nonprofit got a phone call from the CEO requesting an emergency meeting. The board member agreed to the meeting, then called a member of the executive committee to find out if there were any important issues going on. The board member was told that nothing significant was happening, so he concluded that the CEO probably just wanted to talk about issues related to his expertise. Two hours later, the board member met the CEO and was stunned to hear him say as he sat down: "I have been fired, and I need your help!" The CEO then handed over a six-page letter from the "upstairs" executive committee, outlining the reasons for his dismissal.[95]

Whether the "downstairs" board member finds out after the fact about excessive executive director compensation in the morning newspaper or hears about the forced resignation of the executive director only to learn later that her successor was waiting in the wings for three months, "upstairs" executive committees have a reputation for not informing the "downstairs" board of the goings-on until after the fact—no letter, no phone call, no nothing. This denies the board members the very information that they need to accomplish their legal responsibilities.

The board must be very careful in both the Delegation Plan and its bylaws about what powers it delegates to the executive committee. The deciding factor in whether an executive committee is effective has much to do with its authority. An executive committee that has been delegated full authority to act for the board may cause the upstairs–downstairs board that McFarlan describes. An executive committee with a more focused charter may avoid that pitfall.

8.4 OFFICERS

Perhaps no other decisions are as important as those related to the officers. As John Zenger notes in *Leading Teams:*

> Without skilled leadership, teams can easily flounder, get off course, go too far or not go far enough, lose sight of their mission and connection with other teams, lose confidence, get stymied by interpersonal conflict, and simply fall far short of their enormous potential—especially in the early months and years of their development. . . .[96]

The importance of selecting the right people to lead the board team cannot be overstated. The right chair can bring out the best in a board, can help the board become give-and-take in its exchanges. He or she can keep the board on task, allow time for thoughtful reflection, and bring the question to a satisfying conclusion. Part-time keeper, part counselor, the board chair is often the deciding factor between a good board and an extraordinary one.

Expecting the board to manage itself, as some people count on, is unrealistic, as J. Richard Hackman observes in his *Groups that Work:*

> *Managers who hold this view often wind up providing teams with less structure than they actually need. . . . The unstated assumption is that there is some magic in group interaction process and that by working together members will evolve any structures that the team actually needs. . . . It is a false hope; there is no such magic.*[97]

The officers have a challenging job and the board chair in particular must be very skilled. Turning to team literature can be instructive about the responsibilities of team leaders. Jon Katzenbach and Douglas Smith in *The Wisdom of Teams* say to lay out six major ones:

1. Keep the purpose, goals, and approach, relevant and meaningful.
2. Build commitment and confidence.
3. Strengthen the mix and level of skills.
4. Manage relationships with outsiders, including removing obstacles.
5. Create opportunities for others.
6. Do real work.[98]

The authors of *Leading Teams* go even further and outline ten responsibilities:

1. Trust team members and build their trust in you.
2. Focus the team on its mission, goals, measurements, and boundaries.
3. Keep the team energized and moving forward.
4. Help team members bring their knowledge and experience to bear on solving stubborn problems.
5. Expand the team's range of effectiveness.
6. Encourage innovation and measured risk-taking.
7. Share key information with the team.
8. Make team members genuine business partners.
9. Help the team learn and grow from their mistakes.
10. Build the commitment of the team to its own success and to the success of other teams and the whole organization.[99]

Management Consultants for the Arts, which specializes in executive search, planning and organizational analysis, identify the ten characteristics of the most effective board chairs in *The Chair, More Than Just a Title:*

1. The most effective chairs are chosen because they are excellent candidates, not because no one else wants the job.
2. The most effective chairs commit to the position for at lease three or four years and are prepared to devote sufficient time to the business of the board.
3. The most effective chairs are drafted because of their knowledge of, interest in—and we hope, passion for—the organization, and not solely because of their wealth, connections, or other factors.
4. The most effective chairs cultivate a culture of collaboration and collective leadership throughout the organization.
5. The most effective chairs motivate their fellow trustees to make meaningful contributions to the group.
6. The most effective chairs forge ties between the organization and the community in ways that support the organization's mission.
7. The most effective chairs are constantly mindful of technical standards.
8. The most effective chairs consider their individual legacies; they set goals for their tenure, but keep them in perspective.
9. The most effective chairs actively work to develop future generations of leadership.
10. The most effective chairs play a critical role in the selection of a new CEO.

The best place to begin the discussion about officer duties is in the by-laws of the organization. Following this review with brainstorming and affinity grouping leads to a package of typical duties for the four primary officers of the board:

- Chair
  1. Mentor the vice chair.
  2. Provide support and counsel to the executive director.
  3. Represent the single voice of the board to the public.
  4. Chair board meetings.
     a. Develop and coordinate the board's agenda.
     b. Guide the board members to work together efficiently and effectively.
     c. Keep the board focused on important work and on task.
- Vice chair
  1. Serve as the chair elect.
  2. Serve as chair in the chair's absence.

- Treasurer
  1. Ensure that the executive director's financial guidelines are monitored.
  2. Represent the board to the financial community, including the auditors.
- Secretary
  1. Keep the board of directors' documents.
  2. Ensure that the bylaws and Delegation Plan are aligned.

Some boards will have more officers; others will combine the secretary and treasurer positions to have fewer officers. Some boards will be perfectly comfortable with the brevity of these duties; others will want more detail. For those that do, the National Center for Nonprofit Boards provides a tremendous resource for this sort of information, especially as it relates to the board chair. As noted earlier, guidelines for officers are often the same as those for the board and committees:

- Focus talent and time on important work.
- Be a give-and-take board that values the diversity and strength of all its members.
- Govern the organization—don't manage it.

Even though every team must have a team leader, it's never easy to pick the right person. How many of us really use personality profiles to make our choices? But we certainly can consider some attitudes that we know will make success more likely. Katzenbach and Smith concur:

Most team leaders must develop skills after they take the job. Those who succeed have an attitude that they do not need to make all key decisions nor assign all key jobs. Effective team leaders realize that they neither know all the answers, nor can they succeed without the other members of the team. The wisdom of teams lies in recognizing that any person, whether previously an autocrat or a democrat, who genuinely believes in the purpose of the team and the team itself can lead the team toward higher performance.[100]

Zenger agrees:

Leading teams is decidedly not a matter of "You either got it, or you ain't." Being an outstanding team leader is no more a natural talent than being an effective team member. Both roles require new skills and lots of practice.[101]

For the leadership of any board, there will always be inevitable difficulties. Larson and LaFasto identify three common problems. First is that "the team allows individuals to place self-interest above team-interest." Second, there is a "tendency for both team leaders and members to feel that the team is not sufficiently recognized for its accomplishment and that reward and incentive structures are not tied to team performance." Third, "team members, much more so than team leaders, are likely to complain about the absence of open, honest communication."[102]

Anticipating and attending to these customary problem areas is not difficult. To address the first concern about individuals placing self-interest above team interest, the officers in general, and the chair in particular, can regularly reinforce the details contained within the Leadership Plan and the Delegation Plan. Starting each meeting off by reinforcing the duties of the board and those of the board members can be particularly helpful. The board officers and the governance committee can easily address the second concern about recognition, while the third concern of open, honest communication can be met through an agenda that allows enough time for give and take and a chair that facilitates the discussion and is committed to building consensus whenever possible.

8.5 BOARD MEMBERS

Here's what Sharon Percy Rockefeller, CEO of WETA in Washington, says about her experience as a board member:

> When I joined the board of Stanford University, I asked an older, more experienced board member what I was supposed to do. He said to me, "Your main job is to ask why." I'll never forget that. A board member's role is simple. Ask why. Why do we have that priority? Why are we doing that now? Why aren't we doing that now? Board members ask these questions out of duty, but also because they care.[103]

The path to a great board follows that of the outstanding team. The prescription is uncomplicated, according to Larson and LaFasto. To create an effective team:

> First, make sure that the goal is clear, the performance goal crystallized. . . . .Then, select good people, members who possess the essential skills and abilities to accomplish the team's objectives. . . . .Finally, foster high standards of excellence.[104]

The Leadership Plan gives a clear goal and high standards of excellence, but what about good people? In nonprofit boards, "good people" is often not a variable. The board already has most of its members in place and the wait may be a long one for just the right people. Whether it's "wealth, work, and wisdom," "time, treasure, and talent," or the mother of them all, "give, get, or get off," board members are chosen for reasons other than their skill at governing. This is one of the seven realities of nonprofit boards. Often the greatest value that a board member brings to the board is his or her ability to lead the charge on a particular issue or support a need with a large contribution.

Katzenbach and Smith dismiss the concerns about finding just the right members: "We did not meet a single team that had all the needed skills at the outset . . . as long as the skill potential exists, the dynamics of a team cause that skill to develop."[105] Fortunately, the Delegation Plan makes the recruiting process much more effective and efficient. By knowing the duties and guidelines for the board member, potential candidates can be found who at least understand the expectations up front and can answer the call in an informed manner.

Like all duties, the construction process is uncomplicated. First, answer the question of what the board member duties should be. Most boards will give answers similar to those from Child Care Clearinghouse:

attitude of evaluation, speak up, share ideas, expertise, attend meetings, participate, feedback to the board, challenge what you hear, know mission, understand, be prepared, give funds, contribute funds, fundraise, get funds, attend functions (at least half each year), promote the agency, be visible, collaborate with the network, talk up the agency, recruit board members, work on at least one committee, work functions (at least one per year)

Second, affinity group the answers:

POOL OF IDEAS	DUTIES
attitude of evaluation, speak up, share ideas, expertise, attend meetings, participate, feedback to the board, challenge what you hear, know mission, understand, be prepared	Make good decisions.
give funds, contribute funds, fundraise, get funds, attend functions (at least half each year)	Raise money.

continued

POOL OF IDEAS	DUTIES
promote the agency, be visible, collaborate with the network, talk up the agency	Champion the organization.
recruit board members, work on at least one committee, work functions (at least one per year)	Do the board's work.

As with other duties and guidelines, these can be detailed to a greater level. For example, the duty to raise money might look like this:

- Raise money.
  1. Give a generous personal contribution within means ($1,000 level preferred).
  2. Support and attend fundraising events.
     a. Volunteer recognition dinner.
     b. Donor recognition events.
  3. Make fundraising solicitations when called upon.
  4. Support donor recognition.

Guidelines of behavior that are critical for the individual board member will generally include answers similar to those from the Child Care Clearinghouse:

care, be prepared, committee involvement, supportive, volunteer time and money, engaged, active-contributing, read minutes, ethical, loyal, conflicts of interest, obedient, buy into corporate goal, believe in mission, support board decisions, commitment to organization, don't leave it at the door, give-and-take board members, keep promises, follow through, keep confidences, positive with constructive criticism, professional, be supportive, open, no personal agendas, honest, consistent, direct

Affinity grouping brings the final guidelines into focus, which do not vary significantly from board to board:

POOL OF IDEAS	GUIDELINES
care, be prepared, committee involvement, supportive, volunteer time and money, engaged, active-contributing, read minutes, ethical	Use reasonable care, the same care as an ordinarily prudent person would exercise in a like position and under similar circumstances.
loyal, conflicts of interest	Be loyal to the organization.

Be loyal to the organization.

1. Always put the organization's well-being first in decision making and conduct.
2. Reveal any conflicts of interest in appearance or in fact.

| obedient, buy into corporate goal, believe in mission, support board decisions, commitment to organization, don't leave it at the door, give-and-take board members, keep promises, follow through, keep confidences, positive with constructive criticism, professional, be supportive, open, no personal agendas, honest, consistent, direct | Be obedient to the organization. |

Be obedient to the organization.

1. Be faithful to the values and vision contained within the Leadership Plan.
2. Act and speak for the board in an official capacity only if directed to do so by the board.
3. Fully support the board including majority decisions that the individual board member did not personally support.
4. Respect the chain of command between the board, the executive director, and the professional staff.

According to *The Legal Obligations of Nonprofit Boards*, there are three standards of conduct that must be met by board members. These standards are the *duty of care*, the *duty of loyalty*, and the *duty of obedience*. The duty of care says, "A board member owes the duty of 'care that an ordinarily prudent person would exercise in a like position and under similar circumstances.' " The duty of loyalty says that the board member must "give undivided allegiance to the organization when making decisions affecting the organization." Finally, the duty of obedience requires that board members "be faithful to the organization's mission."[106] These are important standards and the guidelines crafted for Child Care Clearinghouse put them solidly in front of the board.

Such explicitly crafted duties and guidelines can be very helpful in the recruiting process for new board members as they tell the board members exactly what will be expected of them. Rather than finding out the expectations after the fact, the prospective board member has most of the needed information to make the commitment to serve. Furthermore, the guidelines and duties offer the recruiter the opportunity to size up the potential candidate against the expectations.

There are people that shouldn't be recruited for the board under any circumstances, no matter how much potential they might have—no matter how much everyone can learn needed skills, no matter how great the ability to "give or get." First, there's the individual who is unwilling or unable to let go of his or her personal agenda when it conflicts with what the board needs. As Larson and LaFasto note:

> *Especially intense among teams that are struggling, but more likely than anything else to be noted as a problem across all teams . . . is that the team allows individuals to place self-interest above team-interest. Tolerating members who are more self-oriented than team-oriented is the most common complaint. . . .*[107]

Independent thinking is not the killer of a board when it's aligned with the needs of the board. It is all right to have a personal agenda that is in support of the team. It's not all right when that personal agenda gets in the way of the team. Says John Kay in *Why Firms Succeed:*

> *In the recent past, basketball was dominated by the Boston Celtics and the Los Angeles Lakers. One or the other of these clubs won more than half the NBA championships since World War II. But whereas baseball success is associated with strong players, basketball success is associated with strong teams. The Celtics and Lakers have had, on average, slightly stronger players than the league's average, but their outperformance has been far greater than the difference in their playing ability would suggest. Both spend an average amount on its players, well below the most flagrant overspenders and the frugal franchisees. In both 1990 and 1991, only one Boston player had a salary ranking in the NBA's top twenty. Rather, the value of the Celtics has rested on their performance as a team in establishing an aggregate worth more than sum of the parts. The written history of the Celtics, most of it not very scholarly, illustrates this. Red Auerbach, the longtime architect of the Celtic's success, is emphatic on this point: "The team is more important than any individual. If some guy couldn't live with that, my philosophy was to let him go and ruin the chemistry of some other team."*[108]

People who let their personal agendas get in the way or who simply can't get along with others may be difficult to identify until after they've spent some time on the board. As a consequence, there may be no way to avoid having these people on the board. It is absolutely vital, however, to deal with them when they are identified.

Second, there's the person who simply can't get along with others no matter how much training or coaching they've been given. In their study of American workers, David Michaelson & Associates identified the most important aspects of a successful team. Top on the list was getting along. Number two on the list was listening to each other.[109] Why is this so important? James Brian Quinn, Philip Anderson, and Sydney Finkelstein provide the answer in their article *Making the Most of the Best:*

> *Information sharing is critical because intellectual assets, unlike physical assets, increase in value with use. Properly stimulated, knowledge and intellect grow exponentially when shared. All learning and experience curves have this characteristic. A basic tenet of communication theory states that a network's potential benefits grow exponentially as the nodes it can successfully interconnect expand numerically. It is not difficult to see how this growth occurs. If two people exchange knowledge with each other, both gain information and experience linear growth. But if both then share their new knowledge with others—each of whom feeds back questions, amplifications, and modifications—the benefits become exponential.[110]*

What experienced board members sometimes forget is that every time someone new joins the board, the board team in essence has been reformed. Allowing time and consideration for building the new board team is an important matter that gives significant import to orientation processes. Starting out with a retreat or social event that brings the new members into the fold can pay handsome dividends. Pairing the new member with a seasoned member in a mentoring relationship can also be quite useful.

8.6 EXECUTIVE DIRECTOR

The job of an executive director is easy to define: Get the job done and help the board do its job as well. Brainstorming in just about any nonprofit will generate a list of answers similar to these:

> *get the job done, run the bus, operations, set program direction, keep vision and goals, facilitate strategic development, manage budget, steward of money and time, program compliance, create budgets, manage staff, delegate, evaluate staff, hire/fire, recruit—match Bigs and Littles, market programs, liaison to national, spokesperson for organization, community resource, schmooze the donors, work fundraisers,*

identify alternative sources of funds, write grants, liaison to United Way, support the board, liaison to board, provide the board with materials, promise steaks for lunch, educate the board, initiate new board members, prepare board meetings

Affinity group the answers and the following duties come into focus:

POOL OF IDEAS	DUTIES
get the job done, run the bus, operations, set program direction, keep vision and goals, facilitate strategic development, manage budget, steward of money and time, program compliance, create budgets, manage staff, delegate, evaluate staff, hire/fire, recruit—match Bigs and Littles, market programs, liaison to national, spokesperson for organization, community resource, schmooze the donors, work fundraisers, identify alternative sources of funds, write grants, liaison to United Way	Implement the Leadership Plan.
support the board, liaison to board, provide the board with materials, promise steaks for lunch, educate the board, initiate new board members, prepare board meetings	Provide support to the board.

Time and again these same answers come up about the job of the executive director. This ignites a debate when it comes to the role of the executive director in helping the board do its work. Some observers say that it is the job of the board to help itself. Others say that the seven realities of the board make this implausible. Robert D. Herman and Richard D. Heimovics are definitive about this matter in their book, *Executive Leadership in Nonprofit Organizations:*

> *Our research shows that board members and staff expect executive directors to take responsibility for success and failure and they do take such responsibility. Thus, we*

argue, the board's performance becomes the executive's responsibility. We can no longer expect boards, in most cases, to improve their performance independently.[111]

This position is repeatedly taken by strategic boards. Even so, in the Herman and Heimovics' executive director–driven approach, the board isn't completely free of responsibility:

Boards are still expected to do much, but they are not expected to do things on their own. Chief executives are expected to provide board-centered leadership. Chief executives do not usurp the board's roles and responsibilities, however. Rather, effective chief executives know that helping their boards to meet their responsibilities is the best way to maximize effectiveness.[112]

The authors go on to summarize their thoughts:

On the one hand, since chief executives are going to be held responsible, perhaps they should assume full control, running things as they think best. The board then becomes either the proverbial rubber stamp or a combination rubber stamp and cash cow. Certainly these patterns are not unknown already. On the other hand, since chief executives are going to be held responsible, and since they do accept responsibility for mission accomplishment and public stewardship, perhaps they should work to see that boards fulfill their legal, organizational, and community roles. We advocate this second option, not only because it is consistent with legal requirements and voluntaristic values, but also because, as our other research findings demonstrate, it is more likely to lead to organizational effectiveness.[113]

The strategic board is not a rubber-stamp board, but it does have high expectations for the executive director. Instead of asking the executive director to read its mind, the strategic board spells its expectations out in advance through the Governance Plan, especially in the Leadership and Delegation Plans.

The elegance of the executive director–driven approach is its simplicity, but the authors may assume too much about the experience of the person at the heart of their philosophy. These full-time professional executive directors are usually early-career, first-time executives with five or fewer years of tenure.[114] With 80 percent of nonprofits having budgets of less than $1 million[115] money is tight, executive salaries low, and tensions high in what has become a very tight market. It may be unrealistic to expect to attract executive directors who have the experience and talent to work with top-rank corporate chief executives and community leaders.

Perhaps the Herman and Heimovics approach works well with larger organizations that have the resources to hold onto talented executives, but smaller organizations will continue to be inviting to rookie executives who will have their hands full with operational duties. This is why a strategic board is such an asset to the organization. Rather than expecting the executive director to have all the answers about what to do, the Governance Plan fills them in through an interactive process where the board and the executive director learn together.

The typical way to start thinking about executive director guidelines is to imagine those things that might keep the board members awake at night. Here are the guidelines generated in brainstorming by the Child Care Clearinghouse board:

> *Internet bad stuff, unethical behavior, don't run off with the money, be legal, don't lose sight of strategic plan, duty of loyalty, report status versus goals, don't talk with other agencies for merger without talking to board first, development, NSFRE, compliance with national and United Way, see lay of land for revenue sources, don't disrespect staff, personnel handbook, turnover, poor morale, poor pay, poor management, complacency, burnout, no surprises, staff changes, serious allegations with Bigs, keep board up to date, don't manipulate board, don't let board waste executive director's time, positive margin from operations without investment income, live within budget, financially prudent, clean audit, deal with management letter, stay on top of budget, lend money, don't invade endowment*

Many of these thoughts are indeed things that should worry the board. The board member understands that he cannot watch over the shoulder of the executive director. Guidelines offer a way for the board to be present in spirit by saying, "Here are the guidelines that you must operate within. If you have a variance, let us know." It is a true risk management approach to delegating accountability and authority to the executive director for implementing the Leadership Plan.

The guidelines shown for the executive director in Exhibit 8.4 are like those for the board, committees, officers, and board members in that there is little variance from organization to organization. That is, almost all organizations will have guidelines that include finance, personnel, board relations, fundraising, and risk management. The degree of detail within the guideline depends upon the particular organization and its circumstances. If at any time the board finds it needs more or less detail in the guidelines for the executive director or, for that matter, the board, committees, officers, or board members, it takes a simple motion to make it so.

Notice that there are no responses in the left column alongside the guidelines for the executive director for endowment funds and risk

POOL OF IDEAS	GUIDELINES
Internet bad stuff, unethical behavior, don't run off with the money, be legal, don't lose sight of strategic plan, duty of loyalty, report status versus goals, don't talk with other agencies for merger without talking to board first	The executive director shall conduct himself or herself with the highest business and professional standards at all times, never causing or allowing any practice that is illegal or unethical or that breaches the terms of this Governance Plan. With regard to interpretation of these guidelines, the executive director shall: 1. Use reasonable interpretation, the same as an ordinarily prudent person would exercise in a like position and under similar circumstances.
development, NSFRE, compliance with national and United Way, see lay of land for revenue sources	With regard to development, the executive director shall: 1. Follow the standards set by the National Society of Fund Raising Executives. 2. Avoid any development practice that could embarrass the organization.
don't disrespect staff, personnel handbook, turnover, poor morale, poor pay, poor management, complacency, burnout	With regard to personnel matters, the executive director shall: 1. Treat the staff and volunteers fairly and respectfully. 2. Establish, communicate, and implement effective personnel policies that are reviewed by independent counsel annually. 3. Establish, communicate, and implement clear accountabilities for staff and monitor performance accordingly. 4. Pay compensation at a level required to attract and retain the qualified staff needed to implement this Governance Plan. 5. Advise the board before making a hire-or-fire change in personnel at the senior level.

Exhibit 8.4   Sample Executive Director Guidelines   (*continued*)

POOL OF IDEAS	GUIDELINES
no surprises, staff changes, serious allegations with Bigs, keep board up-to-date, don't manipulate board, don't let board waste executive director's time	With regard to communication to the board, the executive director shall: 1. Provide information to the board, committees, officers, or board members in a timely manner that could have a significant impact on the organization or in any way cause embarrassment. 2. Send information in advance of board meetings by at least one week. 3. Help the board in its implementation of the Governance Plan. 4. Not burden the board with insignificant issues that divert focus from the Leadership Plan. 5. Inform the board if it is burdening the staff with insignificant issues that divert focus from the Governance Plan. 6. Foster a relationship with the board based on trust and respect.
positive margin from operations without investment income, live within budget, financially prudent, clean audit, deal with management letter, stay on top of budget, lend money, don't invade endowment	With regard to financial matters, the executive director shall: 1. Make no capital acquisition of greater than $10,000. 2. Draw no more than 5 percent income annually from endowment investments. 3. Have and follow an audit-proof procedure for handling income and disbursements. 4. Receive a clean audit and comply with any recommendations outlined in the accompanying management letter. 5. Not take on any debt including lines of credit. 6. Achieve a positive budget surplus annually of income over expenses subject to the following provisions: a. Income shall exclude planned gifts not budgeted and investment

Exhibit 8.4   Sample Executive Director Guidelines   (*continued*)

POOL OF IDEAS	GUIDELINES

	income from endowment funds other than the 5 percent annual draw.
	  b. Expenses shall exclude unfunded depreciation, any incentive package costs for management and contributions to endowment funds.
	7. Present budgets with a probability of occurrence of at least 80 percent.
	8. Not borrow or lend funds.
	
	With regard to endowment funds under management, the executive director shall:
	1. Invest in funds with annual three-year and five-year performance of at least the top quartile.
	2. Invest in any fund with a manager tenure of at least five years.
	3. Invest only in funds that follow the investment guidelines established by the local community foundation.
	
	With regard to risk assessment and management, the executive director shall:
	1. Protect the organization's assets and earning power by using proper risk management techniques. Specifically, the executive director shall:
	  a. Have programs in place to identify risk, quantify risk, minimize, transfer, and/or eliminate risk, monitor risk, and inform the board of directors about programs for risk assessment and management.

management. These particular guidelines were adopted from the guidelines of other organizations, which is a common practice to reassure that the board hasn't forgotten anything important.

Guidelines are ultimately triggers that cause the executive director to bring matters to the board for discussion and perhaps exemption. It is not always possible for the surplus to be met, for example, as circumstances with budgets change unexpectedly. The guidelines implicitly require that the executive director inform the board of variances in a timely fashion; by doing this, confidence and trust are built and the partnership between the board and the executive director is strengthened.

CHAPTER 9

Adding Value

Eighty percent of success is showing up.
—Woody Allen

9.1 INTRODUCTION

The corporate solicitation had come to a close, the memento of thanks presented, and the proposal for the coming year had been discussed. The president of the corporation obviously enjoyed his affiliation as a funder and a board member of Child Care Clearinghouse. His busy schedule of travel had not stood in his way as an active board member and he had missed just one of the last five board meetings. "Bob," he said to the executive director, "I want to do more. I want to be more active on this board, really make a difference, really add value."

Bob couldn't believe his luck: a generous corporate leader and board member willing to do more! "We could certainly use leadership on the performance assurance committee to figure out how to invest our growing endowment," Bob replied, "and someone like you could make a magnificent contribution as a leader of our planned giving initiatives to build our endowment." The corporate president thought for a moment and answered, "Finances have never been of much interest to me and I don't much like asking other people for money. Isn't there something else that I could do?"

That board members want to make a difference and add value to an organization goes without challenge. Most board members sincerely want to help, to make a difference in the organizations that they serve. Nonetheless, boards are not meant to provide entertainment for their members. The board is a means to an end, in the case of the strategic board, it is the achievement of a chosen destiny. If there is a job that the board member can do that adds value, by all means it should be done. Yet making work for the purpose of keeping the board member interested wastes precious resources. Some will say it is a different story if that board member is an important contributor where maintaining connectivity is the objective, but there are better, more effective methods to use than inventing board work.

As elementary as it may seem, 80 percent of what it means to be a good board comes from not being a bad board. The lion's share of being positive is not being negative. Doing no harm seems somehow too simple, too basic to be of value, but it is tremendously significant. Instead of asking themselves how they can do better, good boards often ask what they could do to stop being unproductive.

9.2 BOARDS

How do boards add the most value to the organization? Aside from accomplishing the duties within their guidelines, boards are at their best on the big-ticket items. The mother of all of these is executive director selection. This is because the executive director is often the bearer of the values and vision. Next would be the work done on the Leadership Plan, especially in regard to the selection of new strategies.

Much has been written about how boards add value. Thomas P. Holland and Myra Backmon identify four ways:

Support the Chief Executive
   . . . helping the chief executive determine what matters most. . . . Not every matter is equally important and not all issues can be addressed, so relative priorities must be set.

Serve as a Sounding Board
   These boards create opportunities for the chief executive to think aloud about questions and concerns well before it is necessary to come to conclusions or make recommendations . . . a board must encourage candid discussion of embryonic ideas, ambiguous issues, and unclear challenges in the road ahead.

Encourage and Reward Experimentation
   Effective boards encourage experimentation, trying out new approaches and alternative ways of dealing with issues. . . . Raising critical questions and challenging assumptions stimulate new ideas and creative alternatives for the future of the organization.

Model Effective Behavior
   Most important, effective board model the behaviors they desire in others. . . . Boards that call for accountability of staff have far greater credibility if they show by example how that is to be done.[116]

Ask most executive directors for a specific moment of extraordinary value from their board and it will have a very personal texture to it. The executive director recalls the 30 yellow roses delivered one a day over a month to his terminally ill wife. Another executive director remembers the celebration of her twentieth anniversary complete with commendations from the Governor. Many executive directors will say that the board is at its best when it listens carefully and provides encouragement to the executive director.

9.3 BOARD MEMBERS

Unfortunately, in looking for homeruns board members frequently miss the chance to hit the single that wins the game. The board member misses out on the opportunity to have significant impact by waiting for the big things to come along. The value of a promptly paid pledge pays big dividends to the fundraising staff; an unsolicited invitation to lunch for the executive director "just to see how you're doing" can deliver remarkable results in terms of building self-confidence. If boards are best on the big-ticket things, board members are at their best on a one-to-one basis. Sometimes a few words that may seem small to a veteran corporate leader are career-building to the inexperienced executive director.

Most executives would answer the question of how board members add the most value in very specific terms: "Raise more money." Being ready and willing to assist the organization with the ongoing activities to raise the necessary funds for operations is a critical need. Many executive directors vividly recall that those board members who asked tough questions are some of the best at adding value. A single board member who actively participates in decision making at the full board level can make an immense difference in an organization. Take Child Care Clearinghouse for example.

Julie had always expressed concern to the executive director that she talked too much at board meetings. She had come on the board during a substantial period of growth and she regularly asked what the organization was doing to be a good community citizen. Her vision was that the organization could do more to lend a hand to less-fortunate nonprofits. Time and again Bob, the executive director, reassured Julie that her voice was important and that he wished he had ten other board members that provided the stimulation in a board meeting that she did. Over the years as a board member, Julie continued her tough questioning and slowly other board members began to echo her. Could the organization do more to be a community leader?

In building each new Governance Plan, Bob and the board did not directly identify any opportunities to be a better community citizen. But because Julie had kept the issue in front of the board in a positive way, Bob was more open to the possibilities and the matter finally became a strategy to explore. The rest is history: The first opportunity for helping came to Bob when the board president of another, smaller agency with a similar mission asked for help. Ten months later, a new joint program between the two agencies was launched with an annual price tag of $1 million. This ushered in a new period of dynamic activity for the Clearinghouse that was a direct result of one board member asking tough questions over a period of years.

A single board member can make a difference. Bob recalls having a 20-minute conversation with the president of a large corporation who was a board member wherein he was advised to keep his altitude at 40,000 feet when beginning the discussions for the joint program. "The details are less important now than the vision," the president remarked. This one moment of guidance delivered incredible value to the organization. While the board member would not see this as making a major difference, Bob would most respectfully disagree.

If mentoring the executive director or providing encouragement at full board level delivers such great value, why isn't it a duty of board members? In some boards it is, but in general boards try to stay away from mandating this as a duty because of the potential for abuse on the part of the board members. If the executive director asks for advice from a board member, there is no issue with giving it. Unsolicited advice, however, can pass for instruction and thus dilute accountability.

Being responsive to the executive director who asks for advice is common courtesy and should not breach the chain of command. Because the line is so thin between advice and instruction, however, many boards are loath to prescribe that a board member actively give unsolicited advice. It is often difficult to fulfill the duty of asking tough questions if the board member is also enjoined to be a cheerleader of the executive director. Many times the two are mutually exclusive.

9.4 EXECUTIVE DIRECTOR

Executive directors are significant participants in the process of adding value.

Many executive directors, call them presidents, chief professional officers, or CEOs, live in the world of the traditional model of governance where the board decides what and the staff decide how. This is not how the world works. The executive director has a profound role to play in making the board effective. As Herman and Heimovics observe:

The chief executive is the center of leadership for the organization . . . in most established, staffed nonprofit organizations, chief executives come to be expected by board members, other staff, and themselves to be finally responsible for the successes and failures of the organization. . . . The assertion that organizational effectiveness is enhanced by chief executives taking responsibility, if necessary, for board development and performance is neither unsupported deduction nor wishful thinking. Empirical evidence supports this argument . . . effective executives provided substantially more leadership for their boards than those in the comparison group; that is, they took responsibility for providing board-centered leadership. More specifically, we found that effective executives work with their boards to facilitate interaction both within the board and between themselves and the board. They attend to board members' feelings and needs, envision changes in organizational functioning, promote and reinforce board accomplishments, and provide useful decision-making information to the board.[117]

The truly curious thing is that many executive directors frustrated with their boards fail to recognize their own abilities to make governance better. Like Dorothy in *The Wizard of Oz*, these executive directors have been wearing the ruby slippers all along. Armed with the Strategic Board model of governance, any executive director in partnership with the board can create an environment that fosters great governance. To the executive director that asks "What good is the board?" comes the answer that he or she alone is largely responsible for the answer.

Sample Delegation Plan

The buck stops here.
—Harry S. Truman

This sample Delegation Plan is from Big Brothers-Big Sisters chapter. It is meant only to be an illustration and should not serve as the ideal by which all Delegation Plans are constructed. It is meant to give the reader an impression of what a finished Delegation Plan would look like for many organizations.

BOARD

BOARD DUTIES
I. Decide where to go tomorrow through the Leadership Plan. II. Delegate who does what through the Delegation Plan. III. Determine whether it happened through the Vigilance Plan. IV. Decide what gets done today through the Management Plan. V. Raise funds.

COMMITTEE DUTIES
BOARD COMMITTEES—HELPING THE BOARD DO ITS JOB

I. Executive
    A. Assure performance by setting and ensuring implementation of the vigilance plan.
    B. Ensure that the executive director is selected, supported, reviewed, and managed.

C. Act for the full board in the event of an emergency in which the full board cannot be effectively convened.
D. Act for the full board on routine matters during months when the board does not meet.
E. Determine the board's agenda.

II. Development
A. Recommend fundraising policies.
B. Raise the board portion of the annual campaign.
C. Serve as the board's think tank for innovation in fundraising.
D. Provide qualified prospects.

III. Governance and Nominating
A. Recruit and orient new board members.
B. Ensure that the board is educated.
C. Make sure that the accomplishments of the board are recognized.
D. Recommend the officer slate and committee membership.

IV. Special Events
A. Bowling for Kids
B. Old Time Fun
C. Gourmet Dinner

STAFF COMMITTEES—HELPING THE STAFF DO ITS JOB

I. Program
A. Ensure visible mentoring programs, which appropriately respond to identified community needs.
B. Provide services to waiting-list children.
C. Ensure agency program compliance with the highest professional standards and the national Big Brothers–Big Sisters standards.

II. Marketing
A. Improve community awareness of and exposure to the Big Brothers–Big Sisters program.

III. Recruitment
A. Increase the recruitment of adult volunteers, especially minority males.

OFFICER DUTIES

I. President
   A. Serve as the primary contact between the board and the executive director.
   B. Act as the official spokesperson of the board.
   C. Run effective meetings.
      1. Chair board meetings.
      2. Develop and coordinate the board's agenda.
      3. Keep the board on task.
   D. Encourage participation in a positive atmosphere.
   E. Chair the executive committee.
II. Vice President
   A. Serve as the president elect.
   B. Serve as president in the president's absence.
   C. Chair the governance committee.
III. Secretary/Treasurer
   A. Ensure that the executive director's guidelines that pertain to finances are monitored.
   B. Represent the board to the financial community including the auditors.
   C. Keep the board of directors' documents.
   D. Ensure that the bylaws and delegation plans are aligned.
   E. Chair the development committee.

BOARD, COMMITTEE, AND OFFICER GUIDELINES

I. Focus talent and time on important work.
   A. Center agendas on important work.
   B. Conduct work in an effective and efficient manner, never wasting time.
   C. Ensure that committees and officers respect the board's authority.
      1. Avoid rubber stamping whenever possible.
II. Be a give-and-take board that values the diversity and strength of all its members.
   A. Use *Robert's Rules of Order* to provide a framework for conducting meetings and promoting civility.

B. Exhibit professional decorum at all times.

C. Strive for consensus on important issues.

III. Govern the organization—don't manage it.

A. Delegate responsibility and authority for implementation of the Leadership Plan to the executive director.

1. Ensure that the executive director is the board's sole link to the professional management, its actions, and results.

2. Speak with one voice, recognizing that only decisions made by the board acting as a unified body are binding on the executive director.

B. Ensure that staff committees are accountable to and support the work of the staff.

C. Foster a supportive relationship with the staff.

1. Respect the staff's experience.

2. Be consistent.

BOARD MEMBERS

BOARD MEMBER DUTIES

I. Participate resolutely in decision making.

A. Know the business.

B. Study advance materials.

C. Attend at least 75 percent of scheduled meetings.

D. Ask tough questions.

E. Vote conscientiously.

II. Participate actively in fundraising.

A. Give a generous personal contribution within means.

B. Attend at least half of the fundraising events.

C. Make fundraising solicitations when possible.

III. Champion the organization to and from the community.

IV. Strengthen the board leadership.

A. Recruit new board members.

B. Serve on at least one committee per year.

C. Work at least one function per year.

V. Strengthen the staff leadership.

A. Recruit Bigs and Littles.

BOARD MEMBER GUIDELINES

I. Use reasonable care, the same care as an ordinarily prudent person would exercise in a like position and under similar circumstances.

II. Be loyal to the organization.
  A. Always put the organization's well-being first in decision making and conduct.
  B. Reveal any conflicts of interest in appearance or in fact.

III. Be obedient to the organization.
  A. Be faithful to the values and vision contained within the Leadership Plan.
  B. Act and speak for the board in an official capacity only if directed to do so by the board.
  C. Fully support the board, including majority decisions that the individual board member did not personally support.
  D. Respect the chain of command between the board, the executive director, and the professional staff.

EXECUTIVE DIRECTOR

DUTIES

I. Implement the Leadership Plan.
II. Provide support to the board.

GUIDELINES

I. The executive director shall conduct himself or herself with the highest business and professional standards at all times, never causing or allowing any practice that is illegal or unethical or that breaches the terms of this Governance Plan.

II. With regard to development, the executive director shall:
  A. Follow the standards set by the National Society of Fund Raising Executives.
  B. Avoid any development practice that could embarrass the organization.

III. With regard to personnel matters, the executive director shall:
  A. Treat the staff and volunteers fairly and respectfully.

B. Establish, communicate, and implement effective personnel policies that are annually reviewed by independent counsel.

C. Establish, communicate, and implement clear accountabilities for staff and monitor performance accordingly.

D. Pay compensation at a level required to attract and retain the qualified staff needed to implement this Governance Plan.

E. Advise the board before making a hire-or-fire change in personnel at the senior level.

IV. With regard to communication to the board, the executive director shall:

A. Provide information to the board, committees, officers, or board members in a timely manner that could have a significant impact on the organization or in any way cause embarrassment.

B. Send information in advance of board meetings by at least one week.

C. Help the board in its implementation of the Governance Plan.

D. Not burden the board with insignificant issues that divert focus from the Leadership Plan.

E. Inform the board if it is burdening the staff with insignificant issues that divert focus from the Governance Plan.

F. Foster a relationship with the board based upon trust and respect.

V. With regard to financial matters, the executive director shall:

A. Make no capital acquisition of greater than $10,000.

B. Draw no more than 5 percent income annually from endowment investments.

C. Have and follow an audit-proof procedure for handling income and disbursements.

D. Receive a clean audit and comply with any recommendations outlined in the accompanying management letter.

E. Not take on any debt including lines of credit.

F. Achieve a positive budget surplus annually of income over expenses subject to the following provisions:

1. Income shall exclude planned gifts not budgeted and investment income from endowment funds other than the 5 percent annual draw.

2. Expenses shall exclude unfunded depreciation, any incentive package costs for management, and contributions to endowment funds.

G. Present budgets with a probability of occurrence of at least 80 percent.

H. Not borrow or lend funds.

VI. With regard to endowment funds under management, the executive director shall:

A. Invest in funds with annual three-year and five-year performance of at least the top quartile.

B. Invest in any fund with a manager tenure of at least five years.

C. Invest only in funds that follow the investment guidelines established by the local community foundation.

VII. With regard to interpretation of these guidelines, the executive director shall:

A. Use reasonable interpretation, the same as an ordinarily prudent person would exercise in a like position and under similar circumstances.

VIII. With regard to risk assessment and management, the executive director shall:

A. Protect the organization's assets and earning power by using proper risk management techniques. Specifically, the executive director shall:

1. Have programs in place to identify risk, quantify risk, minimize, transfer, and/or eliminate risk, monitor risk, and inform the board of directors about the programs for risk assessment and management.

IX. With regard to planning, the executive director shall:

A. Operate annually with a Governance Plan containing Leadership, Delegation, Vigilance, and Management

The Management Plan

The best way to make your dreams come true is to wake up.
—Paul Valery

CHAPTER 10

What Gets Done Today?

All our dreams can come true—if we have the courage to pursue them.
—Walt Disney

MANAGEMENT PLAN
What gets done today?

Department Map
Budget Summary

BOARD	**STAFF**
Success Measures	Success Measures
Imperatives	Imperatives
Goals	Goals
	Individual Plans

10.1 INTRODUCTION

The Management Plan answers what gets done today through goals to be accomplished in the next 12 months by the board and staff in their specific departments. It is analogous to an operational or tactical plan as described in *Applied Strategic Planning:*

> Tactical planning *and* operational planning *are synonymous. Both relate to how to get the job done, whereas strategic planning is concerned with what shall be done. That is, both tactical and operational plans are concerned with the setting of specific, measurable objectives and milestones to be achieved by the divisions, departments, work groups, and individuals with the organization, typically in a shorter and more specific time frame.*[118]

The Management Plan accomplishes many of the same purposes, but it adds a strong bias for improvement. At its core, the Management Plan is about doing better, it is definitely not a job description that describes day-to-day operations. Whether it is achieving a success measure target or improving a process, the Management Plan has forward momentum to it, a sense that things will be done better. Thus, it would not be a goal within the finance department of a nonprofit to simply process weekly payroll; it would be a goal to process that weekly payroll with a 25 percent increase in accuracy.

How involved is the board in deciding what gets done today? Does the board actually decide the goals for the staff? As is the case with many of the questions that come up in the Strategic Board model of governance, the answer is "It depends." Some boards with an early-career executive director might have great input into setting goals for staff departments, but this is rare for organizations with seasoned staff. Some boards want to see staff goals in the final presentation of the Governance Plan that is passed by the board; other boards don't. Normally, the board is only involved in setting goals for the board itself and does not monitor the staff portion of the Management Plan. Thus, the Management Plan is generally the work of the staff with the exception of goals that pertain to the board.

As opposed to the highly creative process that characterizes the Leadership Plan, the Management Plan is developed in a more mechanical, step-by-step approach. First a department map is generated to be sure that all function areas are identified. Leadership Plan success measures are then assigned to the departments and additional ones developed where needed. Imperatives are designated and goals and action steps are set for each department. Finally, a budget summary is developed. The place to start is by identifying all of the departments that need to exist to get the work done, not just those that are currently staffed.

10.2 DEPARTMENT MAP

Rather than building goals around job titles and people as is usually the case with traditional approaches, The Governance Plan requires that goals be built around function area departments that must exist for the organization to be successful, even if these departments do not have staff members. As a consequence, job titles and department boundaries have less meaning because people have job duties that often cross function areas. Since nonprofit organizations are lean and flat in terms of hierarchy, it is not uncommon for people to do many different jobs. The finance person does the budgets and answers the phones; the executive director handles governance, fundraising, and programming.

If a carefully considered department map is not done, there is a chance that some function areas will be neglected. In an organization with a budget of less than $500,000, it is unlikely that there will be a development director on staff, but fundraising must still get done. By making sure that there is a development department in the department map and Management Plan, it is much more likely that important matters won't drop through the cracks. Whether the people who work in the department are staff, board members, or volunteers, having a clearly identified department makes it likely that goals will be developed that can move the department ahead.

As with so many elements of the Governance Plan, the process for developing the department map is easy to do by using the brainstorming– affinity grouping tools. The staff generates the tasks that have to be done on a daily basis. These tasks are then grouped together to form the departments for the map. Exhibit 10.1 is a sample from a Big Brothers–Big Sisters chapter.

POOL OF IDEAS	DEPARTMENTS
support staff, governance, success celebrations, planning, pulling it all together, mentoring, liaison to the board, lead the organization	Executive
administration, office, budgets, payroll, insurance, credit union, human resources, FICA, order supplies, handle the mail, receptionist, telephone service, computers, technology	Administration
marketing, community awareness, educate other professionals, educate public, fund development, sponsorship fundraising, annual fund campaign, employee giving, board giving, get the money we need	Development
special events, the bowling event, the golf tournament, the annual roast,	Special Events
Bigs and Littles, recruit of little girls	Recruiting

core match program, Community University, University Medical	Core Match
	  Core Match
	  Community University
	  University Medical

high school mentoring program	High School Mentoring
teen mothers	Teen Mothers

Exhibit 10.1   Building a Department Map

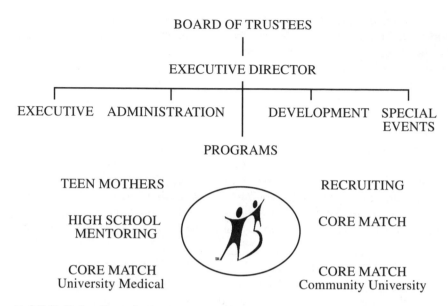

Exhibit 10.2   Sample Department Map

Once the departments are described, a chart is created that becomes the department map, like the one seen in Exhibit 10.2.

10.3 BUDGET SUMMARY

The budget summary is the last element to be finished in a Management Plan. Its place near the top of the list is only for information-access purposes. Board members are likely to page through the Governance Plan from front to back. Thus, while the budget is the last to be constructed, its placement near the top is indicative of its interest to board members.

There is tremendous variety in the budget formats that are used for the summary and there is no right or wrong style to use. A budget summary should not be longer than one or two pages, three at the most. Because it is information that the board needs, it is advisable to take counsel from the board treasurer about the format. So often the budget format is drawn at the convenience of the staff or may have been driven by just one individual, many times an executive director who has long since departed. The danger in asking too many people for their opinions is that the format may end up being too complicated; what should have been a simple three- or four-column presentation turns into something impossibly confusing.

In general, the budget format for a new fiscal year that is brought to the board for approval as part of a Governance Plan ought to have at least three columns. The first column should contain the projected results for the current year, the second column should contain the budget for the year coming up, and the third column should be a variance between the first two:

Income	Projection Ye 6/30/00 as of 4/30/00	Budget 6/30/01 proposed	Variance Column 2 minus Column 1
Earned Income			
Direct client payments	3,312	3,517	205
Third-party reimbursements	2,131	1,116	−1,015
Referral commissions	73	73	0
Regular commissions	31	44	13
Contract services	1,119	869	−250
Investments	224	257	33
Other earned	191	207	16
Earned Income total	7,081	6,083	−998

At the midyear forecast, the same format would be used, but with column headings adjusted accordingly and a column added for year-to-date activity:

Income	Year-to-Date as of 9/30/00	Budget Ye 6/30/01 as passed 7/1/00	Projection Ye 6/30/01 as of 9/30/00	Variance minus Column 3 minus Column 2
Earned Income				
Direct client payments	1,215	3,517	3,602	85
Third-party reimbursements	285	1,116	999	−117
Referral commissions	24	73	73	0
Regular commissions	11	44	46	2
Contract services	262	869	902	33
Investments	68	257	261	4
Other earned	52	207	201	−6
Earned Income Total	1,917	6,083	6,084	1

This format does not answer every question that a board member might have. It does not compare last year's year-to-date results against this year's, it does not contain elegant percentage comparisons. With the addition of another column, this basic format can be enhanced to do more:

	Year-to-Date as of 9/30/99	Year-to-Date as of 9/30/00	Budget Ye 6/30/01 as passed 7/1/00	Projection Ye 6/30/01 as of 9/30/00	Variance Column 4 minus column 3
Income					
Earned Income					
Direct client payments	999	1,215	3,517	3,602	85
Third-party reimbursements	187	285	1,116	999	−117
Referral commissions	22	24	73	73	0
Regular commissions	14	11	44	46	2
Contract services	301	262	869	902	33
Investments	88	68	257	261	4
Other earned	42	52	207	201	−6
Earned Income Total	1,653	1,917	6,083	6,084	1

Generally, the more information that is added and provides value to the board, the better, but there is always a limit that must respect the seven realities of nonprofit boards. Where that limit occurs is going to be different for every board, but there is real peril in providing too much information. The danger is that the board will not be able to wade through the details to find the truth. The best place to begin a discussion of the right format is at the absolute minimum, not the maximum. As a minimum rule of thumb, any budget presented to the board should give enough information to answer at least these three questions:

1. What has been spent so far this fiscal year?
2. What is the budget for the current fiscal year?
3. What is the projection for how the current fiscal year will end?

By having at least these three perspectives, the board can understand the basic financial position. Regrettably, the most common format revolves around year-to-date comparisons complete with percentages and extensive detail. This approach has arisen primarily because publicly held corporations use quarter-to-quarter comparisons and board members are comfortable with this format. In a nonprofit, however, such information can be largely distracting and is very time-consuming to develop. Above all else, the board must be able to easily get a clear picture of the anticipated surplus or deficit that will occur at the end of the fiscal year.

General Dillman Rash, a wizened community volunteer and sought-after board member in Louisville, Kentucky, used to call the surplus or deficit the "southeast corner of the budget," referring to the lower-right corner of the financial statement where he said, "The sun goes up or down on the executive director." It was, he said, "about the only number that any board member worth his salt should care about."

CHAPTER **11**

Building the Management Plan

The human tendency to regard little things as important has produced very many great things.
—**G. C. Lichtenberg**

MANAGEMENT PLAN
What gets done today?

Department Map
Budget Summary

BOARD	**STAFF**
Success Measures	Success Measures
Imperatives	Imperatives
Goals	Goals
	Individual Plans

11.1 INTRODUCTION

The department map in the Management Plan is a tool that is used to identify all of the departments that need to exist to get the work done. Nonprofit organizations are chronically understaffed, and it is inevitable that some jobs go undone because they are forgotten or not identified in the first place. The department map consequently guides the creation, revision, or elimination of departments throughout the organization. Once defined, the departments are where goals are set for the work that gets done.

In some respects, the department map could be discarded and not shown in the Management Plan since the departments themselves are clearly outlined in the document. The map is shown because it can help the board and staff quickly understand how the things are organized.

The same can be said of the budget summary, which is presented in the Management Plan as a matter of convenience for the board and staff. This puts all of the important materials that the board might require in one simple place so that they are easily accessible to everyone and can be approved by the board. The real work of the Management Plan is at the department level in the success measures, imperatives, and goals.

11.2 DEPARTMENT SUCCESS MEASURES

Success measures are the first step in helping people decide what gets done today through goals and action steps. Determining success measures begins with assigning each success measure from the Leadership Plan to appropriate departments. Mission success measures are almost always assigned to the board.

Once all of the Leadership Plan success measures are assigned, additional success can be developed for departments that do not have any or to augment those departments that need more. It is not a requirement that every department in an organization have success measures; remember that all success measures have a cost to them in terms of time and effort. A facilities department that maintains heating and air-conditioning equipment, mows the lawn, and keeps the building clean is unlikely to have any Leadership Plan success measures and it may have a tough time figuring out what success measures to use, let alone manage the tracking.

Success measures, whether assigned from the Leadership Plan or developed specifically for a particular department, have a distinct purpose to help people decide what goals to pursue in the coming 12 months. Success measures should never be an end in themselves. It could be a waste of time to develop success measures for the facility department of a small nonprofit. Imperatives, which are discussed later, will do the trick for designing that department's goals.

As with the facilities department, it is unlikely that a development department will have any Leadership Plan success measures assigned to it. Even so, there are abundant opportunities to develop meaningful success measures. From the total amount of funds raised to renewal rates, there are many possibilities. Here is what a Big Brothers–Big Sisters Chapter chose for its development department:

	'97	'98	'99	'00 Budget	'00 7/5 YE Forecast	'00 12/31 YE Final	'01
Total funds raised	72,824	125,629	120,958	118,000			125,000
Annual fund: Friends	26,544	14,243	20,808	23,000			25,000
Firms	7,752	15,003	15,144	15,000			17,500
Foundations	7,854	17,171	16,350	15,000			15,000
Grants	30,683	79,212	68,656	65,000			67,500

Up until its first Governance Plan, the chapter tracked this development information, but it had never consolidated it into one department where it could be easily utilized for making decisions about goals. A development department in a different organization might choose another array of success measures as illustrated by the following:

	'96–'97	'97–'98	'98–'99	Budget	'99–'00 12/31 YE Forecast	Final	'00–'01 Budget	'01–'02
Sponsorship	237K	1.01M	1.02M	950K	1.07M	1.07M	950K	975K
Annual fund: Funds	842K	253K	280K	295K	310K	332K	350K	368K
Repeat rate	.67	.73	.76	.77	.77	.77	.78	.79
Documented legacies	7	13	18	20	20	20	22	24
Expense ÷ contributed	.14	.14	.13	.13	.12	.11	.11	.11
Contributed ÷ income	.23	.21	.25	.23	.24	.24	.27	.27

Is documented legacies the correct measure? Is it measured correctly? Should documented legacies be measured by the estimated amount of the legacy as opposed to the number of legacies that are known? These are all appropriate questions, which are best decided by the development staff and executive director.

The degree of involvement from the board in deciding staff success measures and the eventual imperatives and goals is customarily very limited. In some nonprofits, the board never sees the staff portion of the Management Plan, while in others the board is given this information as matter of practice, but is not invited to comment on it. In smaller organizations with limited staff, the board may be very involved. Whatever fits for the organization at its particular time and place is agreeable, but there needs to be careful consideration of the fine line between advice and instruction and the covenant to respect the chain of command between the board, the executive director, and the professional staff.

Many executive directors have found that sharing the staff portion of the Management Plan with the board has few if any negative consequences. It heightens the board's understanding of the complexity of the organization and builds its confidence in the staff through knowing that a well-thought-out Management Plan is in place. Some executive directors invite board members, officers in particular, to sit in at staff progress reviews as a way to make the process more significant (e.g., give it teeth) and to provide the board members with a direct opportunity to observe the executive director's performance.

Assigning the Leadership Plan success measures to departments and developing any additional success measures is a highly interactive process that is best done with all of the key staff present. This provides the added benefit of building a greater understanding of what other team members do within the organization.

11.3 IMPERATIVES

Imperatives are the second step in helping people decide what work gets done. Overall, imperatives are obstacles that impede success. The easiest way to identify imperatives is by addressing the following points:

- Problems
- Weaknesses
- Threats

The department is in search of obstacles to its success in the same manner as was done earlier for the organization in the Leadership Plan. Each department should list as many answers to these questions as possible, affinity group the answers to eliminate duplication, and prioritize the imperatives down to two or three at the most. Given the fact that some departments will not have full-time staff assigned to the department, and in the interest of building an understanding of the total organization, it is best to identify department imperatives with all of the key staff present. Here is how a Big Brothers–Big Sisters chapter answered the board question of imperatives for the administration department:

Problems: Fear that system is skewed and others will get special favors (i.e., "best" volunteers and/or children); new employees "paying" for the "sins" of past employees; low level of optimism among staff; lack of respect for diversity and strengths among staff; redundant paper and tracking systems; mistrust among staff and/or management inability to network program; lack of official training; lack of teamwork, low visibility of organization in the community, need for better marketing

Weaknesses: Some reluctant to assist others; more interest in affixing blame than in helping problem-solve; high expectation of staff without guidelines; unwillingness to share information

Threats: Lack of cooperation among staff; withholding information

With this information, the staff picked those items that were the most actionable. For example, redesigning agency operations and fixing redundant paper and tracking systems are both actionable obstacles, but the first is a much more difficult assignment compared with the second. Through discussion and debate, the number of imperatives from this department's list were reduced to just two:

1. Redundant paper and tracking systems
2. Low visibility

The first is a very addressable problem that can be executed immediately; the second is a bigger issue that will pay handsome dividends over time. Here is another example from the same organization for the development department:

Problems: Lack of a strategic plan for operations and planned giving; lack of total board involvement and commitment to raising money; missing the tremendous transfer of wealth to take place over the next few years

Weaknesses: Limited staff time and resources; no formal fund development training or experience within existing staff; no truly wealthy and/or highly positioned patrons or volunteers

Threats: All other 501(c)(3) organizations; United Way funding allocation decreases

These responses are then distilled down into just one imperative: lack of a plan for operations.

Boards also set imperatives, which can be a valuable and stimulating exercise. This is where self-assessment can be a very useful tool in terms of identifying those areas of board structure or process that should be addressed.

With the success measures and the department imperatives in place, the staff is ready to construct the goals that will constitute the work that gets done today.

11.4 GOALS

Call it an objective, tactic, or target, a goal is meant to do just one thing: achieve a result. In the case of the Management Plan, that result is an improvement or innovation for the organization. Goals do not describe the day-to-day activities of the organization, but do deliver results that will make those day-to-day activities better.

It is unusual for any department to have more than two or three goals in any given year. While goals in the Strategic Board model of governance are never about day-to-day operations, goals must respect the reality that the regular work of the organization must get done. The time needed to implement a goal must be found in the same work week that existed before the goal was decided. Thus, a department with seven meaningful and challenging goals may fail with five due to lack of time. In fact, it is not uncommon for one or two departments or one or two board committees within the organization to have no goals at all for a particular year. This situation might arise because of new staff, because day-to-day activities in a particular department are currently too time-consuming, or because the department has just concluded a major improvement project.

At this point in the process of building the Management Plan most departments have the success measures in place and all departments have imperatives identified. The departments now have the information needed to decide the goals for the coming 12 months. It is very important that the goals that are chosen have the highest probability of succeeding:

> Goals can be implicit or explicit, vague or clearly defined, and self-imposed or externally imposed. Whatever their form, they serve to structure employee time and effort. Two key attributes of goals are particularly important for individual goal setting:
>
> - *Goal clarity.* Goals must be clear and specific if they are to be useful for directing effort. The employee thus will know what he or she is expected to accomplish—and not have to guess.
> - *Goal difficulty.* Goals should be moderately challenging. If they are too easy to attain, the employee may procrastinate or approach the goal lackadaisically.

The employee may not accept a goal that is too difficult and thus not try to meet it.[119]

Hellriegel, Solcum, and Woodman summarize their thinking about goal setting in this manner:

In general, clear and challenging goals lead to higher performance than do vague or general goals. For example, it would be better to set a salesperson's goal at a specific amount to be sold than to set a goal of "trying to increase sales" or "doing your best." Goals that are difficult—but attainable—will lead to higher performance than will easy goals. Unrealistically high goals that can't be reached may not be accepted or may lead to high performance in the short run. Employees eventually get discouraged and stop trying.[120]

Making sure that those who do the work are involved in setting the goals is also important:

Setting clear and challenging, but not impossible, goals may be thought of as necessary but not sufficient for gaining high performance and focused efforts from individuals. Goal acceptance is also necessary. Goal acceptance is the extent to which a goal is approved, favored, and recognized by the employee. The degree of acceptance could range from a deep personal commitment to the goal to rejection of and hostility toward it. . . . In general, positive goal acceptance is more likely if employees participate in setting goals.

The expected incentives for achieving goals play an important role in the degree of goal acceptance and commitment. The greater the extent to which employees believe that positive incentives (merit pay raises, bonuses, promotions, opportunities to perform interesting task, and the like) are contingent on achieving goals, the greater is the likelihood of goal commitment and acceptance.[121]

Goals are always constructed with the needed simplicity to ensure that they are accomplished. The process for crafting goals is straightforward, highly interactive, and starts with the success measures. Most success measures have a texture of growth or improvement built into them. Thus, increasing a success measure target from last year's results to a higher number this year is a very credible goal. The departments can also look to the imperatives and consider addressing them directly as a way to select goals. The administration department from a Big Brothers–Big Sisters chapter offers a good example of goals for a department with no success measures, but with imperatives (see Exhibit 11.1).

Notice in the format that people are assigned responsibility to accomplish the goal by a certain time. In this case, LB will be the primary person in charge and will be assisted by MP. The goal is to be completed by January 1.

IMPERATIVES

- Redundant paper and tracking systems
- Low visibility

GOALS

	Who-When
I. Implement plan of action for improving visibility so that more Bigs and Littles can be recruited.	CA, 10/1/00
II. Fix paper and tracking systems so that more time can be spent on serving Bigs and Littles.	LB, MP, 1/1/01

Exhibit 11.1   Sample Goals from a Department with Imperatives Only

Goals always start with an action verb, which is followed by a noun and a *so that* statement. The *so that* statement provides justification for the goal and also provides information to determine success. That is, there's no point for fixing paper and tracking systems unless more time is spent on serving the Bigs and Littles. A *so that* statement essentially describes the expected results that will occur as a result of accomplishing the goal. Like so many logic models that have become common in recent years, the success

Success Measures

	'97	'98	'99	Budget	'00 7/5 YE Forecast	12/31 YE Final	'01
Bigs: Inquiries	352	319	610	400	400		400
Applications completed	120	176	229	200	200		200
Littles: Inquiries	54	33	50	75	75		100
Applications completed	33	42	42	60	70		85

Imperatives

- Not enough Bigs
- Not enough Little Sisters
- Need more Littles in Greene County

Goals

	Who-When
I. Implement a plan of action to improve Little Sisters inquiries so that there are more core matches.	CA, 1/1/01
II. Implement plan to recruit more minority Bigs so that there are more core matches.	CA, 1/1/00

Exhibit 11.2   Sample Goals from a Department with Success Measures and Imperatives

measures and imperatives provide information to define the need or problem to be addressed, the goal is the intervention, and the *so that* statement
is the expected result. Exhibit 11.2 is an example of a department with both
success measures and imperatives in a Big Brothers–Big Sisters chapter.

The Management Plan is not just about the staff departments. The
board itself is treated as a department as well and must follow the same
discipline. Generally this occurs within the committee structure. These
are the goals from a typical strategic board:

Goals

	Who-When
Executive committee	
I. Ensure Governance Plan is implemented so that results are achieved.	MG, 3/1/00
II. Address the issue of low attendance at meetings and events so that good decisions are made.	MG, 3/1/01
III. Investigate the feasibility of an incentive plan so that performance is maximized.	JT, 1/1/01
Development Committee	
I. Implement plan for planned giving program so that more money is raised.	JW, 1/1/01
II. Establish a fundraising policy manual so that fundraising complies with standards.	MP, 3/1/01
Governance and Nominating Committee	
I. Execute a review of the bylaws so that the Governance Plan and bylaws are aligned.	MP, 2/1/01
II. Improve the recruitment orientation process to attract higher-profile board members so that more money is raised, the profile is raised, and good decisions are made.	JT, 2/1/01

Building goals starts with looking at the success measures (if they are
available) and the imperatives. Goals are drafted to address each success
measure and imperative. The goals are then prioritized in importance and
the top two or three are selected. There are other ways to proceed as well,
including frank discussion between the department leaders and the executive director about the success measures and imperatives.

Having developed the goal provides an opportunity for the individuals
or teams responsible for implementation to flesh out the details at the action step level. Action steps are simply the next step down in detail from
the goal. Typically action steps are not shown in the presentation of a Governance Plan, but are done off line between managers and their direct reports when necessary. Because goals are generally about either doing

something new or improving something that currently exists, templates can be used to ensure that the goals are executed appropriately:

I. Doing something new
  A. Find existing alternatives.
  B. Create new or improved alternatives.
  C. Decide best alternatives.
  D. Determine what could go wrong.
  E. Draft implementation plan.
  F. Test plan.
  G. Check results and revise accordingly.
  H. Finalize plan and implement.
	II. Improving something
	  A. Clarify current problems.
	  B. Determine true causes of the problems.
	  C. Find existing alternatives to solve the problems.
	  D. Create new or improved alternatives.
	  E. Decide best alternatives.
	  F. Determine what could go wrong.
	  G. Draft implementation plan.
	  H. Test plan.
	  I. Check results and revise accordingly.
	  J. Finalize plan and implement.

11.5 INDIVIDUAL PLANS

Peter Drucker says, "Executives spend more time on managing people and making people decisions than on anything else. . . . No other decisions are so long lasting in their consequences or so difficult to unmake."[122] Individual plans are the final element of the Management Plan and help make it possible to manage people more effectively.

The style and manner of individual planning is a matter of choice and unique to most organizations. The important thing is that a reasonable process exists for the employee and his or her manager to work together to answer the following questions for the coming 12 months:

- What are your basic job duties?
- What are your job goals?
- What is your team member goal?

Often these questions will be formed into a standard individual plan that is used throughout the organization. Such plans generally can address a number of different issues including past performance and compensation review. What follows is just one approach to individual planning. This particular tool has two key elements: the past and the future.

The Past

The section on the past is used to describe the results achieved by the employee during the previous year. It consists of three simple questions:

1. What were your basic job duties and how well did you accomplish them?
2. What were your job goals and how well did you accomplish them?
3. What was your team member goal and how well did you accomplish it?

These questions are contingent upon an individual plan being completed a year earlier; a new employee would simply skip this section.

Job duties are essentially the job description for the employee, nothing less, nothing more. Job goals are what the employee will do to help his or her department achieve its goals. The team member goal is what the employee intends to do to improve his or her interactions with team members.

All of these goals are set a year in advance at the tail end of the Governance Plan process. If the new Governance Plan is approved by the board for a fiscal year beginning January 1, the job duties, job goals, and team member goal would be set in December.

The Future

There are six questions in this section:

1. What are your basic job duties?
2. What are your job goals?
3. What is your team member goal?
4. What are the manager's comments?
5. What is the compensation adjustment?
6. When are the four quarterly meetings scheduled for the coming year?

The first three questions are to be answered by the employee working with his or her manager. The manager alone answers the last three.

Describing the job duties is an important step in thinking about the future. They are described in the individual plan as follows:

Taking a moment to look at your current job duties is very important. It allows you and your manager to discuss whether your job duties have changed and to resolve any misunderstandings. Job duties have a tendency to shift over time and it is a good idea to be sure that you are on the right track.

Job goals are described as follows:

Job goals are what you will do to help your department achieve its goals. Examples could include doing your job faster, learning a new skill, reducing the number of errors, or specifically addressing a department goal. The manager that you directly report to will tell you about your department's goals and help you choose appropriate job goals. Remember that your job goals should be measurable, challenging, and make an important difference for your department.

Team member goals are described this way:

Everyone in this organization at one time or another works as a team member. Most of the time, you work within your department team. In this section you will decide your team member goal. Team member goals are about how you interact with fellow team members.

One place to begin thinking about your team member goal is to evaluate yourself against our values in action. For example, one of our values in action is "Lending a hand without asking." Ask yourself if your fellow team members would say that you are always, sometimes, or rarely described by this statement. You might also ask your manager and fellow team members to evaluate you against these values in action statements.

You could be more general and simply ask what you could do to be a more effective team member. Finally, your manager can tell you about other feedback tools available including 360-degree feedback.

The team member goal is always restricted to just one because it is such a personal matter and it can be quite difficult to confront. Simply put, one is enough. Dealing with a job goal like learning a new computer program or being more responsive to the client is much easier to discuss than controlling your temper, being a better listener, or lending a hand to others without being asked.

It takes sensitivity on the part of the manager to handle these discussions with delicacy. Even so, the team member goal should not be avoided simply because it is difficult to do. A well-thought-out team member goal accomplished successfully can make a career-changing difference, whether it is advancing an employee to a higher level of responsibility, paying higher compensation, or moving the employee out of the organization. So frequently the long-overdue discussion about an employee's insensitivity to others or errant temper are never brought to his or her attention, but still hold the person back.

The manager's comments are the response to the individual plan. These comments can be focused on both the past and the future. They should be written after the manager and employee have worked together on developing the job duties, job goals, and team member goal. Frequently the manager can include department success measures in the comments if the employee hasn't already done so, as Exhibit 11.3 shows.

There is both good news and challenging news in these success measures, which were easily adapted from the Governance Plan. On the upside, almost everything about program 1 and 3 is positive, on the downside, almost everything about program 2 is negative. Using success measures from the Governance Plan for employees who have accountability and authority for impacting them is very legitimate and helpful in the personal performance planning process.

The next-to-last element in the future section of the individual plan is the compensation adjustment. While some managers prefer that this be a separate matter, it is convenient to include it, which ensures that it gets done. Some managers are very uncomfortable or downright negligent about confronting compensation adjustments, so by including the issue in the individual plan, it gets done.

The final element is the schedule of quarterly meetings that should occur between the manager and the direct report. Organizations using The Strategic Board Model of governance usually make a commitment to mandate these quarterly meetings, which are used to discuss the

		'99–'00		'98–'99 to '00–'01	'99–'00 Budget to Forecast
	'98–'99	Budget	6/15 YE Forecast		
Program 1:					
Total usage	104K	103.9K	106.6K	+	+
Direct	14,708	14,400	14,525	−	+
Indirect	15,790	17,500	19,423	+	+
Program 2:					
Total usage	25,336	18,650	16,720	−	−
Direct	2,379	2,500	2,397	+	−
Indirect	13,440	6,150	4,735	−	−
Program 3:					
Total usage	28,111	26,900	29,055	+	+
Direct	2,322	2,250	2,370	+	+
Indirect	4,891	4,400	5,355	+	+

Exhibit 11.3   Tying Employee Success Measures to Department Measures

individual plan from beginning to end. Rather than waiting a whole year to have a conversation about progress, scheduling quarterly meetings in advance forces discipline into the system. Managers and their employees grow to value these meetings as they become opportunities to build bridges of communication. How nice it is for an employee to be the focus of his or her manager four times a year! These meetings often give the manager the chance to ask the employee what he or she can do to help the employee succeed. Exhibit 11.4 is an actual format for an individual plan.

Exhibit 11.4   Sample Model Individual Plan Document

Name: _____

Position: _____

Manager: _____

Period Covered: _____

Date: _____

Directions

1. Schedule a meeting with your manager to review your individual plan.
2. Fill out sections I and II. Be sure to get your manager's input before completing section II.
3. Give the individual plan to your manager at least five business days in advance of your meeting so that he or she can complete sections III and IV.
4. If you disagree with the manager's comments, you may provide a written response to your manager with a copy to the executive director.

I. The Past

A. What were your basic job duties and how well did you accomplish them?

_____

_____

_____

_____

B. What were your job goals and how well did you accomplish them?

_____

_____

_____

_____

C. What was your team member goal and how well did you accomplish it?

_____

_____

_____

_____

II. The Future

A. Job duties—What is your job?

Taking a moment to look at your current job duties is very important. It allows you and your manager to discuss whether your job duties have changed and to resolve any misunderstandings. Job duties have a tendency to shift over time and it is a good idea to be sure that you are on the right track.

Working with the manager that you directly report to: What are your basic job duties?

_____

_____

_____

_____

B. Job goals—What will you do to help your department achieve its goals?

Job goals are what you will do to help your department achieve its goals. Examples could include doing your job faster, learning a new skill, reducing the number of errors, or specifically addressing a department goal. Your manager will tell you about your department's goals and help you choose appropriate job goals. Remember that your job goals should be measurable, challenging, and make an important difference for your department.

Working with the manager that you directly report to: What job goals will you accomplish to help your department achieve its goals? What steps will you take to achieve these goals? When will these steps be completed?

_____

_____

_____

_____

C. Team member goals—What will you do to be a better team member?

Everyone in this organization at one time or another works as a team member. In this section you will decide your team member goal. Your team member goal should improve how you interact with your team members.

One place to begin thinking about your team member goal is to evaluate yourself against our values in action. For example, one of our values in action is "Lending a hand without asking." Ask yourself if your fellow team members would say that you are always, sometimes, or rarely described by this statement. You might also ask your manager and fellow team members to evaluate you against these values in action statements.

You could be more general and simply ask what you could do to be a more effective team member. Finally, your manager can tell you about other feedback tools available including 360-degree feedback.

Working with the manager you directly report to: What is your *one* team member goal for the new season? What steps will need to be accomplished to achieve the goal? When will these steps be completed?

_____

_____

_____

_____

III. Manager's Comments

_____

_____

_____

_____

IV. Compensation Adjustment

Compensation adjustment, if any, will be effective only with completed signatures.

A. Recommended compensation _____

B. Effective date _____

C. Next review for compensation adjustment will occur on or by _____

V. Quarterly Meetings

You will need to meet with your manager at least four times in the coming season to discuss your progress on this individual plan.

A. First meeting: No earlier than October 1,
        no later than November 1 Date: _____

B. Second meeting: No earlier than January 1,
        no later than February 1 Date: _____

C. Third meeting: No earlier than April 1,
        no later than May 1   Date: _____

D. Fourth meeting: No earlier than July 1,
        no later than August 1   Date: _____

VI. Signatures

The employee's signature means that this individual plan was reviewed with him or her. It does not necessarily indicate that the employee agrees with the manager's comments.

Employee _____

Manager _____

Executive Director _____

Date _____

A P P E N D I X   1 1 . 1

Sample Management Plan

If one advances confidently in the direction of his dreams, and endeavors to live the life which he has imagined, he will meet with a success unexpected in common hours.
—Thoreau

What follows is a sample Management Plan from a Big Brothers–Big Sisters chapter early in its experience with The Strategic Board model of governance.

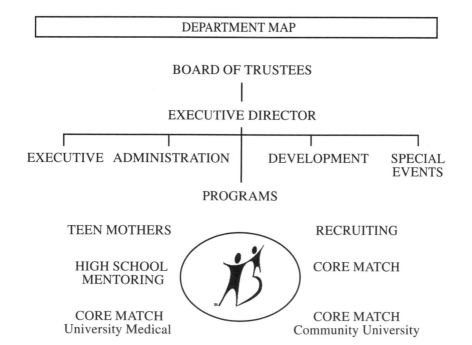

DEPARTMENT MAP

BOARD OF TRUSTEES

EXECUTIVE DIRECTOR

EXECUTIVE ADMINISTRATION   DEVELOPMENT   SPECIAL
                                                    EVENTS

PROGRAMS

TEEN MOTHERS   RECRUITING

HIGH SCHOOL   CORE MATCH
MENTORING

CORE MATCH   CORE MATCH
University Medical   Community University

BUDGET SUMMARY			
			Variance Column 3
Income	'99 As Passed	'99 Projected	'00 Budget Minus Column 2
CONTRIBUTIONS	52,500	52,328	50,000	−2,328
LITHOS	500	0	586	586
OLD TIME NEWSIES	55,000	55,366	57,500	2,134
"304" DINNER	29,750	29,751	29,000	−751
BOWL FOR KIDS	100,000	90,124	95,000	4,876
BUY.COM GOLF OUTING	0	2,242	12,000	9,758
GRANTS	65,000	68,416	66,000	−2,416
UNITED WAY	127,535	129,954	130,000	46
INTEREST INCOME	2,500	3,633	3,000	−633
MISC. INCOME	8,500	11,543	5,000	−6,543
BB/BS FOUNDATION	0	0	0	0
IN-KIND	3,972	3,972	0	−3,972
TOTAL	445,257	447,329	448,086	757

Expenses

	'99 As Passed	'99 Projected	'00 Budget	Variance
SALARIES	280,590	260,249	266,254	6,005
HEALTH/LIFE INS.	43,090	34,017	44,267	10,250
RETIREMENT	10,141	7,515	10,041	2,526
PAYROLL TAXES	22,018	21,459	20,624	−835
AUDIT/ACCOUNTING	2,200	2,169	3,500	1,331
LIABILITY INSURANCE	13,500	12,202	13,500	1,298
RECREATION-PROG.	4,000	4,584	4,500	−84
MAINT. & REPAIRS	1,200	1,358	1,200	−158
OFFICE & COPIES	4,500	5,284	5,500	216
TELEPHONE	7,500	7,812	7,500	−312
POSTAGE	3,500	3,873	4,000	127
RENT	26,124	24,881	27,500	2,619
OUTSIDE PRINTING	6,500	6,461	6,500	39
SUBSCRIPTIONS/DUES	250	539	500	−39
ADVERTISING	4,700	5,205	10,000	4,795
MILEAGE	4,000	4,026	4,500	474
OTHER STAFF EXP.	1,500	1,241	1,500	259
CONFERENCES	1,000	50	1,200	1,150
PROGRAM RES./CONSUL.	1,250	7,778	2,500	−5,278
MISC. EXPENSE	500	321	500	179
BB/BS FOUNDATION	0	25,000	0	−25,000
NATIONAL DUES	7,194	7,224	7,500	276
TOTAL	445,257	443,248	443,086	162
DEPRECIATION	−4,060	−5,140	−5,000	0
NET INCOME/LOSS	−4,060	−1,059	0	0

BOARD GOALS

Success Measures

	'97	'98	'99	Budget	'00 7/5 YE Forecast	12/31 YE Final	'01
Average total matches	269	237	234	245	245		257
Total income	384K	473K	447K	451K	451K		450K
Operating margin percent	3.8	5.5	6.9	0	0		2.0

Imperatives

- Low attendance at meetings
- Board members that can open doors to fundraising
- Plan of action for planned giving

Goals

	Who-When
Executive Committee I. Ensure Governance Plan is implemented so that results are achieved.	MG, 3/1/01
II. Address the issue of low attendance at meetings and events so that good decisions are made.	MG, 3/1/01
III. Investigate the feasibility of an incentive plan so that performance is maximized.	JT, 1/1/01
Development Committee I. Implement plan for planned giving program so that more money is raised.	JW, 1/1/01
II. Establish a fundraising policy manual so that fundraising complies with standards.	MP, 3/1/01
Governance and Nominating Committee I. Execute a review of the bylaws so that the Governance Plan and bylaws are aligned.	MP, 2/1/01
II. Improve the recruitment orientation process to attract higher profile board members so that more money is raised, the profile is raised, and good decisions are made.	JT, 2/1/01

STAFF GOALS

EXECUTIVE

Imperatives

- Current personnel practices

Goals

	Who-When
Program Committee I. Complete five-year national program audit so that the organization is in compliance.	MP, 5/1/01
II. Revise personnel policies so that policies comply with standards, are fair, clear, and concise.	MP, 1/1/01

ADMINISTRATION

Imperatives

- Redundant paper and tracking systems
- Low visibility

Goals

	Who-When
I. Implement plan of action for improving visibility so that more Bigs and Littles can be recruited.	CA, 10/1/00
II. Fix paper and tracking systems so that more time can be spent on serving Bigs and Littles.	LB, MP 1/1/01

DEVELOPMENT

Success Measures

	'97	'98	'99	Budget	'00 7/5 YE Forecast	12/31 YE Final	'01
Total funds raised	72,824	125,629	120,958	118,000	120,000		125,000
Annual fund: Friends	26,544	14,243	20,808	23,000	22,000		25,000
Firms	7,752	15,003	15,144	15,000	14,700		17,500
Foundations	7,854	17,171	16,350	15,000	15,250		15,000
Grants	30,683	79,212	68,656	65,000	66,000		67,500

Imperatives
• Lack of a plan for operations

Goals

	Who-When
Goals will be determined later because of Board Development Committee draft plan due 1/1/00.	

SPECIAL EVENTS

Success Measures

	'97	'98	'99	Budget	'00 7/5 YE Forecast	12/31 YE Final	'01
Bowling for Kids	88,385	101,990	90,489	90,000	95,783	95,783	104,000
Old Time Fun:							
Pins	15,754	20,881	30,934	20,000	22,000		25,000
Party			2,195	5,000	5,000		7,500
Races	30,454	41,354	48,876	30,000	30,000		35,000
Gourmet dinner	32,771	29,751	29,405	30,000	30,000		32,000

Imperatives
• Agency Board involvement
• Size of committees
• Better volunteer recognition

Goals

	Who-When
I. Improve agency board involvement so that more money is raised.	MP, 9/1/00
II. Increase committee size so that more money is raised.	MP, 9/1/00

RECRUITING

Success Measures

	'97	'98	'99	Budget	'00 7/5 YE Forecast	12/31 YE Final	'01
Bigs: Inquiries	352	319	610	400	400		400
Applications completed	120	176	229	200	200		200
Littles: Inquiries	54	33	50	75	75		100
Applications completed	33	42	42	60	70		85

Imperatives

- Not enough Bigs
- Not enough Little Sisters
- Need more Littles in Greene County

Goals

	Who-When
I. Implement a plan of action to improve Little Sisters inquiries so that there are more core matches.	CA, 1/1/01
II. Implement plan to recruit more minority Big Brothers so that there are more core matches.	CA, 1/1/01

CORE MATCH

Success Measures

	'97	'98	'99	Budget	'00 7/5 YE Forecast	12/31 YE Final	'01
December total matches: Boys	144	134	133	150	150		160
Girls	121	125	118	135	135		140
Avg. new matches: Boys	4.0		6.25	5.0	5.0		
Girls	3.75		6.83	5.0	5.0		
Avg. active matches length			1.6	1.5	1.5		2.0
United Way initial:							
Bigs want to keep match		97.4%	98.4%	95%	95%		95%
Littles want to keep match		99.1%	99.5%	95%	95%		95%
United Way 6 months:							
Bigs-Littles goals set			94%	100%	100%		100%

Imperatives

- Opportunity to make core matches better

Goals

	Who-When
I. Fix paper and tracking systems so that more time can be spent on serving Bigs and Littles.	LB, MP 1/1/01

CORE MATCH—COMMUNITY UNIVERSITY

Success Measures

	'97	'98	'99	Budget	'00 7/5 YE Forecast	12/31 YE Final	'01
December total matches	29	33	31	35	35		35

Imperatives

• No curriculum

Goals

	Who-When
I. Implement a new curriculum so that more matches occur because Bigs will know what to do.	LB, 8/1/00

CORE MATCH—UNIVERSITY MEDICAL

Success Measures

	'97	'98	'99	Budget	'00 7/5 YE Forecast	12/31 YE Final	'01
December total matches		15	22	33	33		40

Imperatives

• Improve monitoring processes
• Opportunity for 1-to-1 matching

Goals

	Who-When
I. Implement a plan to improve the monitoring process for compliance with standards so that matches endure.	LL, 1/1/01

HIGH SCHOOL MENTORING

Success Measures

	'97	'98	'99	Budget	'00 7/5 YE Forecast	12/31 YE Final	'01
December total matches: North High				15	15		30
Catholic	13	27	21	24	24		24
Colonel	7	23	24	20	20		20
National			21	25	25		30
Program outcome evaluation						TBA 1/1/01	TBA 1/1/01

Imperatives

- Lack of transportation at North High, Catholic, Colonel
- Lack of nine-month curriculum at National

Goals

	Who-When
I. Implement plan to solve the transportation problem so that more matches occur.	MP, 10/1/00
II. Implement a nine-month curriculum so that the program flow is smooth and more matches occur.	GD, 9/1/00
III. Implement a success measure tool for program outcome evaluation of the high school mentoring so that effectiveness can be determined to improve the program.	MP, 1/1/01

TEEN MOTHERS

Success Measures

	'97	'98	'99	Budget	'00 7/5 YE Forecast	12/31 YE Final	'01
Average total matches	6	27	18	10	7		0

Imperatives

- Loss of collateral support
- Training aspects of mentoring discontinued
- Loss of interest from remaining participants
- Inability to contact frequently relocated teen mothers
- Poor follow-through and documentation from prior case manager
- Legal liability for poorly supervised matches
- Little or no opportunity for program expansion exists

Goals

	Who-When
No goals; teen mothers will be phased out in 2000.	

The Vigilance Plan

What gets measured gets done.
—**Maison Haire**

CHAPTER **12**

Did It Happen?

The secret to success is constancy to purpose.
—Benjamin Disraeli

VIGILANCE PLAN
Did it Happen?

BOARD	**STAFF**
Reporting Schedule	Reporting Schedule

12.1 INTRODUCTION

The Vigilance Plan is where the Governance Plan is put to the test of *Did it Happen?* It is about scheduling the reviews that will determine whether the desired results are on track or were achieved. From executive director performance to the cycle for making a new Governance Plan, the Vigilance Plan is more than just a monitoring schedule. It becomes "agenda central" for the board and the staff and creates a common platform for planning activities for an entire year.

12.2 THE REPORTING SCHEDULES

Evaluation of performance is very important in ensuring that the Governance Plan is effectively implemented. Frequently, however, boards and staff simply cannot decide what should be monitored, when it should be monitored, and by whom. The Vigilance Plan is a reporting schedule that addresses these issues quickly and practically.

189

The timing of the process to develop the next Governance Plan plays a dramatic role in the reporting schedules. While monitoring of performance is vital on its own, this information can be extraordinarily helpful in developing the next Governance Plan. In order to be done on time, the process is paced to fall into the following schedule:

WHEN	WHAT
First quarter	Leadership Plan drafted
Second quarter	Leadership Plan finalized
Third quarter	Delegation, Management, and Vigilance Plans drafted
Fourth quarter	Delegation, Management, and Vigilance Plans finalized

The board's reporting schedule is layered in by priority and should include the major reviews for the board in the coming fiscal year:

WHO	WHEN	WHAT
	First quarter	Leadership Plan drafted
Board		• Review last year final results—except audit
	Second quarter	Leadership Plan finalized
Board		• Review last year final results—audit
	Third quarter	Delegation, Management, and Vigilance Plans drafted
Board		• Review midyear forecast
	Fourth Quarter	Delegation, Management, and Vigilance Plans finalized
Board		• Approve new Governance Plan

There are essentially only two major reviews each year. The first is a review of last year's results, and it is broken into two stages. The first stage is a review of last year's results, but without benefit of the audit, which generally cannot be ready in the first quarter if done by independent auditors.

The second stage of the review of last year's results is a presentation of the audit by the organization's auditors. The reader will ask why not just wait until the audit is finished and do the last year's results including audit all at one time. The answer is that the board must begin formulating the new Leadership Plan in the first quarter in order to stay on track for getting the new Governance Plan approved in the fourth quarter. There is no point in having the board and staff dig into a new Leadership Plan only to find out on closer examination that the actual results from last year can't support the vision.

The second review is the midyear forecast that takes place in the third quarter. Even though the for-profit sector is accustomed to quarterly reviews, nonprofit organizations using the Strategic Board model of governance have found this difficult to do, especially in light of both the seven realities of nonprofit boards and the precious resources of time and effort within the professional staff.

A variety of factors can affect the timing of reviews, including availability of the board and the organization's activities. Whether the review of the midyear forecast occurs in the third quarter or early in fourth quarter is at the discretion of the board.

The final step in drafting the board's reporting schedule is to fill in the work of the committees and the fine detail of what needs to be done to finish the new Governance Plan (See Exhibit 12.1).

The staff reporting schedule simply takes the board's work and adds to it the things that the staff must do to be prepared as shown in Exhibit 12.2.

The two reporting schedules shown above are neither complex nor difficult to construct. In most organizations, it takes less than an hour to put together the Vigilance Plan. What makes the Vigilance Plan so remarkable is the fact that most organizations don't do it. Yes, boards will almost always set meetings a year in advance and some will set committee meetings that far out as well. Few boards, however, set the agendas in advance and instead default to a show-and-tell reporting style that uses the same agenda for each meeting. The strategic board takes the bull by the horns and decides what work needs to be done in advance. Purely a form-follows-function approach, the Vigilance Plan builds the board's work around the Governance Plan. Thus, the board and its work are a means to an end: achieving the chosen destiny.

WHO	WHEN	WHAT
	First quarter	Leadership Plan drafted
Executive		• Review last year results—executive director's duties • Executive director's individual plan including compensation review
Board		• Review last year's final results—except audit • Review current season preliminary forecast • Begin new Leadership Plan
	Second quarter	Leadership Plan finalized
Executive		• Executive director's individual plan
Governance		• Review last year's results—board duties and guidelines • Begin recruitment process for new class
Performance Assurance		• Review last year's results—executive director's guidelines • Review last year's results—audit
Development		• Committee business
Board		• Review last year's results—audit • Finalize new Leadership Plan
	Third quarter	Delegation, Management, and Vigilance Plans drafted
Executive		• Executive director's individual plan
Board		• Educate—socialize
	Fourth quarter	Delegation, Management, and Vigilance Plans finalized
Executive		• Review midyear forecast—executive director's duties • Review executive director's duties for possible revisions • Executive director's individual plan
Governance		• Review midyear forecast—board duties and guidelines • Review board duties and guidelines for possible revisions • Finalize recruitment process for new class
Performance Assurance		• Review midyear forecast—executive director's guidelines • Review executive director guidelines for possible revisions
Development		• Committee business
Board		• Review midyear forecast • Review first draft Governance Plan
Executive		• Executive director's individual plan
Board		• Approve next year's final Governance Plan • Annual meeting

Exhibit 12.1   Sample Board Reporting Schedule

192

WHO	WHEN	WHAT
	First quarter	Leadership Plan drafted
Staff		• Finalize last year final results • Draft ideas for strategies and imperatives
	Second quarter	Leadership Plan finalized
Staff		• Expand basic Leadership Plan to first draft
	Third quarter	Delegation, Management, and Vigilance Plans drafted
Staff		• Finalize current season midyear forecast • First draft next season Governance Plan
	Fourth quarter	Delegation, Management, and Vigilance Plans finalized
Staff		• Final draft Governance Plan

Exhibit 12.2   Sample Staff Reporting Schedule

12.3 MONITORING

It is all well and good to set up a schedule for monitoring, but what reports should be used? As with all the elements of the Governance Plan, less is more, simple is better. There are essentially just three ways to evaluate performance: The executive director does it, the board does it, or an independent third party does it. In most cases, it is agreeable for the executive director to evaluate performance, especially when it comes to success measures as shown in Exhibit 12.3.

SUCCESS MEASURES REPORT

To: Board of Trustees

Date: September, 2000

Reason: Last Season Results—Midyear Forecast Report—Success Measures

The following success measures show last season results and midyear forecast. The numbers are firm with the exception of financials, which are still out for audit with our independent auditors.

Last season results are shown in the 99–00 column and are final except for financial numbers, which are pre-audit. The current season preliminary forecast is shown in the 00–01 column along with basic trend analysis (= stable and no concerns, ↑ up and looks promising, ↓ down and with concerns).

Success Measures

Mission

	'96–'97	'97–'98	'98–'99	'99–'00	'00–'01 Budget	'00–'01 8/31 YE Forecast	'01–'02
						trend =	
Total attendance	279K	288K	284K	284K	269K	263K	285K
Total income	6.17M	6.99M	7.75M	8.78M	7.76M	7.68M	7.89M
Earned to contributed	76/24	79/21	80/20	81/19	78/22	78/22	78/22
Net income	148K	99K	−79K	99K*	0	−38K	0

*Subject to Audit

Broadway

	'96–'97	'97–'98	'98–'99	'99–'00	'00–'01 Budget	'00–'01 8/31 YE Forecast	'01–'02
						trend =	
Total attendance	107.3K	101.0K	104.0K	106.6K	106.5K	106.5K	103.0K
Subscriptions	15,727	14,421	14,708	14,525	15,000	15,000	14,700
Single tickets	13,000	14,500	15,790	19,423	16,500	16,500	14,800
Gross sales	2.60M	2.78M	3.07M	3.39M	3.62M	3.63M	3.68M
Renewal rate	.86	.80	.90	.85	.87	.87	.86

Next Stage

	'96–'97	'97–'98	'98–'99	'99–'00	'00–'01 Budget	'00–'01 8/31 YE Forecast	'01–'02
						trend ↓	
Total attendance		24,509	25,336	16,720	14.900	13,100	15,300
Subscriptions		2,237	2,379	2,397	2,600	2,150	2,900
Single tickets		13,324	13,440	4,735	4,500	4,500	3,700
Gross sales			691K	414K	359K	310K	406K
Renewal rate			.70	.73	.63	.62	.68

Theatre for the Young at Heart

	'96–'97	'97–'98	'98–'99	'99–'00	'00–'01 Budget	'00–'01 8/31 YE Forecast	'01–'02
						trend ↓	
Total attendance	31,150	24,583	24,778	26,113	14,900	14,100	22,400
Subscriptions	4,400	3,562	4,220	4,380	3,100	2,900	3,900
Single tickets	4,750	3,211	3,684	4,213	2,500	2,500	2,900
Gross sales	193K	157K	173K	225K	141K	131K	141K
Renewal rate	.62	.64	.82	.72	.54	.55	.70

Exhibit 12.3   Example of a Success Measures Report

The executive director reporting on guidelines is also acceptable provided that the executive director indicates the rationale behind the evaluations. It is generally not enough to indicate compliance to guidelines; board members will want to be reassured about how the executive director arrived at his or her conclusion, as shown below in an example with three guidelines:

I. With regard to risk assessment and management, the executive director shall:
   A. Protect the company's assets and earning power by using proper risk management techniques. Specifically, the executive director shall:
      1. Have programs in place to identify risk, quantify risk, minimize, transfer and/or eliminate risk, monitor risk, and inform the Board of Trustees about the company's programs for risk assessment and management.

→ Fall report—October 15, 2000: In compliance. Held meeting with Task Force on Risk Management August 21 to hear presentation from our insurance broker and to review risk management protocols. We received a clean bill of health.

II. With regard to endowment funds under management at the community foundation, the executive director shall:
   A. Invest in funds with annual three-year and five-year performance of at least top quartile.
   B. Invest in funds with a manager tenure of five years or more.
   C. Invest in funds that follow the investment guidelines established by the community foundation.
   D. Review the investment mix with independent financial counsel annually, using a 50-year long-term perspective.

→ Fall report—October 15, 2000: In compliance. The Performance Assurance committee met in April with representatives from the community foundation and reviewed report from our fund evaluation firm. Our endowment funds are performing well within our guidelines.

III. With regard to financial matters, the executive director shall:
   A. Achieve at least a two-percent surplus annually of income over expenses, subject to the following provisions:
      1. Income shall exclude planned gifts not budgeted and investment income from endowment funds other than the five percent annual draw.
      2. Expenses shall exclude unfunded depreciation, any incentive package costs for management, and contributions to endowment funds by the company.

195

→ Fall report—October 15, 2000: Not in compliance. The board passed a motion on June 2, which changed the surplus from 2% to 0. This allowance was given due to our commitment to bringing new strategies on line.

Boards wanting more reassurance than that shown in the above example should always be offered the opportunity to examine the backup, including correspondence where available. Boards uncomfortable with accepting the executive director's evaluation on its own can always undertake to do the evaluation itself or invite an independent third party audit usually using the organization's auditing firm. While a third party auditor may be unable to evaluate softer guidelines such as those related to relations with the board, it will certainly be capable of ascertaining the condition of the financial numbers.

12.4 MAINTAINING

As shown in the reporting schedules, the Governance Plan is part and parcel of the board's work. Rather than doing a retreat every few years to build a new plan, the reporting schedules make this the ongoing regular work of the board. Thus, the board shown in Exhibit 12.4 is maintaining its Governance Plan in a schedule of five meetings a year.

The Strategic Board model of governance respects the seven realities of nonprofit boards, but a board with more time to give will find ample opportunities to enhance the quality of the Governance Plan. Time can be spent exploring best practices, meeting with stakeholders, educating the board about the organization and its strategies, or building team cohesion. In some boards, adding education components to the board agenda is done to enhance the quality of meetings. In a strategic board, the board is always educating itself since almost all meeting time is spent discussing and learning about the organization as the Governance Plan is built, implemented, and then monitored.

Sample Vigilance Plan

The best way out is always through.
—Robert Frost

BOARD		
WHO	**WHEN**	**WHAT**
First quarter		Leadership Plan drafted
Executive duties	Early September	• Review last year's results—president's • President's individual plan including compensation review
Board audit	September 13 Dinner meeting 5:30–8:30 PM	• Review last year's final results—except • Review current season preliminary forecast • Begin new Leadership Plan
	Second quarter	Leadership Plan finalized
Executive	Late October	• President's individual plan
Governance	Late October	• Review last year's results—board duties and guidelines • Begin recruitment process for new class
Performance assurance	Late October	• Review last year's results—president's guidelines • Review last year's results—audit
Development	Late October	• Committee business
Board	November 8 11:30–1:30 PM	• Review last year's results—audit • Finalize new Leadership Plan
	Third quarter	Delegation, Management, and Vigilance Plans drafted
Executive	Mid January	• President's individual plan
Board	January 25	• Educate—Socialize

197

WHO	Lunch meeting 11:00–1:00 PM WHEN	WHAT
	Fourth quarter	Delegation, Management, and Vigilance Plans finalized
Executive	Mid-April	• Review midyear forecast—president's duties • Review president's duties for possible revisions • President's individual plan
Governance	Mid-April	• Review midyear forecast—board duties and guidelines • Review board duties and guidelines for possible revisions • Finalize recruitment process for new class
Performance assurance	Mid-April	• Review midyear forecast—president's guidelines • Review president's guidelines for possible revisions
Development	Mid-April	• Committee business
Board	April 26	• Review midyear forecast

STAFF		
WHO	WHEN	WHAT
	First quarter	Leadership Plan drafted
Staff	By September 6	• Finalize last year's final results • Draft ideas for strategies and imperatives
	Second quarter	Leadership Plan finalized
Staff	By November 1	• Expand basic Leadership Plan to first draft
	Third quarter	Delegation, Management, and Vigilance Plans drafted
Staff	By April 1	• Finalize current season midyear forecast • First draft next season Governance Plan
	Fourth quarter	Delegation, Management, and Vigilance Plans finalized
Staff	By June 13	• Final draft Governance Plan

PART VI

Endings

You campaign in poetry. You govern in prose.
—Mario Cuomo

CHAPTER **13**

Closing Thoughts

The main thing is to make sure the main thing is still the main thing.
—James Barksdale

In a recent *Opera in Trust* article, Thomas P. Holland, an acknowledged expert on boards, commented about how to build the team:

> *Building a high-performing board team means building a team that is ready, willing, and able to focus on the main thing—a team that isn't hobbled by inefficient or unproductive procedures or distracted by trivial issues that will have little impact on your board's ability to achieve its vision for the organization.[123]*

Ready, willing, and able to focus on *what* main thing? Which comes first: the main thing or the structure that helps the board decide the main thing? The strategic board advocates the former. Structure follows values and vision; the Delegation Plan follows the Leadership Plan. Management follows leadership. Paul Valery's "The best way to make your dreams come true is to wake up" follows Walt Disney's "If you can dream it, you can do it." As Holland noted in the same article:

> *The idea is to determine what the big ideas are, to find the whales in the pool and not be distracted by the paramecium, to ask yourself what is of such overwhelming imprint that it requires the board's attention for the foreseeable future.[124]*

The Strategic Board model of governance answers Holland's call to converge on the big ideas. Its focus is on answering the four questions, not on dictating the answers, which makes it very usable and very flexible for the large majority of nonprofits including the 80 percent that have budgets of less than a million dollars.

One way to fix problems within an organization is to yell at the people who cause them. Someone puts the letter in the wrong envelope or forgets to turn out the lights when leaving. Yelling can produce meaningful short-term results, but it fades over time. Wouldn't it be better to simply get window envelopes and install motion sensors to automatically turn off the lights? Like Deming says, "Workers are responsible for only 15 percent of the problems, the system for the other 85 percent."[125]

Board members are part of a system too. They're on a manufacturing line that should be making the chosen destiny come true for the organization that they govern. Many nonprofits not only don't know what that chosen destiny is, they don't know the product they're supposed to be making. Imagine walking into a completely dark building for the first time, being taken to a spot on a manufacturing line you have never seen, given tools you've never held, and then being told to get to work making something you have never seen before. Imagine being a new board member walking into his or her first meeting.

The strategic board turns on the lights in that dark building and provides itself with the tools it needs to be productive. Imagine being a new member of a strategic board. Imagine being part of something special, an organization bringing a dream to life. Imagine. . . .

Victoria Theatre Association Governance Plan

LEADERSHIP PLAN

EXECUTIVE SUMMARY

VISION SUMMARY

The Victoria Theatre Association's 1999–2000 season was planned to consolidate the recent growth that brought Next Stage to life, launched the Victoria Children's Festival, and welcomed the Dayton Opera to its family. In general, it was a record-breaking season ending solidly in the black. In addition, operating results for the Dayton Opera put that organization solidly on plan. While there were continuing disappointments with Next Stage and there are new concerns about softness in our family series, the combined operations of the Victoria Theatre Association and Dayton Opera gave an outstanding performance.

Building a resilient organization that can handle the breadth of current activity and be ready for new opportunities that will arise when the Benjamin and Marian Schuster Performing Arts Center opens in 2003 is vitally important. Thus, the Governance Plan for 2000–2001 concentrates again on consolidating gains, building the Dayton Opera, and fixing problem areas in Next Stage and Theatre for the Young at Heart. The vision summary for this Governance Plan is simple: Set the stage for 2003.

IMPERATIVES

Imperatives are issues that are of vital importance to the Association. The two imperatives for the 1999–2000 season were to improve organizational infrastructure and stabilize the Next Stage Series. For 2000–2001, the Association will continue to work on these imperatives and add revitalization of the Theatre for the Young at Heart Series.

The focus on improving organizational infrastructure in the 1999–2000 season was to make operations more effective and efficient. The results of these efforts are beginning to show. In finance, for example, the books are being closed now on a quarterly basis in order to ensure a smooth audit in the fall. Even so, there are pockets of weakness in the company due to staffing changes and the breadth of activity. The organization is not up to standard with technology, especially in web access for ticketing. Thus, for 2000–2001, the organization will continue to work on this imperative.

Next Stage continues to struggle. The 1999–2000 season was particularly difficult with very low attendance for the opening production, Shakespeare's *As You Like It*. Total Attendance was down 34 percent over the previous season to 16,720. Single Tickets were off 65 percent to 4,735 and Gross Sales were down 41 percent to $412K. Next Stage is now executing a complete revamp of the programming focus and campaign strategy in an effort to bring the losses on this series into a more acceptable range. 2000–2001 losses for the series are expected to drop 4 percent to $168K. The objective is to reduce losses to an acceptable level in the low to mid-$100K range while maintaining subscribership. Ways to do this include reducing the number of shows in the series to four and doing all shows in the Loft Theatre where it is more cost-effective to operate and expectations are lower. In addition a four-production series makes cross-selling to Broadway attenders easier.

There are new concerns about the health of the Theatre for the Young at Heart Series. Subscribership is expected to drop nearly 30 percent and the renewal rate is expected to reach a low of 54 percent, the worst in four seasons. This is why revitalizing the series is an imperative for the new season. An empirically valid marketing survey will be conducted in the late summer to determine causes after which a plan for corrective action will be developed.

STRATEGIES

The concentration for 2000–2001 strategies is on maintaining most existing strategies while modestly boosting the Victoria Children's Festival, stabilizing Next Stage, and revitalizing the Theatre for the Young at Heart Series. With no new strategies being brought on line or studied, it will be a relatively quiet season for growth; however, there is an expectation that the new Schuster Center will provide much opportunity for the future. While this summary should not take the place of a careful reading of the rest of the Governance Plan, the following items stand out:

In general:
- '99–'00 Total Revenues were up nearly 10 percent to a record-breaking $8.8M. Adding in Dayton Opera revenues of $1.26M brings the combined revenues under management up 9 percent to $10M. Contributed Income was up 8 percent to $1.68M with sponsorship setting a new record of $1.07M and the Annual Fund breaking through to a new top at $332K, up 19 percent. Net income was $99K, a positive margin of 1.1 percent, and a solid improvement over 1998–99 when a loss of $79K was recorded.
- '00–'01 Earned Income will be down 14 percent because of a drop in Star Extras income.

About the Broadway Series:
- '99–'00 Broadway Single Tickets were up 23 percent to a record-breaking 19,423 tickets. Gross Sales were up 10 percent to $3.39M. That the Broadway Series Gross Sales is in good health is counter to the decline nationally of 18 percent in '99–'00, 9 percent in '98–'99, and 4 percent the season before.
- '00–'01 Broadway Single Tickets will be off 15 percent, due to 97 performances versus 98 last season and conservative budgeting, but Gross Sales are expected to rise 7 percent to $3.62M. Broadway is the engine that drives the rest of the organization given that Gross Revenues for every other activity equals just 27 percent of what the Broadway Series does on its own.

About Star Extras:
- '99–'00 Star Extras Total Attendance was up 63 percent to 26,647 due to two blockbusters on the series, *Les Miserables* and *Cats,* at Memorial Hall with a total capacity of 40,000 seats. Gross Sales were up 13 percent to $1.14M.
- '00–'01 Star Extras Total Attendance will be down 68 percent. Only one blockbuster, *Joseph and the Amazing Technicolor Dreamcoat,* will be presented and it will be at the Victoria Theatre at a total capacity of 9,000 seats. Consequently, Gross Sales will drop 84 percent to $185K.

About Next Stage:
- '99–'00 Next Stage Total Attendance was down 34 percent to 16,720. Single Tickets were down 65 percent to 4,735. Gross Sales declined 40 percent to $414K.

- '00–'01 Next Stage Subscriptions will be up 8 percent to 2,600 based on new programming and marketing strategies, but the Renewal Rate will be down 14 percent to 63 percent for the same reasons. Next Stage Total Attendance will be down 11 percent to 14,900 because of a reduction from five productions to four, but on a per-show basis, Total Attendance is expected to be up 11 percent to 3,725 per show. Gross Sales will continue declining with a drop of 13 percent to $359K or roughly half of where the series stood in '98–'99.

About Hot Times–Cool Films:
- '99–'00 Gross Sales were up 19 percent to $57K.

About Theatre for the Young at Heart:
- '99–'00 Gross Sales were up 31 percent to $226K due to *Winnie the Pooh* and *Sleeping Beauty on Ice.*
- '00–'01 Young at Heart Subscriptions will be down nearly 30 percent to 3,100 and the Renewal Rate will be down a quarter to 54 percent. Gross Sales will decline accordingly, dropping 38 percent to $141K. Much of the decline in sales is due to a reduction of productions from five in '99–'00 to four.

About Discovery:
- '99–'00 Discovery Total Attendance was down 17 percent to 61,240, but a change in the ticketing mix to 65/35 paid/free allowed Gross Sales to remain steady at $160K. Discovery Workshop Attendance was up 50 percent to 3,000.
- '00–'01 Discovery Total Attendance will be up 17 percent to 71,910. Discovery Paid Attendance will be up 18 percent to set a record at nearly 47,000 tickets. Gross Sales will rise accordingly by 20 percent to $192K.

VALUES

Our customer is the star.
Delivering what our customer wants.
Fixing problems with yes and
common sense.
Always appreciating.

Win and lose together.
Optimistic.
Listening well, speaking up.
Lending a hand without asking.
Celebrating success.

<table>
<tr><td>

Trust.
Actively truthful.
Keeping promises.
Taking responsibility for actions.
Doing the right thing—fair.
Golden Rule, consistent.

</td><td>

The best we can be.
Self-confident.
Self-aware
Proactive.
Persistent.

</td></tr>
</table>

VISION

VISION SUMMARY
Set the stage for 2003.

MISSION
You are the star!

Enriching life on behalf of our diverse Miami Valley community
for adults, families, and school children throughout our region
by making our customer the star.

STRATEGIES

Broadway Series
Sit back and enjoy
for adults

Star Extras
Blockbuster memories
for adults

Next Stage
Theatre for your mind
for adults

Jubilee
A sense of belonging
for everyone

Young at Heart
Quality Play Time
for families with
children grades K–4

*Hot Times–Cool
Films*
Remember when
for older adults

*Victoria Children's
Festival*
I had fun!
for families with
children ages 4–13

Discovery
Enriched classrooms
for school children and
teachers in grades K–8
• Education Series
• In-School
  Workshops
• Muse Machine
  Tickets

*Facilities
Management*
A downtown source of
pride for the Miami
Valley
• Main Street
  Theatre
• Community Arts
  Center

Strategies to Explore
Setting the stage for
future audiences
• Summer Stages
• Dayton Comedy
  Festival
• Camp Broadway
• New diversity
  initiatives
• New education
  initiatives
• New hall
  management

IMPERATIVES

- Improve organizational infrastructure.
- Stabilize the Next Stage Series.
- Revitalize Theatre for the Young at Heart.

SUCCESS MEASURES
Mission

	'96–'97	'97–'98	'98–'99	Budget	'99–'00 12/31 YE Forecast	Final	'00–'01 Budget	'01–'02
Total attendance	279K	288K	284K	294K	292K	284K	269K	285K
Total income	6.17M	6.99M	7.75M	7.95M	8.38M	8.78M	7.76M	7.89M
Earned to contributed	76/24	79/21	80/20	81/19	80/20	81/19	78/22	78/22
Net income	148K	99K	−79K	0	164K	99K*	0	0

*Subject to audit.

Broadway

	'96–'97	'97–'98	'98–'99	Budget	'99–'00 12/31 YE Forecast	Final	'00–'01 Budget	'01–'02
Total attendance	107.3K	101.0K	104.0K	103.9K	104.7K	106.6K	106.5K	103.0K
Subscriptions	15,727	14,421	14,708	14,400	14,525	14,525	15,000	14,700
Single tickets	13,000	14,500	15,790	17,500	17,500	19,423	16,500	14,800
Gross sales	2.60M	2.78M	3.07M	3.10M	3.39M	3.39M	3.62M	3.68M
Renewal rate	.86	.80	.90	.84	.85	.85	.87	.86

Star Extras

	'96–'97	'97–'98	'98–'99	Budget	'99–'00 12/31 YE Forecast	Final	'00–'01 Budget	'01–'02
Total attendance	24,143	23,498	16,389	30,700	26,647	26,647	8,500	8,500
Gross sales	741K	867K	1.01M	1.13M	1.14M	1.14M	185K	190K

Next Stage

	'96–'97	'97–'98	'98–'99	Budget	'99–'00 12/31 YE Forecast	Final	'00–'01 Budget	'01–'02
Total attendance		24,509	25,336	18,650	16,985	16,720	14,900	15,300
Subscriptions		2,237	2,379	2,500	2,397	2,397	2,600	2,900
Single tickets		13,324	13,440	6,150	5,000	4,735	4,500	3,700
Gross sales		566K	691K	495K	412K	414K	359K	406K
Renewal rate			.70	.67	.73	.73	.63	.68

Hot Times–Cool Films

	'96–'97	'97–'98	'98–'99	Budget	'99–'00 12/31 YE Forecast	Final	'00–'01 Budget	'01–'02
Total attendance	30,878	23,165	28,111	26,900	29,055	29,055	29,350	29,850
Subscriptions	2,655	1,901	2,322	2,250	2,370	2,370	2,375	2,420
Single tickets	4,328	4,155	4,891	4,400	5,355	5,355	5,600	5,650
Gross sales	47K	42K	48K	48K	57K	57K	58K	61K
Renewal rate	.87	.42	.66	.69	.61	.61	.65	.67

Jubilee

	'96–'97	'97–'98	'98–'99	Budget	'99–'00 12/31 YE Forecast	Final	'00–'01 Budget	'01–'02
Jubilee Diversity %:								
Broadway	.02	.01	.06	.03	.03	.03	.03	.03
Young at Heart	.03	.01	.02	.02	.02	.02	.02	.03
Discovery	.72	.75	.70	.65	.65	.65	.65	.65

Theatre for the Young at Heart

	'96–'97	'97–'98	'98–'99	Budget	'99–'00 12/31 YE Forecast	Final	'00–'01 Budget	'01–'02
Total attendance	31,150	24,583	24,778	25,875	26,150	26,113	14,900	22,400
Subscriptions	4,400	3,562	4,220	4,325	4,380	4,380	3,100	3,900
Single tickets	4,750	3,211	3,684	4,250	4,250	4,213	2,500	2,900
Gross sales	193K	157K	173K	219K	226K	225K	141K	141K
Renewal rate	.62	.64	.82	.62	.72	.72	.54	.70

Victoria Children's Festival

	'96–'97	'97–'98	'98–'99	Budget	'99–'00 12/31 YE Forecast	Final	'00–'01 Budget	'01–'02
Ticketed attendance			6,666	7,500	7,500	6,040	7,500	6,900
Street attendance						5,000	5,000	5,000
School attendance			4,100	6,150	6,150	3,637	3,870	6,100
Percentage paid			.61	.65	.65	.57	.65	.65
Gross sales			53K	69K	69K	56K	77K	50K

Education

	'96–'97	'97–'98	'98–'99	Budget	'99–'00 12/31 YE Forecast	Final	'00–'01 Budget	'01–'02
Total attendance	81,002	91,118	73,736	74,500	76,175	61,240	71,910	80,000
Gross sales	169K	184K	160K	198K	182K	160K	192K	202K
Percentage paid	.52	.47	.56	.65	.65	.65	.65	.65
Renew rate	.68	.71	.73	.75	.78	.78	.80	.80
Workshop attendance	240	1,920	2,010	3,000	2,250	3,000	3,000	3,000

Facilities Management

	'96–'97	'97–'98	'98–'99	Budget	'99–'00 12/31 YE Forecast	Final	'00–'01 Budget	'01–'02
Venue Performances: Victoria	310	303	287	298	303	313	305	310
Loft	121	136	117	116	128	130	148	143
Days of use: Victoria	282	285	273	267	265	262	277	268
Loft	299	294	318	315	318	321	298	307
Facility net income: Victoria Theatre	−943K	−931K	−1.1M	−1.34M	−1.32M	−1.36M	−1.36M	−1.42M

DELEGATION PLAN

BOARD

BOARD DUTIES

I. Ensure that the Association's chosen destiny is achieved.
   A. Decide where to go tomorrow through the Leadership Plan.
   B. Delegate who does what through the Delegation Plan.
   C. Determine if it happened through the Vigilance Plan.
   D. Define what gets done today through the Management Plan.

COMMITTEE DUTIES

I. Executive
   A. Ensure effective delegation from the board to the president.
      1. Manage the selection process.
      2. Manage the individual planning process, including quarterly meetings.
      3. Manage the performance review process, including the compensation program.
      4. Mentor the president.
   B. Determine the board's agenda.
   C. Recommend committee membership.
   D. Recommend revisions to the President's Duties.
II. Performance Assurance
   A. Recommend revisions to the President's Guidelines.
   B. Assess the president's performance against the President's Guidelines.
   C. Serve as the audit and finance committee of the board.
III. Governance
   A. Recruit, welcome, and orient new board members.
   B. Recommend the officer slate.
      1. Nominate the chair.
      2. In concert with the chair, propose the other officers.
   C. Assess performance against the Delegation Plan excluding the President's Duties and Guidelines.

D. Recommend revisions to the Delegation Plan excluding the President's Duties and Guidelines.
E. Make sure that the accomplishments of the board are recognized.
F. Ensure alignment between the Governance Plan and the by-laws.
IV. Development
A. Conduct the board member portion of the annual fund campaign.
B. Provide qualified prospects.
C. Serve as a think tank for development innovation.

OFFICER DUTIES

I. Chair
A. Ensure that the Governance Plan is effectively implemented.
B. Chair the Executive Committee.
C. Chair board meetings.
1. Develop and coordinate the board's agenda.
2. Guide the board members to work together efficiently and effectively.
3. Keep the board focused on important work and on task.
D. Serve as the board's official spokesperson.
II. Vice chair
A. Chair a committee if asked.
B. Serve on the Executive Committee.
C. Serve as chair in the chair's absence.
D. As the chair elect, prepare to succeed the chair.
III. Treasurer
A. Chair a committee if asked.
B. Serve on the Executive Committee.
C. Represent the board to the financial community.
IV. Secretary
A. Chair a committee if asked.
B. Serve on the Executive Committee.
C. Ensure an accurate recording and archival process of the board's work.

BOARD, COMMITTEE, AND OFFICER GUIDELINES

I. Focus talent and time on important work.
   A. Conduct work in an effective and efficient manner.
   B. Center agendas on important work.
II. Be a give-and-take board that values the diversity and strength of all its members.
   A. Use *Robert's Rules of Order* to provide a framework for conducting meetings and promoting civility.
   B. Strive for consensus on important issues.
III. Govern the organization—don't manage it.
   A. Adhere to the Governance Plan.
   B. Ensure that committees, officers, and board members are accountable to the board, helping the board to perform its duties effectively.
   C. Respect the chain of command between the board, the president, and the professional staff.

BOARD MEMBERS

BOARD MEMBER DUTIES

I. Make good decisions.
   A. Keep the Leadership Plan in focus.
   B. Know the business.
      1. Subscribe.
      2. Study advance materials.
   C. Attend at least 75 percent of scheduled meetings.
   D. Participate resolutely and ask tough questions.
   E. Vote conscientiously.
II. Raise money.
   A. Give a generous personal contribution within means.
      1. Annual Fund (President's Circle preferred)
   B. Support and attend fundraising events.
      1. Volunteer Recognition event and donor recognition events.
   C. Make fundraising solicitations when possible.
   D. Support donor recognition.
      1. Write 30–40 thank-you letters each season.
III. Champion the organization to and from the community.

IV. Do the board's work.
  A. Serve on at least one committee.
  B. Accept tasks on behalf of the Board.

BOARD MEMBER GUIDELINES

  I. Use reasonable care, the same care as an ordinarily prudent person would exercise in a like position and under similar circumstances.
  II. Be loyal to the organization.
   A. Always put the organization's well-being first in decision making and conduct.
   B. Reveal any conflicts of interest in appearance or in fact.
  III. Be obedient to the organization.
   A. Be faithful to the values and vision contained within the Leadership Plan.
   B. Act and speak for the board in an official capacity only if directed to do so by the board.
   C. Fully support the board, including majority decisions that the individual board member did not personally support.
   D. Respect the chain of command between the board, the president, and the professional staff.

PRESIDENT

PRESIDENT'S DUTIES

  I. Implement the Leadership Plan.
  II. Provide management support to the board for its work.

PRESIDENT'S GUIDELINES

  I. Controlling standard.
   A. The president shall conduct himself or herself with the highest business and professional standards at all times, never causing or allowing any practice that is illegal, or unethical, or that breaches the Values or Vision contained in the Leadership Plan.

II. With regard to interpretation of these guidelines, the president shall:

   A. Use reasonable interpretation, the same interpretation as an ordinarily prudent person would exercise in a like position and under similar circumstances.

III. With regard to risk assessment and management, the president shall:

   A. Protect the organization's assets and earning power by using proper risk management techniques. Specifically, the president shall:

      1. Have programs in place to identify risk, quantify risk, minimize, transfer and/or eliminate risk, monitor risk, and inform the Board of Trustees about programs for risk assessment and management.

IV. With regard to endowment funds under management at the Dayton Foundation, the president shall:

   A. Invest in funds with annual three-year and five-year performance of at least top quartile.

   B. Invest in funds with a manager tenure of five years or more.

   C. Invest in funds that follow the investment guidelines established by the Dayton Foundation.

   D. Review the investment mix with independent financial counsel annually using a 50-year long-term perspective.

V. With regard to planning, the president shall:

   A. Operate annually with a Governance Plan containing Leadership, Delegation, Vigilance, and Management Plans.

   B. Ensure that all employees have individual plans that are updated at least annually and reviewed quarterly.

VI. With regard to financial matters, the president shall:

   A. Make capital acquisitions of less than $50,000.

   B. Draw a maximum of 5 percent income annually from endowment investments.

   C. Have and follow an audit-proof procedure for handling income and disbursements.

   D. Receive a clean audit and comply with any recommendations outlined in the accompanying management letter.

   E. Keep the Association debt-free including lines of credit.

   F. Achieve at least a 2 percent surplus annually of income over expenses subject to the following provisions:

      1. Income shall exclude planned gifts not budgeted and investment income from endowment funds other than the 5 percent annual draw.

2. Expenses shall exclude unfunded depreciation, any incentive package costs for management and contributions to endowment funds.

G. Present budgets with a probability of occurrence of at least 80 percent.

H. Maintain separate deposit accounts for the Dayton Opera and the Victoria Theatre Association.

VII. With regard to personnel matters, the president shall:

A. Treat the staff and volunteers fairly and respectfully.

B. Establish, communicate, and implement effective personnel policies that are reviewed by independent counsel annually.

C. Establish, communicate, and implement clear accountabilities for staff and monitor performance accordingly.

D. Pay compensation at a level required to attract and retain the qualified staff needed to implement the Leadership Plan, Governance Plan, and Management Plan.

VIII. With regard to communication to the board, the president shall:

A. Provide information in a timely manner to the board, committees, officers, or board members that could have a significant impact on the organization or in any way cause embarrassment.

B. Send information in advance of board meetings by at least five days.

IX. With regard to the Victoria Theatre Association's 403(b)(7) plan, the president shall

A. Have a 403(b) policy document covering all administrative particulars including a provision for independent financial counsel for investment decisions.

B. Review the 403(b) policy document with independent legal and independent financial counsel annually.

X. With regard to development, the president shall:

A. Follow the standards set by the National Society of Fund Raising Executives.

VIGILANCE PLAN

BOARD

WHO	WHEN	WHAT
	First quarter	Leadership Plan drafted
Executive	Early September	• Review last year's results—president's duties • President's individual plan including compensation review
Board	September 13 Dinner meeting 5:30–8:30 P.M.	• Review last year's final results—except audit • Review current season preliminary forecast • Begin new Leadership Plan
	Second quarter	Leadership Plan finalized
Executive	Late October	• President's individual plan
Governance	Late October	• Review last year's results—board duties and guidelines • Begin recruitment process for new class
Performance Assurance	Late October	• Review last year's results—president's guidelines • Review last year's results—audit
Development	Late October	• Committee business
Board	November 8 11:30–1:30 P.M.	• Review last year's results—audit • Finalize new Leadership Plan
	Third quarter	Delegation Management, and Vigilance Plans drafted
Executive	Mid-January	• President's individual plan
Board	January 25 Lunch meeting 11:00–1:00 P.M.	• Educate—socialize
	Fourth quarter	Delegation, Management, and Vigilance Plans finalized
Executive	Mid-April	• Review midyear forecast—president's duties • Review president's duties for possible revisions • President's individual plan
Governance	Mid-April	• Review midyear forecast—board duties and guidelines • Review board duties and guidelines for possible revisions • Finalize recruitment process for new class

WHO	WHEN	WHAT
Performance Assurance	Mid-April	• Review midyear forecast—president's guidelines • Review president's guidelines for possible revisions
Development	Mid-April	• Committee business
Board	April 26 11:30–1:30 P.M.	• Review midyear forecast • Review first draft Governance Plan
Executive	Late June	• President's individual plan
Board	June 27 5:30–7:30 P.M.	• Approve next year final Governance Plan • Annual meeting

STAFF

WHO	WHEN	WHAT
	First quarter	Leadership Plan drafted
Staff	By September 6	• Finalize last year's final results • Draft ideas for strategies and imperatives
	Second quarter	Leadership Plan finalized
Staff	By November 1	• Expand basic Leadership Plan to first draft
	Third quarter	Delegation, Management, and Vigilance Plans drafted
Staff	By April 1	• Finalize current season midyear forecast • First draft next season Governance Plan
	Fourth quarter	Delegation, Management, and Vigilance Plans finalized
Staff	By June 13	• Final draft Governance Plan

MANAGEMENT PLAN

DEPARTMENT MAP

VICTORIA THEATRE ASSOCIATION
Board of Trustees

PRESIDENT

MANAGING
DIRECTOR

DEVELOPMENT   MARKETING   EXECUTIVE   ADMINISTRATION
- Finance
- Technology
- Ticketing

FACILITIES
MANAGEMENT
- House Management
- Licensing
- Property Management

PROGRAMMING
- Public
- Education
- Artistic Administration

PRESENTING

DAYTON OPERA

BUDGET SUMMARY—VICTORIA THEATRE ASSOCIATION

VARIANCE REPORT

ITEM	+/− $		REASON
Income			
Subscriptions	+	204,350	Broadway +318,000
			Young at Heart −64,240
			Next Stage −49,410
Single Tickets	−	1,015,220	Broadway −90,000
			Young at Heart −19,700
			Discovery +32,200
			Children's Festival +21,885
			Star Extras −955,410
Tenant	+	12,645	Rent Increase—Dayton Ballet
Contract Services	−	250,750	Dayton Opera Management Fees +27,000
			MAC operating reimbursables −294,178
			Ticket Center fees and reimbursables
			+14,800
Investments	+	33,000	Interest from Dayton Foundation
Other Earned	+	16,100	Program book advertising +15,400
Sponsorship	−	122,895	Budget based on known sponsors
Membership	+	18,000	New strategies being implemented
Government	+	104,500	City of Dayton funding eliminated
			−17,080
			Montgomery County +108,480
			City of Vandalia +15,000

EXPENSES

Artistic—Theatre	+	770,000	Broadway −22,100
			Young at Heart −47,250
			Next Stage −57,000
			Star Extras −653,500
Support—Development	+	43,000	Salary increases and new position +26,000
Support—Marketing	+	61,250	Salary increases and new position
Support—Ticket Center	+	37,000	Salary increases and new position
Education	+	28,850	Salary increases +17,000
			Education material increase +9,000
Facilities—Victoria	+	15,000	Increase due to wage increases
Facilities—Met Arts	−	294,500	Decrease due to Uno's project

BUDGET SUMMARY
(In Thousands)

INCOME EARNED INCOME	Projection YE 6/30/00 as of 4/30/00	Budget 6/30/01 proposed	Variance Column 3 Minus Column 2
Subscriptions	3,312	3,517	204
Single Tickets	2,131	1,116	−1,015
Production	0	0	0
Venue	73	73	0
Tenant	31	44	13
Contract Services	1,119	869	−251
Investments	224	257	33
Other earned	191	207	16
Earned Income Total	7,082	6,082	−1,000

CONTRIBUTED INCOME

Sponsorship	1,073	950	−123
Membership	332	350	18
Government	277	382	104
Endowment	0	0	0
Planned Giving	0	0	0
Events	0	0	0
Other Contributed	0	0	0
Contributed Income Total	1,682	1,682	0
Income Total	8,765	7,764	−1,001

EXPENSE ARTISTIC

Theatre	3,286	2,516	−770
Scouting	54	61	7
Film	21	25	4
Music	4	5	0
Artistic Total	3,365	2,606	−758

PRODUCTION

Stage	646	646	0
House	255	259	5
Production Total	900	906	5

221

	Projection YE 6/30/00 as of 4/30/00	Budget 6/30/01 proposed	Variance Column 3 Minus Column 2
SUPPORT			
Administration	822	813	−9
Development	246	289	43
Marketing	1,312	1,363	51
Ticket Center	610	647	37
Support Total	2,990	3,112	122
EDUCATION			
Education	147	176	29
FACILITIES			
Victoria	505	507	2
Met Arts Center	623	326	−297
Facilities Total	1,127	833	−295
ACCRUALS			
Accruals/Funded Depreciation	137	132	−5
EXPENSE TOTAL	8,666	7,764	−901
SURPLUS/(DEFICIT) FROM OPERATIONS	**99**	**0**	**−99**

BOARD GOALS

Success Measures

	'96–'97	'97–'98	'98–'99	Budget	'99–'00 12/31 YE Forecast	Final*	'00–'01 Budget	'01–'02
Total attendance	279K	288K	284K	294K	292K	284K	269K	285K
Total income	6.17M	6.99M	7.75M	7.95M	8.38M	8.78M	7.76M	7.89M
Earned-to-contributed	76/24	79/21	80/20	81/19	80/20	81/19	78/22	78/22
Net income	148K	99K	−79K	0	164K	99K*	0	0

*Subject to audit.

Imperatives

- Organization success

Goals

	Who - When
Executive	
I. Evaluate the Victoria Theatre Association–Dayton Opera alliance so that the future of the alliance may be determined.	ML, 6/1/01
II. Evaluate the compensation program for senior leadership so that the highest-quality people can be attracted and retained.	SS, 6/1/01
Governance	
I. Improve orientation and education practices so that the board is more engaged, more prepared, and educated.	DM, ML 2/1/01

STAFF GOALS

EXECUTIVE

Imperatives

- Poor coordination across departments, especially on subscription campaign
- Limited time for president to spend on governance, big picture

Goals

	Who - When
I. Develop and implement standard operating procedures for all phases of subscription processing so that the campaigns reach their fullest potential.	SS, DK 11/1/00
II. Reorganize reporting relationships so that day-to-day operations are more effectively coordinated.	ML 10/1/00
III. Determine cost-benefit of adding an executive-level assistant for the president so that he can spend more time focused on strategic issues.	ML, 11/1/00

DEVELOPMENT
Success Measures

	'96–'97	'97–'98	'98–'99	Budget	'99–'00 12/31 YE Forecast	Final	'00–'01 Budget	'01–'02
Victoria								
Sponsorship	237K	1.01M	1.02M	950K	1.07M	1.07M	950K	975K
Annual fund: Funds	242K	253K	280K	295K	310K	332K	350K	368K
Renewal rate	.67	.73	.76	.77	.77	.77	.78	.79
Documented legacies	7	13	18	20	20	20	22	24
Opera								
Sponsorship	incl.↓	114K	204K	191K	290K	316K	352K	370K
Annual fund: Funds	293K	148K	130K	120K	105K	116K	130K	137K
Renewal rate			.58	.65	.60	.85	.81	.82
Documented legacies			11	14	14	14	20	25
Combined*								
Expense ÷ contributed	.14	.14	.13	.13	.12	.11	.11	.11
Contributed ÷ income	.23	.21	.25	.23	.24	.24	.27	.27

*Figures prior to 1998–99 are for the Victoria only.

Imperatives
- Department has reached its capacity to take on new growth.
- Board will be smaller, or less of "give, get, or get off" in the future.

Goals

	Who–When
I. Develop and test plan to address connectivity issues in 2000–2001 so that giving is sustained and increased.	LF, 6/1/01
II. Implement plan to increase capacity so that the department can handle more fundraising opportunities.	LF, 10/1/00

ADMINISTRATION—FINANCE

Imperatives
- Depth of team
- Meeting back-office deadlines in finance

Goals

		Who–When
I.	Close general ledger and maintain schedules monthly to eliminate delays in completion of year-end so that the annual audit may be completed in a more timely and efficient manner.	TL, SS 11/1/00

ADMINISTRATIVE—TECHNOLOGY

Imperatives
- Lack of penetration of technology to all areas of the organization.

Goals

		Who–When
I.	Improve telephone systems for ticket center use to route more callers to information detail before speaking with an agent so that call-waits may be reduced for ticket buyers.	DH, CZ 11/1/00
II.	Improve fault tolerances on the network so staff members experience less downtime.	DH, CZ 1/1/01

ADMINISTRATION—TICKET CENTER

Success Measures

	'96–'97	'97–'98	'98–'99	Budget	'99–'00 12/31 YE Forecast	Final	'00–'01 Budget	'01–'02
Customer satisfaction (1–4, 4 is best)								
Friendliness	3.97	3.89	3.99	3.88	3.96	3.98	3.99	
Knowledge	3.94	3.89	3.97	3.88	3.96	3.98	3.99	
Accuracy	3.97	3.86	3.99	3.88	3.96	3.98	3.99	
Overall satisfaction	3.99	3.91	3.99	3.80	3.96	3.98	3.99	
Thank you	4.00	4.00	4.00	4.00	4.00	4.00	4.00	

Imperatives

- Coordination issues with marketing and other departments.
- Instability in quality of subscription processing.
- Ticket agent knowledge is hit-or-miss.

Goals

		Who–When
I.	Implement a process to review marketing/performance calendar so that ticket center personnel may be scheduled accordingly to cover peak times and curtains.	CB, DH 9/1/00
II.	Document Standard Operating Procedures for the subscription department so that subscribers are served more effectively and subscription/donation processing/ tracking is accurate.	PH, DH 11/1/00
III.	Establish, improve, and document a consistent program for training and testing ticket center agents so that customers may be served more accurately and efficiently.	DH, 9/1/00
IV.	Establish and document subscription rollover processes, time line, and cross-department requirements so that subscription rollovers may be completed accurately and in a period consistent with the marketing calendar.	MR, DH 11/1/00

MARKETING
Success Measures

	'96–'97	'97–'98	'98–'99	Budget	'99–'00 12/31 YE Forecast	Final	'00–'01 Budget	'01–'02
Broadway:								
Total attendance	107.3K	101.0K	104.0K	103.9K	104.7K	106.6K	106.5K	103.0K
Subscriptions	15,727	14,421	14,708	14,400	14,525	14,525	15,000	14,700
Single tickets	13,000	14,500	15,790	17,500	17,500	19,423	16,500	14,800
Star Extras:								
Total attendance	24,143	23,498	16,389	30,700	26,647	26,647	8,500	8,500
Next Stage:								
Total attendance		24,509	25,336	18,650	16,985	16,720	14,900	15,300
Subscriptions		2,237	2,379	2,500	2,397	2,397	2,600	2,900
Single tickets		13,324	13,440	6,150	5,000	4,735	4,500	3,700
Hot Times:								
Total attendance	30,878	23,165	28,111	26,900	29,055	29,055	29,350	29,850
Subscriptions	2,655	1,901	2,322	2,250	2,370	2,370	2,375	2,420
Single tickets	4,328	4,155	4,891	4,400	5,355	5,355	5,600	5,650
Jubilee Diversity %:								
Broadway	.02	.01	.06	.03	.03	.03	.03	.03
Young at Heart	.03	.01	.02	.02	.02	.02	.02	.03
Discovery	.72	.75	.70	.65	.65	.65	.65	.65
Young at Heart:								
Total attendance	31,150	24,583	24,778	25,875	26,150	26,113	14,900	22,400
Subscriptions	4,400	3,562	4,220	4,325	4,380	4,380	3,100	3,900
Single tickets	4,750	3,211	3,684	4,250	4,250	4,213	2,500	2,900
Children's Festival:								
Ticketed attendance			6,666	7,500	7,500	6,040	7,500	6,900
Street attendance						5,000	5,000	5,000
Opera series:								
Total attendance	14,846	15,442	13,730	12,550	14,329	15,476	16,700	17,800
Subscriptions	3,249	2,716	2,639	2,700	2,743	2,743	2,900	3,100
Single tickets: Paid	5,099	7,294	4,004	2,450	2,450	3,370	4,500	5,500
Comps	incl.↑	incl.↑	2,016	2,000	3,650	3,877	3,500	3,000

Imperatives
- Softness in all lines except Broadway Series

Goals

		Who–When
I.	Fix external list management challenge so that our direct mail campaigns are restored.	KP, SB 9/1/00
II.	Implement department reorganization department so that future opportunities can be taken on.	KP, 8/1/00

PROGRAMMING—PUBLIC

Success Measures

	'96–'97	'97–'98	'98–'99	Budget	'99–'00 12/31 YE Forecast	Final	'00–'01 Budget	'01–'02
Broadway:								
Gross sales	2.60M	2.78M	3.07M	3.10M	3.39M	3.39M	3.62M	3.68M
Renewal rate	.86	.80	.90	.84	.85	.85	.87	.86
Star Extras:								
Gross sales	741K	867K	1.01M	1.13M	1.14M	1.14M	185K	190K
Next Stage:								
Gross sales		566K	691K	495K	412K	414K	359K	406K
Renewal rate			.70	.67	.73	.73	.63	.68
Hot Times:								
Gross sales	47K	42K	48K	48K	57K	57K	58K	61K
Renewal rate	.87	.42	.66	.69	.61	.61	.65	.67
Young at Heart:								
Gross sales	193K	157K	173K	219K	226K	225K	141K	141K
Renewal rate	.62	.64	.82	.62	.72	.72	.54	.70
Children's Festival:								
Gross sales			53K	69K	69K	56K	77K	50K
Opera series:								
Gross sales	507K	490K	366K	450K	446K	453K	523K	607K
Renewal rate	.72	.68	.81	.74	.80	.80	.73	.80

Imperatives
- Softness in all lines except Broadway Series

Goals

		Who–When
I.	Program pre-performance activities for at least two Young at Heart productions so that the Young at Heart experience may be enhanced.	TM, 10/1/00
II.	Develop financial scenarios for Broadway programming in the new PAC so that we can determine Victoria Theatre Association's expected usage for that facility.	DK, 10/1/00

PROGRAMMING—EDUCATION
Success Measures

	'96–'97	'97–'98	'98–'99	Budget	'99–'00 12/31 YE Forecast	Final	'00–'01 Budget	'01–'02
Discovery:								
Total attendance	81,002	91,118	73,736	74,500	76,175	61,240	71,910	80,000
Gross sales	169K	184K	160K	198K	182K	160K	192K	202K
Percentage paid	.52	.47	.56	.65	.65	.65	.65	.65
Renew rate	.68	.71	.73	.75	.78	.78	.80	.80
Workshop attendance	240	1,920	2,010	3,000	2,250	3,000	3,000	3,000
Children's Festival:								
School attendance			4,100	6,150	6,150	3,637	3,870	6,100
Percentage paid			.61	.65	.65	.57	.65	.65
Opera Education:								
Total attendance	13,000	13,000	9,653	0	0	0	22,000	27,700
Maniacs attendance							18,500	21,400
Workshop attendance							3,500	3,600
Opera Outreach:								
Total attendance			935	950	2,305	2,305	2,570	2,760
Girls Scouts attendance			320	240	168	168	170	170
Overtures attendance			240	335	337	337	500	600
Previews attendance			375	375	1,800	1,800	1,900	2,000
Muse Machine:								
Broadway tickets	1,631	1,114	1,443	1,250	1,441	1,113	1,250	1,250
Next stage tickets	NA	1,065	701	1,100	729	729	600	750
Young at Heart tickets	0	0	0	300	0	0	400	400
Opera tickets	1,852	1,086	757	1,850	940	733	1,850	1,850

Imperatives
- Decline in attendance

Goals

		Who–When
I.	Launch Opera Maniacs, the opera education program so that 22,000 customers are served.	TM, PE 9/1/00
II.	Improve Discovery penetration into Montgomery County K–8 classrooms by 10%.	AT, JY 6/1/01
III.	Increase knowledge of department software so that we do not rely on systems department for help.	AT, JY 10/1/00
IV.	Artistically develop and produce an Artist-in-Residence program and workshops so that Opera Maniacs may be launched.	TB, PE 2/1/01

PRESENTING

Imperatives

- Demand for services extending to new performing arts hall

Goals

		Who–When
I.	Upgrade camera for the lobby monitor so that latecomers are afforded the best possible view from the lobby.	JC, 12/1/00
II.	Include the house steward and electrician on the LAN so that we may ensure a steady, efficient flow of communication.	JD, 6/1/01
III.	Implement transfer of all Victoria Theatre Association technical drawings to the Auto CAD system to improve communication so that the audience is presented the best show possible.	JD, 6/1/01
IV.	Implement transfer of Discovery responsibilities to production coordinator so that the production manager has a back-up.	MP, 6/1/01
V.	Investigate and test the use of interoffice e-mail for Green Lites so that the process becomes more efficient and cost saving.	MP, 12/1/00

FACILITY MANAGEMENT—HOUSE MANAGEMENT

Success Measures

	'96–'97	'97–'98	'98–'99	Budget	'99–'00 12/31 YE Forecast	Final	'00–'01 Budget	'01–'02
Volunteers: Number	1,104	1,188	1,211	1,200	1,150	1,273	1,300	1,300
Renewal rate	.71	.75	.92	.95	.95	.98	.90	.90
Hours	23,500	30,275	N/A	31,000	31,000	35,508	36,000	36,000

Imperatives

- Inconsistent quality of house management from performance to performance

Goals

	Who–When
I. Plan Victoria Theatre Association gift shop so that it can be built in summer of 2001.	RF, DH 6/1/00
II. Improve volunteer performance so that we may better serve the customer.	BF, 3/1/00
III. Improve consistency of operations during performances so that we may always provide standing ovation customer service.	RF, 10/1/00

FACILITY MANAGEMENT—LICENSING

Success Measures

	'96–'97	'97–'98	'98–'99	Budget	'99–'00 12/31 YE Forecast	Final	'00–'01 Budget	'01–'02
Venue performances:								
Victoria	310	303	287	298	303	313	305	310
Loft	121	136	117	116	128	130	148	143
Days of use:								
Victoria	282	285	273	267	265	262	277	268
Loft	299	294	318	315	318	321	298	307
Facility net income:								
Victoria Theatre	−943K	−931K	−1.1M	−1.34M	−1.32M	−1.36M	−1.36M	−1.42M

Imperatives

- Increasing demands for services with new performing arts hall

Goals

	Who–When
I. Design and create an informational packet about our venues so that we can provide necessary information to potential licensee's who are not familiar with our venues.	JB, 6/1/01
II. Implement department reorganization so that increased demand for services is met in both licensing and property management.	JB, ML 11/1/00

FACILITY MANAGEMENT—PROPERTY MANAGEMENT

Imperatives

- Depth of staff to handle increased load from new performing arts center

Goals

	Who–When
I. Finalize plans to unify the Victoria Theatre and Metropolitan Arts Center as an arts center so that our customers may have the most convenient experience possible when attending either venue.	JB, 6/1/01
II. Investigate the feasibility of booster seats for our Young see the stage.	TM 2/1/01
III. Investigate the feasibility of replacing the balcony seats with the same size seats as the orchestra seats.	TM 2/1/01
IV. Research, write, and implement a "What Do You Do If" book for the Metropolitan Arts center so that the tenants will have the necessary information in the absence of Victoria Theatre Association staff.	JB, 6/1/01
V. Implement plan for necessary interior restoration of the stairwell, third, and fourth floors of the Metropolitan Arts Center so that the facility will continue to be maintained at our usual standards.	HB, 12/1/01

Endnotes

[1]Richard L. Moyers and Kathleen P. Enright, *A Snapshot of American's Nonprofit Boards* (Washington, DC: National Center for Nonprofit Boards, 1997), p. 5.

[2]*Ibid.*, p. 4.

[3]Jon R. Katzenbach and Douglas K. Smith, *The Wisdom of Teams* (Boston: Harvard Business School Press, 1993), pp. 45–46.

[4]Richard L. Moyers and Kathleen P. Enright, *A Snapshot of American's Nonprofit Boards* (Washington, DC: National Center for Nonprofit Boards, 1997), p. 4.

[5]*Ibid.*, p. 12.

[6]Top Position is One-Time Shot for Many Executive Directors, *Board Member*, November/December 1999, p. 6.

[7]*Ibid.*, p. 6.

[8]*Ibid.*, p. 6.

[9]William G. Bowen, Thomas I. Nygren, Sarah E. Turner, and Elizabeth A. Duffy, *The Charitable Nonprofits* (San Francisco: Jossey-Bass, 1994), p. 24.

[10]*Ibid.*, p. 24.

[11]William G. Bowen, *Inside the Boardroom* (New York: Wiley, 1994), p. 110.

[12]*Board Member*, January 1996, p. 11.

[13]Top Position is One-Time Shot for Many Executive Directors, *Board Member*, November/December 1999, p. 6.

[14]*What You Should Know about Nonprofits* (Washington, DC: National Center for Nonprofit Boards, Independent Sector, 2000), p. 4.

[15]William G. Bowen, *Inside the Boardroom* (New York: Wiley, 1994), p. 1.

[16]Jacqueline C. Leifer and Michael B. Glomb, *The Legal Obligations of Nonprofit Boards* (Washington, DC: National Center for Nonprofit Boards, 1997), p. 5.

[17]John Carver, *Boards That Make a Difference* (San Francisco: Jossey-Bass, 1997), p. xiii.

[18]Peter F. Drucker, *On the Profession of Management* (Boston: Harvard Business School Press, 1998), p. 156.

[19]Richard P. Chait, Thomas P. Holland, Barbara E. Taylor, *Improving the Performance of Governing Boards* (Phoenix, AZ: Oryx Press, 1996), p. 1.

[20]Richard L. Moyers and Kathleen P. Enright, *A Snapshot of America's Nonprofit Boards* (Washington, DC: National Center for Nonprofit Boards, 1997), p. 13.

[21]Paul C. Light, *Making Nonprofits Work* (Washington, DC: Brookings Institute, 2000), p. 44.

[22]*Ibid.*, p. 46.

[23]*Ibid.*, p. 46.

[24]*Ibid.*, p. 47.

[25]*Ibid.*, p. 53.

[26]*Ibid.*, p. 54.

[27]*Ibid.*, pp. 58–59.

[28]*Ibid.*, p. 62.

[29]*Ibid.*, p. 63.

[30]*Ibid.*, p. 63.

[31]*Ibid.*, p. 68.

[32]*Ibid.*, p. 70.

[33]*Ibid.*, p. 69.

[34]*Ibid.*, p. 69.

[35]United We Stand: How to Make Your Board Work Like a Championship Team, *Board Member,* January 2000, pp. 3–6.

[36]Carl E. Larson and Frank M. LaFasto, *Teamwork: What Must Go Right/What Can Go Wrong* (Newbury Park, CA: Sage Publications, 1989), pp. 33–34.

[37]Peter F. Drucker, *Managing the Non-Profit Organization* (New York: HarperCollins, 1990), p. 152.

[38]Stephen R. Covey, *The 7 Habits of Highly Effective People* (New York: Simon and Schuster, 1989), pp. 70–71.

[39]*Ibid.*, p. 76.

[40]Mary Walton, *The Deming Management Method* (New York: Perigee Books, 1986), p. 55.

[41]Thomas J. Peters and Robert H. Waterman Jr., *In Search of Excellence* (New York: Harper and Row, 1982), p. 13.

[42]Paul C. Light, *Sustaining Innovation* (San Francisco: Jossey-Bass, 1998), p. 16.

[43]James C. Collins and Jerry I. Porras, *Built to Last* (New York: HarperCollins, 1994), p. 9.

[44]Karl Albrecht, *The Northbound Train* (New York: AMACOM, 1994), p. viii.

[45]Stephen R. Covey, *The 7 Habits of Highly Effective People* (New York: Simon and Schuster, 1989), p. 76.

[46]Paul Charles Light, *Sustaining Innovation* (San Francisco: Jossey-Bass, 1998), p. 23.

[47]*Ibid.*, pp. 254–255.

[48]Karl Albrecht, *The Northbound Train,* (New York: AMACOM, 1994), p. 105.

[49]Laying the Foundation, *Board Member,* May 2000, p. 6.

[50]Raising Money: Tips for Start-Up Organizations, *Board Member,* May 2000, p. 5.

[51]Cyril O. Houle, *Governing Boards* (San Francisco: Jossey-Bass & Washington: National Center for Nonprofit Boards: 1989), p. xvi.

[52]Glenn Van Ekeren, *The Speaker's Sourcebook, Quotes, Stories and Anecdotes for Every Occasion* (Englewood Cliffs, NJ: Prentice Hall, 1988), p. 188.

[53]Max DePree, *Leadership Is An Art* (New York: Doubleday, 1987), p. 9.

[54]Stephen R. Covey, *The 7 Habits of Highly Effective People* (New York: Simon and Schuster, 1989), p. 101.

[55]Warren Bennis, *On Becoming a Leader* (New York: Addison-Wesley, 1989), p. 194.

[56]John P. Kotter, *A Force for Change* (New York: Free Press, 1990), p. 6.

[57]Ibid., p. 6.

[58]*Ibid.,* p. 10.

[59]Stephen R. Covey, *The 7 Habits of Highly Effective People* (New York: Simon and Schuster, 1989), p. 101.

[60]Conversations about Leading and Managing Change, *National Arts Stabilization Journal,* Spring 2000, pp. 3–6.

[61]Carl E. Larson and Frank M. LaFasto, *Teamwork: What Must Go Right/What Can Go Wrong* (Newbury Park, CA: Sage Publications, 1989), p. 27.

[62]Jon Winokur, *Friendly Advice* (New York: Penguin Group, 1992), p. 194.

[63]http://www.starwars.com/characters/c-3p0.

[64]Michael Brassard and Diane Ritter, *The Memory Jogger ™II,* (Methuen, MA: GOAL/QPC: 1994), pp. 19–20.

[65]*Ibid.,* pp. 12–14.

[66]Burt Nanus, *Visionary Leadership* (San Francisco: Jossey-Bass, 1992), pp. 8–9.

[67]*Ibid.,* pp. 28–29.

[68]Jerry Bowles and Joshua Hammond, *Beyond Quality* (New York: Berkley Books, 1991), pp. 108–109.

[69]Ken Blanchard, Sheldon Bowles, *Raving Fans* (New York: William Morrow and Company, 1993), pp. ix–x.

[70]John P. Kotter, "Leading Change: Why Transformation Efforts Fail," *Harvard Business Review,* March/April 1995, p. 63.

[71]John Kay, *Why Firms Succeed* (Oxford: Oxford University Press, 1995), p. 268.

[72]Burt Nanus, *Visionary Leadership* (San Francisco: Jossey-Bass, 1992).

[73]Mary Walton, *The Deming Management Method* (New York: Perigee Books, 1986), p. 94.

[74]*Ibid.,* p. 191.

[75]Carl E. Larson and Frank M. LaFasto, *Teamwork: What Must Go Right/What Can Go Wrong* (Newbury Park, CA: Sage Publications, 1989), p. 27.

[76]Cyril O. Houle, *Governing Boards* (San Francisco: Jossey-Bass & Washington: National Center for Nonprofit Boards: 1989), p. 88.

[77]*Ibid.*, p. 89.

[78]William G. Bowen, *Inside the Boardroom* (New York: Wiley, 1994), p. 9.

[79]*Ibid.*, p. 127.

[80]J. Sterling Livingston, "Pygmalion in Management," *Harvard Business Review*, September/October 1988, p. 126.

[81]*Ibid.*, p. 126.

[82]Philip B. Crosby, *Quality Is Free* (New York: Penguin Books USA, 1980), p. 114.

[83]Paul C. Light, *Making Nonprofits Work* (Washington, DC: Brookings Institute, 2000), pp. 72–73.

[84]*Measuring Program Outcomes, A Practical Approach* (Washington, DC: United Way of America, 1996), p. 8.

[85]Paul C. Light, *Making Nonprofits Work* (Washington, DC: Brookings Institute, 2000), pp. 72–73.

[86]Karl Mathiasen, III, *Board Passages: Three Key Stages in a Nonprofit Board's Life Cycle* (Washington: National Center for Nonprofit Boards, 1992), p. 17.

[87]Carl E. Larson and Frank M. LaFasto, *Teamwork: What Must Go Right/What Can Go Wrong* (Newbury Park, CA: Sage Publications, 1989), pp. 55–58.

[88]Robert C. Andringa and Ted W. Engstrom, *Nonprofit Board Answer Book* (Washington: National Center for Nonprofit Boards, 1997), p. 4.

[89]*Ibid.*, p. 4.

[90]*Ibid.*, pp. 4–5.

[91]*Ibid.*, pp. 4–5.

[92]*Board Member,* January 1996, p. 10.

[93]F. Warren McFarlan, "Don't Assume the Shoe Fits," *Harvard Business Review*, November/December 1999, p. 74.

[94]*Ibid.*, p. 74.

[95]*Ibid.*, p. 74.

[96]John H. Zenger (et al.), *Leading Teams* (Burr Ridge, IL: Zenger-Miller, 1994), pp. 12–15.

[97]J. Richard Hackman, editor, *Groups That Work (and Those That Don't)* (San Francisco: Jossey-Bass, 1990), p. 498.

[98]Jon R. Katzenbach and Douglas K. Smith, *The Wisdom of Teams* (Boston: Harvard Business School Press, 1993), pp. 139–144.

[99]John H. Zenger (et al.), *Leading Teams* (Burr Ridge, IL: Zenger-Miller, 1994), p. 16.

[100]Jon R. Katzenbach and Douglas K. Smith, *The Wisdom of Teams* (Boston: Harvard Business School Press, 1993), pp. 85–86.

[101]John H. Zenger (et al.), *Leading Teams* (Burr Ridge, IL: Zenger-Miller, 1994), pp. 12–15.

[102]Carl E. Larson and Frank M. LaFasto, *Teamwork: What Must Go Right/What Can Go Wrong* (Newbury Park, CA: Sage Publications, 1989), pp. 134–135.

[103]*Board Member,* January 1996, p. 10.

[104]Carl E. Larson and Frank M. LaFasto, *Teamwork: What Must Go Right/What Can Go Wrong* (Newbury Park, CA: Sage Publications, 1989), pp. 133–134.

[105]Jon R. Katzenbach and Douglas K. Smith, *The Wisdom of Teams* (Boston: Harvard Business School Press, 1993), p. 48.

[106]Jacqueline Covey Leifer and Michael B. Glomb, *The Legal Obligations of Nonprofit Boards* (Washington, National Center for Nonprofit Boards: 1995), pp. 31–33.

[107]Carl E. Larson and Frank M. LaFasto, *Teamwork: What Must Go Right/What Can Go Wrong* (Newbury Park, CA: Sage Publications, 1989), p. 134.

[108]John Kay, *Why Firms Succeed* (Oxford: Oxford University Press, 1995), pp. 16–17.

[109]David Michaelson, *Performance,* December 1995, p. 4.

[110]"Information sharing is critical . . .," *Harvard Business Review,* March/April 1996, p. 75.

[111]Robert D. Herman and Richard D. Heimovics, *Executive Leadership in Nonprofit Organizations* (San Francisco: Jossey-Bass, 1991), p. xiii.

[112]*Ibid.,* p. 59.

[113]*Ibid.,* p. 56.

[114]"Top Position is One-Time Shot for Many Executive Directors," *Board Member,* November/December 1999, p. 6.

[115]William G. Bowen, Thomas I. Nygren, Sarah E. Turner, and Elizabeth A. Duffy, *The Charitable Nonprofits* (San Francisco: Jossey-Bass, 1994), p. 24.

[116]Thomas P. Holland and Myra Blackmon, *Measuring Board Effectiveness* (Washington, National Center for Nonprofit Boards: 1995), p. 7.

[117]Robert D. Herman and Richard D. Heimovics, *Executive Leadership in Nonprofit Organizations* (San Francisco: Jossey-Bass, Inc., 1991), pp. 54–56.

[118]Leonard Goodstein, Timothy Nolan, and J. William Pfeiffer, *Applied Strategic Planning* (New York: McGraw-Hill, 1993), p. 4.

[119]Don Hellreiegel, John W. Slocum, Jr., and Richard W. Woodman, *Organizational Behavior* (St. Paul: West, 1989), p. 407.

[120]*Ibid.*, p. 408.

[121]*Ibid.*, p. 408.

[122]Peter H. Drucker, "Strategic Humor," *Harvard Business Review,* November/December 1995, p. 130.

[123]"United We Stand," *Opera in Trust,* Summer 2000, p 6.

[124]*Ibid.*, p. 6.

[125]Mary Walton, *The Deming Management Method* (New York: Perigee Books, 1986), p. 94.

Index